How to Win
the Love You Want

Effective Techniques and Tactics
for Finding and Keeping
the One You Love

How to Win
the Love You Want

TWO BESTSELLING WORKS COMPLETE IN ONE VOLUME

THOMAS W. McKNIGHT
& ROBERT H. PHILLIPS

GALAHAD BOOKS
NEW YORK

First Galahad Books edition published in 1998.

Galahad Books
A division of BBS Publishing Corporation
386 Park Avenue South
New York, NY 10016

Galahad Books is a registered trademark of BBS Publishing Corporation.

Published by arrangement with Avery Publishing Group.

Library of Congress Catalog Card Number: 97-77419

ISBN: 1-57866-018-1

Printed in the United States of America.

Contents

LOVE
TACTICS

Contents

Acknowledgments

To Charles and Alois McKnight, whose commitment and love for one another has shown the way; to Rudy Shur, without whose confidence this message of hope might never have been so widely shared; and most of all, to God, who is the true and ultimate source of all love.

T.W.M.

This book is dedicated to all those wonderful people—family and friends—who have always been there for me, providing love and support when I needed it, and sharing progress and growth together.

I must acknowledge the participation of Sharon Balaban and Jacqueline Balla for their patience and expertise in processing, editing, and preparing this project.

R.H.P.

Preface

Whether this book ever becomes a best seller remains to be seen, but it really ought to be! Why? The answer is painfully obvious to anyone who has ever felt the agonizing frustration of not having their love reciprocated!

Isn't it ironic that, in spite of the many technological advances made within the last century, people today are still as frustrated as ever in their quest for true love? Our society is full of individuals who have disappointedly abandoned their idealistic dreams of romantic fulfillment. It almost seems a law of nature that the one *you* want never wants you back, while the ones who *are* interested in you are simply incapable of stirring your emotions! Love forever looms on the horizon, but is just out of reach.

Many have given up, deciding that nothing can be done to alter an apparently loveless destiny. They have resigned themselves to going through life, taunted by the prospects of love, but never truly possessing it. You may have experienced such feelings of helplessness yourself! If so, then this book is the answer to your prayers.

Love Tactics demonstrates why there is a very real reason not to give up hope. Love is *not* the mere result of chance meetings determined by pure luck. Believe it or not, love is a *predictable human response!* It results whenever a person's key psychological needs are satisfied. It's true that, on occasion, love does seem to occur accidentally. But even in these cases, such relationships still conform to the principles of romantic behavior outlined in this book! Anyone who chooses to consciously apply these rules of love in an intelligent manner need not go through life unloved! Succeeding in romance, then, only requires becoming aware of your ability to modify and influence the emotional moods, attitudes, and behaviors of others through well-proven psychological techniques. We're not talking about taking unfair advantages—just using strategic common sense!

As you can probably imagine, it would be impossible to include all the different strategies, techniques, and tips that can possibly be used in winning the one you want. Rather, *Love Tactics* provides the basic formula from which you will be able to derive your own solution to your particular circumstances. As you read the book, you'll find yourself becoming more enthusiastic, confident, and eager to approach others in an effort to win the person of your dreams.

Of the many lessons you'll learn in *Love Tactics*, however, remember this important truth above all else: *The way to true love is not to sit back and wait for the person of your dreams to magically appear. Rather, it involves choosing the one you want above all others, and then winning them over using known principles of human romantic behavior.*

Yes, you *can* win the one you want! You don't have to settle for anything (or anyone) less! The dream is in sight! It's merely a matter of psychology. *Love Tactics* will acquaint you with the science of human behavior as it relates to love and romance, and teach you how to *win the one you want!*

1

An Introduction: General Strategy

The general strategy behind *Love Tactics* is quite simple. It is based on the premise that romantic love has three essential parts: 1. *Friendship* 2. *Respect* and 3. *Passion*. Because love will fail if it lacks one or more of these necessary ingredients, the only way you can be successful in winning the one you want is by learning how to cultivate *all three feelings* in their heart for you.

THE HOUSE OF LOVE

We can compare a love relationship to a housing unit. As long as it is complete and functions the way it should, it makes a pleasant abode. There is no incentive to move out, since all one's needs for shelter and comfort are being adequately met.

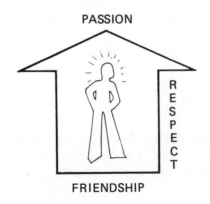

PASSION

RESPECT

FRIENDSHIP

But what if the resident came home, night after night, only to discover that there was no roof? Or floor? Or walls? It wouldn't be long before they would be looking for a new home!

FRIENDSHIP

Sometimes, out of desperation, a person may jump prematurely into a situation that meets some of their more immediate needs. But if this situation doesn't satisfy their other emotional requirements as well, they will eventually realize their mistake (and move out)!

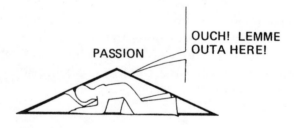

AN EMPTY HOUSE

Why does love sometimes fail? In most cases it can be traced to the absence of one or more of these three essential elements. Together, these elements contain all the ingredients necessary for the development of romantic fulfillment. Just as a house would be incomplete without a roof, walls, or foundation, so would a relationship be unfulfilling without friendship, respect, and passion. If just one of these components fails to germinate and develop, then the person lacking these feelings for the other cannot help but feel a little dissatisfied (yes, even cheated!). The relationship would be about as rewarding as sitting down on a three-legged stool and finding out (too late) that it only has two legs!

The basic strategy, then, to win *and* keep the one you want is to cultivate *friendship, respect,* and *passion* in your relationship with that person. *Only* when all three of these essential elements are present can you hope to enjoy love at its very best!

FRIENDSHIP

Before you can truly win someone's heart, you must first become friends with that person. Although this may appear easy, it really is not. True friendship meets a person's deep, emotional needs. A wise person once defined *a friend* as "someone you can think out loud in front of." In light of this definition, then, we might all find ourselves reevaluating who we really consider to be our true friends!

To become a true friend, you must learn to meet that person's basic human emotional needs. These include:

1. *Attention.* You'll need to show the other person that you are consciously aware of his or her existence.

2. *Understanding.* Just communicating your awareness that the person exists isn't enough. You also need to show that you're aware of how *they feel* about—and perceive—the world around them.

3. *Acceptance.* This means showing the person that you still value being with them, even though at times their behavior or attitudes may be less than praiseworthy.

4. *Appreciation.* You can satisfy this need by recognizing those redeeming qualities that the other person possesses.

5. *Affection.* This is easily shown by reassuring the person that, regardless of comparisons with others, he or she is still very special to you and, therefore, very important. Sometimes this can be communicated by no more than a *simple touch.*

As you begin to meet a person's five basic emotional friendship needs, you'll be helping that person along the road to greater happiness. In return, he or she will develop a subconscious emotional dependence on you. This dependence is an essential part of any romantic relationship. In order to encourage them to voluntarily place this trust in you, however, you must first prove worthy of their trust.

Behavior Principle #1:
People Subconsciously Grow Dependent Upon
Those Who Satisfy Their Emotional Needs

The first objective of *Love Tactics* is to show you how to satisfy the emotional friendship needs of the one you want—and to do it better and more completely than anyone they have ever met before! The various techniques described in this book will help you to easily accomplish this.

RESPECT

While it is true that pure *friendship* is the engine of romantic love, *respect* is the gas that makes it go! People are motivated to be with, and to associate themselves with, those persons whom they truly respect.

How do we come to respect someone? Respect is an acquired attitude. For the most part, it is usually based on our perception of a person's independence and self-reliance. The more capable a person seems to be of getting along in life without having to rely on us, the more likely we are to actually feel drawn towards that person. The opposite also holds true. The more easily a person becomes dependent upon us, the more "turned off" we become. When people act possessive towards us and show an inclination to "cling," our degree of respect for them declines. It is quite normal to feel a need to escape from such persons.

Behavior Principle #2:
People Are Most Attracted To Those Who Exhibit Some Degree Of Aloofness and Self-Reliant Independence

So if we want to win someone's heart fully and completely, we must be perceived (by that person) as being capable of surviving quite well without him or her. At the same time, however, we cannot neglect their very real psychological need for friendship. This presents us with the task of performing a delicate balancing act. Again, *Love Tactics* will show you how to accomplish both objectives!

PASSION

The crowning experience of romantic love is the ultimate sensation we know as *passion*. We can only enjoy something in life to the degree that we truly long for it. Therefore, levels of romantic desire must be raised to a fever pitch if the romantic experience is really going to satisfy our need for a fulfilling relationship and become the ecstasy we always dreamed of. This brings us to one of the most widely-known principles of human behavior.

Behavior Principle #3:
People Want What They Can't Have!

What happens when people become overly confident that a desirable object is "theirs for the taking?" They'll almost always take such a treasure for granted. (Frequently, they'll even abuse it!) Therefore, if you want to successfully build a romantic relationship with someone, it is imperative that you not ignore this principle. Otherwise, you will wind up forfeiting the rewards that you would ultimately have reaped!

By using the tactics discussed in the remainder of this book, you can build a romantic fire in someone else's heart that will blaze exclusively for *you*. Once begun, this fire will burn so brightly that the remaining embers will continue to glow for a lifetime! So there is no time like the present to concentrate on fueling that fire with the appropriate elements.

The secret to building passion in another person can be expressed in the form of a mathematical equation:

$$HOPE + DOUBT = PASSION$$

COMMITMENT

Falling in love is ultimately a rational, conscious act. It's a willful decision to let down our last remaining emotional barriers and become wholly vulnerable to another human being. But even though this final decision is a conscious and rational act, it is actually based upon emotional feeling, despite the natural tendency to deny this. As J. Pierpont Morgan reportedly once quipped, "Every man has two reasons for doing, or not doing, a thing: One that sounds good, and a real one."

Behavior Principle #4:
People Make Conscious Decisions Based On Subconscious Feelings, Then Justify Their Decisions With Reasons That Sound Good

It doesn't matter how logical it seems that a particular person should be in love with you. If the proper emotional attitudes have not been cultivated inside that person, then a meaningful commitment to you in a relationship simply will not occur. It is true that a person may commit himself to you based on sheer will power alone, but that person would always feel a void and emptiness inside. This would undermine the strength of anyone's commitment to you in the long run, no matter how sincere it might be at first.

On the other hand, if the proper feelings of friendship, respect, and passion have been appropriately cultivated in the relationship, it would be practically impossible for the person to resist making such a commitment to you, regardless of other "logical" reasons why it shouldn't happen.

If it's your desire to truly be loved by the one you want—if you want a complete, fulfilling, and totally reciprocated commitment from the person of your dreams—then get smart! Use the understanding of human behavior you will acquire from this book to your advantage! Cultivate friendship, respect, and passion in your relationship, and you will see how commitment to you will follow as naturally as day follows night!

Simply put, the general strategy of this book is based on the philosophy, *"love begets love."* The key is to communicate that love. It begins with your commitment to love another human being. It results in that person's commitment to love you back.

2

Acting With Self-Assurance

Principle: People are most readily drawn to you when you radiate a positive self-image!

Now you're ready to begin! You're willing to give it a try and go after the one you want! You're hopeful that this book will finally unravel the mystery of how to do it! But deep down you're still wondering if you've got what it takes. You have self-doubts. You're afraid.

Let those fears be dispelled! True enough, *you* are where this whole process begins. But *we* have faith in you! We know from our own personal experience that you (whoever you are) have within you capacities for greatness yet untapped! We haven't the slightest doubt that you, in fact, are *already* great— however hidden from view this side of you may have been until now.

This chapter contains a number of tactics that will help you to feel more confident about yourself. As this confidence grows, you will become more emotionally prepared to suc- cessfully win the one you want. Additionally, you will radiate more charm to help enchant and draw the one you want *to you.*

Whitney Houston sings that "learning to love yourself is the greatest love of all . . . " It is understandable that, unless a person feels good about himself, then he will not be able to show much love to another person. Therefore, it's important for you to learn to *like yourself* as much as possible. Our whole focus here can be summed up in the words *positive self-image.*

VIBES

Have you ever noticed that people tend to pick up vibes from others they are with? Think about the people you enjoy being with the most. You undoubtedly pick up positive vibes from these people, and that's why you enjoy being with them. So it makes sense for you to try to radiate these same types of positive vibes to others. But how is this done? Again, *by feeling better about yourself.* A positive self-image gives off positive vibes. This will be apparent in your face, your speech, and your behavior in general.

The vibes you give off will become an "aura" that brightens the atmosphere around you, engulfing and captivating those individuals with whom you come in contact. Others will enjoy being with you because of your positive attitude. This is the true source of that personal magnetism we know of as *charisma.*

LOVE TACTIC #1 Be Nice To Number One (Yourself)!

Before you can begin to glow with increased self-confidence, you must practice treating yourself with kindness, tolerance, and mercy! Research has indicated that many people are harder on themselves than they need be. They are too negative and self-critical in their private thoughts. Constantly bad-mouthing yourself will only serve to keep your self-image low. And, consequently, such self-deprecation can also diminish a person's ability to win the one they want.

So cut it out! As a first step toward winning the one you want, commit yourself here and now to break any such patterns of self-abuse. Make up your mind to no longer put yourself down. From now on, it is essential that you *go easier on yourself and be nice to Number One (yes, that's you!)* True, you may not be perfect, but it is vital to the overall plan that you at least treat yourself with respect.

How do you begin, if such self put-downs are already a habit with you? First, become consciously aware of exactly how much you do this. Take note of when you say something negative to yourself. Mentally keep track of your personal thoughts and self-dialogues. What did you say? What were your reasons for being upset with yourself?

Even if you get angry at something you've done, realize that you can learn from your mistakes. You *can* change. Criticize your *behavior* instead of blaming *yourself*. Emphasize the action rather than the person. How much better it is to say, "I did a dumb thing" than "I'm dumb!" Turn those negatives around! You can always find something positive in yourself.

Sure, this requires letting yourself off the hook sometimes when you blow it. But who doesn't deserve a good dose of mercy from time to time? And we promise that the improvement you will see in yourself because of this will surpass any results you hope to achieve by self-chastisement! In this way, you'll gradually improve the way you feel about yourself. As you feel more confident, it will begin to show and the people around you will respond to the aura that you radiate.

This is not to say that you should engage in the practice of excusing your faults, or bragging to others. Just realize that everyone has faults. Making mistakes does not make you a "bad" person. In fact, being human can actually work in your favor. As one young single person explained, "I don't want someone who is *too* perfect!"

Second, realize that nobody is perfect. Everyone (absolutely *everyone*) makes mistakes and, heck, you are certainly entitled to your share of them! Mistakes do not make a person inferior—only human!

Third, don't become discouraged if you're having a hard time shaking your feelings of inferiority, even after what we've just told you in the paragraph above! Be aware that if you are plagued with a bit of an inferiority complex, you are not alone. In fact, *most* people in the world secretly feel inferior to others, though they obviously don't go around broadcasting this. So your feelings of inadequacy are *not* the end of the world. You can *still* win the one you want, in spite of this. Millions of others have! But the more accepting you are of yourself, *without putting yourself down*, the greater an advantage you will have.

Fourth, realize that no matter what frailties you may have exhibited in the past, if you are capable of *recognizing* them as faults then you possess the capacity to improve yourself. This is a very important point.

Last, control your inner thinking. Indulging in negative thoughts can be one of the most destructive things you do. How do you know you're thinking negatively? By your feelings! Whenever you're feeling depressed, angry, guilty, lonely, sad, hopeless, or another upsetting emotion, you can be sure you have negative thoughts on your mind. These may sometimes be subconscious, however. Get those feelings out in the open! Ask yourself, "What exactly am I feeling? Why am I feeling this way? What specific incidents are making me feel this way?" You can't stop feelings and impressions from popping into your head, but you can certainly control how you react to them! Practice the "red flag" approach. Identify negative thoughts as soon as they appear in your mind—in essence, "red flagging" them. As soon as you're aware that they exist, defuse them. Squarely face up to them, examine them, and analyze them for what they are. Be thorough. Be exhaustive. Take several days to do this, if necessary, and then *write those thoughts down!* Ask yourself which of those things can be changed. Ask yourself which ones cannot. Then attempt to change the ones that can be changed, and accept the ones that cannot. You may be depressed because you can't change everything in your life, but you'll be surprised at how much better you'll feel about your life just by changing the few things you *do* have control over. This will greatly increase your self-esteem and heighten your ability to win the one you want!

GIVE YOURSELF CREDIT

Of course, the *best* thing you can do to boost your self-esteem is to realize the many good things you *already* have going for you. What *are* your good qualities? What are the positive aspects of you, the person? Every person has some. Think about yours. Again, sit down with a pencil and paper and compile a list of your good qualities. At first, you might feel like you don't have any (or very few). That's not true. Every person has positive traits that they should be given credit for. You, too, should get your share. You'll be surprised how your list will continue to grow, once you get started!

Think about the positive things you're able to do, the positive things you've accomplished in your life. Identify the people who like you, the people who look up to and respect you. Write down those things that you actually *like* about yourself: *character traits, talents, achievements*. Write down the nice things you've done for others; any acts of kindness you can remember showing someone else. Write down the skills you possess naturally or have developed. You'll be surprised at the effect that this list will have on your self-esteem! You'll feel better about yourself than you have in a long time!

Even after you've completed this exercise and have moved on to other parts of this book, there's no reason not to continue adding to your list of positives as you become aware of them. Make this ongoing list a regular part of your life, which you tuck away in a drawer to review and revise from time to time. (This is one way Benjamin Franklin always kept his life improving!) In this way, even when you're feeling down or suffering from a shaky self-image, you can review this list. It can help you to feel better about yourself. Remember: *Identifying your positive characteristics, as well as thinking more positively, are two of the most important ways you can help to improve your self-image.* And as your acceptance of yourself manifests itself to others, they, too, will follow your lead and become more accepting of you.

LOVE TACTIC #2 Identify Your Goals

Something very strange happens when you start to center your life—and happiness—around another person. It gets out of kilter. It gets out of whack. Oddly enough, even though there is no greater joy than that of being loved by another person, as soon as the gratification of that particular need becomes the primary focus of our life's existence it will elude us. It is paradoxical, but true, that in order to successfully win someone's love and devotion, you must first learn how to be happy *without their love and devotion*—at least to some degree. Happy relationships seldom result from joining two unhappy people together. Happy relationships arise from the union of *two happy individuals!* What this means is that your best chances for possessing the love you've always dreamed of come from pursuing your own individual destiny and attempting to find as much personal satisfaction and happiness as you can on your own—alone. As you do this, love will follow *you*. In this regard, love is like a shadow. It runs from you when chased directly, but when you give up on it and turn to walk away, it will always be found tagging along behind you!

Not long ago, one of the authors prodded a friend about when he and his girlfriend were going to get around to "tying the knot." The friend suddenly became very sober and frankly admitted that something was lacking in his attitude towards her. "She's a great girl," he said, "but it's like she has no goals in life other than to get married. I think I need somebody more goal-oriented than that!"

Whether you realize it or not, most of us subconsciously want someone who is goal-oriented and heading someplace—

even without us! You, too, must establish a course of direction if you hope to attract the one you want.

To pursue your own destiny, though, requires identifying your own set of personal goals and planning ways of achieving them. Having a plan of action—having goals and anticipating the particular steps necessary to achieve each goal—is one of the most essential processes for happy and successful living.

Goal-setting can be a very positive experience. It focuses on your positive potential, rather than your negative deficiencies. This, in itself, will reassure you of your true limitless value and help you to convey greater self-confidence to others. Have you ever been concerned that the one you want might not desire you because you lack certain qualities? Then among the goals you can establish for yourself are ways to improve in these areas! Your self-confidence will be further increased as you have the experience of feeling yourself actually improve, as you acquire some of the qualities and characteristics that you so admire in others!

But perhaps the greatest benefit of identifying goals and planning ways to achieve them is the sense of power that comes from actively taking steps to assume control of your own life! Think about the times when you've felt good about your own life and compare them to the times when you haven't. You'll realize that, in most cases, you were feeling good when you were actively taking steps to achieve something in your life. On the other hand, when you sat around doing nothing, being bored, or hoping for something to happen, you probably felt much less positive about yourself. Without definite goals to work towards, you'll stagnate and lose confidence in yourself, floundering aimlessly. (Just what you need to impress the one you want, right?) Goals help you to determine the exact direction you want to move in, so you can proceed with confidence!

Picture the following scenario: Your car is filled with gas. You start the ignition, shift into gear, and pull out of your parking space. All of a sudden you realize, "I don't know where I'm going!"

Sound strange? Yet how many of us are content to do this day after day with a vehicle so much more precious than any car—our very lives!! Don't you fall into this trap! *Love Tactics* demands that you take a more active role in the management of your own life! By identifying personal goals and taking steps to achieve them, your love life will fall into place naturally. Indeed, it may surprise you how naturally!!

1. Decide what you want. Think about your present wishes and desires. Dream big, but break your dream down into small enough steps so that you always have something to do next. Ask yourself, "What exactly do I want to accomplish in the near future? What do I want to achieve?" Make sure your goals consist of things that you, personally, can work towards. Don't depend on the whims of others to help you achieve your goals. Remember, you can't depend on somebody else to accomplish your goals for you. You're the only one you can count on to implement your plan!

2. Write down your goals. For some reason goals become real the moment they are written down. You then have a record of what you've decided to shoot for, which will help you to keep track of your progress. Otherwise, it's far too easy to forget your goals and not follow through.

3. Know your priorities. Of the many things you would like to accomplish, decide which ones are the most important. Determine which goal you want to work towards first.

4. Attach a time frame. The difference between a goal and a wish is that a goal has a definite time frame attached to it, within which we intend to do certain things to help accomplish that goal.

5. Break down your goals into daily tasks. When we talk about setting goals, we're not just talking about life-long ones. We're also talking about goals for your day-to-day

existence. What good would any business person be if he or she didn't know what had to be accomplished at work each day? How effective could a teacher be if he only thought about the semester exam and neglected planning the daily lessons? You will be most effective by breaking down your long-term goals into daily sub-goals.

Deciding on a specific plan of action—forming goals and planning the steps necessary to achieve each one—is one of the most essential processes for happy and successful living. Do it! As you will eventually discover, it will assist you in winning the one you want!

LOVE TACTIC #3 Relax!

Anyone who has ever had a really serious crush on someone is aware of the tension and anxiety associated with even being in the same room with that person! You think you're just about going to die, right? Your legs feel like putty, and you're afraid to speak because you're sure you'll only be able to manage a hoarse whisper (with a couple of squeaks thrown in for good measure!). Your instincts tell you to hide this nervousness, while your good sense tells you you can't—which only heightens the tension you are feeling! What's a self-respecting person supposed to do in a situation like this? Why, *relax*, of course!

Up until now, however, nobody's really been able to tell you how to accomplish that feat, have they? Today, though, you are going to learn something that will be more helpful to you than all the relaxation exercises in the world. Are you ready? Here it is: *It's o.k. to be nervous!* Did you get that? Let's go over it one more time, because it's a hard concept to grasp: *It's o.k. to be nervous!* That's right! The very thing we go around trying to avoid all our lives is not so terrible after all!

The real problem isn't our nervousness, but our unwillingness to forge ahead with our plans as long as we think it shows! Actually, the power to succeed is in us all along, but we are deceived into not using it. So relax! Realize that it's o.k. to be nervous! You'd be surprised to learn how many people will actually be *more* attracted to you when they sense your courage to act in spite of your fears. A shaky voice is music to their ears and a greater compliment than you can imagine! This doesn't mean you have to discuss your feelings of nervousness. Just be willing to go with the flow. Don't go to any unnatural extremes one way or the other, to either suppress your nervousness or to enhance it.

You might as well enjoy it while you can, in fact, because it won't last. Once you start acting in spite of your fears, they will soon begin to dissipate. Would you like to know the most effective cure for nervousness? It's *experience!*

Now why might it be important to learn to relax as part of your quest for the one you want? Well, you obviously want to feel that you're making the best possible impression, right? You want to come across as a confident person, don't you? Well, being able to relax can be a very important tool to help you feel like you're in control of the situation. By finding an inner calm and peace in your quiet, reflective moments alone, you'll realize that your entire world doesn't depend on a single encounter with another person. You'll find inner resources of self-confidence that you can fall back on whenever your anxiety level would otherwise be reaching the "red zone."

There's another reason, too, why it's good to be relaxed when you're with others. When you convey a cool, calm demeanor, it helps others to follow your lead and feel calm and relaxed *with you!* On the other hand, if you place too much importance on every rendezvous with another person, and convey nervous desperation continuously, it will produce uneasiness in the person you're with and may cause them to be a little more "on guard" and defensive.

The more carefree and relaxed you are, the more free your subconscious mind will be to guide your actions in social settings. And, like an automatic homing device, you'll find that trusting your intuitive powers will lead you where you want to go.

Of course we perform best when we are free of anxiety and relaxed. But how, you ask, can you possibly keep from freezing up in the most important situation of your entire life? The answer: You can't! So don't feel so overly distraught when you do! The compensation for all this is that once you really blow a situation badly, you'll feel amazingly more confident in similar encounters in the future. So don't ever be afraid of blowing a situation. There will always be a benefit to you, either way, no matter what the outcome. You always win, either by accidentally coming off just like you wanted, or by gaining experience that will make you ever so much more suave and cool in future encounters. So, relax! You just can't lose!

LOVE TACTIC #4 Talk With Confidence

Wouldn't you like to be able to talk to the one you want with confidence? Then it's important that you be accepting of yourself. Don't inhibit your efforts to converse with him or her because of your fears of what they might think of you. *What you say* is not nearly as important as the fact that you say *something*. As you become accustomed to not letting your fears prevent you from speaking, your ability to make more sense and to be more entertaining will improve.

STARTING A CONVERSATION

What is the best way to start a conversation with someone new? People are more uncomfortable with this aspect of social interaction than any other. There is not only pressure on the person trying to initiate the conversation, but also on the person being approached. The person being approached may be put "on the spot" because he or she is concerned that their response will appear inadequate or foolish. However, a few key techniques can put everyone at ease. Starting a conversation need not be that difficult. In fact, once you get over your initial reluctance, you'll find making conversation an effective instrument to help you win the one you want.

You must first realize that conversation involves more than words. It also includes eye contact and, to a lesser extent, body language. Realize, too, that facial expressions are a crucial part of the conversation process. If you continue smiling even as you stumble over your words, you can be assured that you'll make a good impression.

CONVERSATION ANXIETIES

Now let's get down to basics. One of the main reasons why you might feel uncomfortable starting a conversation with someone new is the fear of rejection. You may fear that if you don't come across in just the right way you'll be rejected. How humiliating! How shameful! You can just picture yourself slinking off in embarrassment. Let such thoughts be dispelled, though! The key to successful conversation isn't the use of fancy words in an attempt to make a good impression. The secret is to come across as a warm, caring person! And as long as you are making a sincere effort to communicate by putting yourself on the line for someone, that's exactly how you'll come across! If you're sincere, you'll never make a bad impression. It's when we try to be *impressive* that we get ourselves into trouble.

WHAT TO SAY

Is there anything you can say to get the ball rolling? Yes, just about *anything!* For lack of something better, even old hackneyed phrases that indicate you've been watching old movies will do! You might feel funny walking up to somebody you've never met and saying something like, "Excuse me, but haven't I seen you somewhere before?," but such efforts work! It's part of human nature to be flattered by such attention, and the people you approach in this fashion will eat it up!

SMALL TALK

Making small talk is the usual way to break the ice and meet new people. This is because such talk focuses on non-threatening, non-personal subjects such as the weather, surrounding location, or other people. The advantage of small talk is that it gives a person a chance to warm up to you a bit and learn to trust you *before* making themselves vulnerable to you. A gentle, slow approach is better than coming on like a gangbuster! However, small talk alone won't get you very far in developing a deep relationship! It merely serves as a temporary transition to more meaningful conversation.

"BIGGER" TALK

As soon as it's appropriate, you need to personalize the conversation. You need to discuss feelings and attitudes that are normally missing in small talk. Once small talk has gotten the ball rolling, gradually direct the conversation towards the other person. Ask questions that show an interest in their opinions. Ask about their experiences. Mention something about yourself occasionally, but do so only as it relates to the other person (to show you can identify with what they are saying). Quickly turn the spotlight back on them. If the other person asks you some sincere questions about yourself, answer them without getting carried away. Remember that their interest has its limits! In the early stages, especially, you only want to reveal enough about yourself to whet their appetite and make them want to know more! Always maintain some mystery about yourself. This will keep them coming back around. Think of your conversations as a great banquet, in which *they* are the main course and you are the seasoning. You don't want the main course to be *too* spicy!

Of course, we hardly need mention here that you must avoid even the *appearance* of bragging. Nothing is as repulsive as the person who seems to get "high" on recounting endless facts about himself. Another no-no involves speaking negatively of others. Unfortunately, some people like to make conversation by putting other people down in some way. Uniting themselves with anyone who will join them in such backstabbing ventures gives them a false sense of acceptance. But don't you fall into this trap! All it does is sow seeds of distrust in everyone you meet. If you would put down someone else, how can they be sure you won't do the same thing to them? So avoid this as well as other forms of negative gossip! It will leave a bad impression on the one you want. It's better to speak positively and supportingly of others. As the saying goes, "If you can't say somethin' nice, don't say nothin' at all!"

In conclusion, then, realize that you must accept the responsibility for initiating and maintaining successful conversation if you hope to win the one you want. You can't leave such a vital element of a developing relationship to chance. *You must be in control.* This doesn't mean you should be doing most of the talking. *You keep control largely by listening and asking questions.* Invite the other person to do most of the talking, but make sure that you have plenty of fuel available to feed the fire when the flame looks like it's dying out! A little preplanning can help out here. Have some ideas ahead of time regarding topics you can *ask them about.* (Many years ago, one of the authors of this book was quite nervous about an upcoming date and how he could keep the conversation flowing comfortably. He finally resorted to writing down a list of possible topics on a 3" x 5" index card and secretly referring to it throughout the evening. It worked great!) But don't get hung up on the particulars. Just remember to be warm and caring. Even if you're not totally confident of your conversational abilities, you can show that you care by being a good listener. Others like that! Remember—people don't care how much you *know* until they know how much you *care!*

LOVE TACTIC #5   Know What You Want (In A Prospective Mate)!

Before going on to the rest of the love tactics in this book, you'll need to have a clear idea of what characteristics and qualities you're looking for in the one you want. At times, the going will get quite tough, and being sure that the one you want is the one you *really* want will be the only source of strength and motivation you'll have to fall back on. When your goal is more defined, you'll be more committed to following through and doing what is necessary to win them over.

Some people don't realize that they are attracted by certain qualities. They've never really analyzed their *reasons* for becoming enamored in the first place. For them, love remains a mystery. They are like a ship in the midst of an ocean without a map to guide them, drifting to whatever isle fate happens to choose, and having no control whatsoever over their own destiny.

But you must be different! For those who understand the forces that guide them, and who know where they want to go, it is possible to chart their own course! And that's exactly what we expect *you* to do!

First, you should make a list of all the people you can remember having crushes on in your life. Then, next to each name, write down all the things you remember liking about that person. What exactly attracted you to them? Was it their smile? Their eyes? The way they laughed? Think of the kind of person they were. Were they kind? Self-assured? Intelligent? Did they have a good sense of humor? These are the kinds of things you'll want to ask yourself. Then review this list and ask yourself what other qualities you would like the person of your dreams to have. This will take a lot of careful thought. Soon you should come up with a pretty good profile of your ideal person. Now don't panic just because you don't think such a person exists! This is just a starting point.

Knowing what characteristics you'd like in a person will better prepare you to begin your search. This doesn't mean, however, that your expectations will remain inflexible. You'll be surprised at how easy it will be to adjust your wants according to the real live prospects available. Your list is just a frame of reference for starting out. Obviously, you may revise your list if you like, and you will discover that you are still attracted to many people who don't meet up to all your initial, ideal expectations. But knowing what that ideal is will give you power in your search!

LOVE TACTIC #6   Plan Out Where To Hunt

As much help as *Love Tactics* can be when you have actually found someone you want, it wouldn't be complete without some suggestions as to *where* you may find a prospective mate. This section will briefly discuss a few settings where you might plant a few romantic seeds.

ON THE JOB

This may be one of your very best sources of meeting people, for a couple of reasons. First, you spend a lot of time there and can become intimately acquainted with customers, clients, and co-workers. Second, because your activities are focused around other business, it can take some of the pressure off male/female relationships.

Countless couples have met through work-related circumstances! Although some people feel it is risky to become romantically involved with someone you associate with at work, others state that it is worth the risk! Only you can decide if the gamble is worth it in your particular situation.

SPECIAL INTEREST GROUPS

Another gold mine for potential romance lies in special hobby groups. A photography club, skiing club, health club, etc. probably exists not far from your home. You might obtain a catalogue from an adult education program, or a community college with continuing education courses, and browse through topics of interest. This will give you an idea of the types of clubs and organizations that may already exist in your community. And, if not, you can always take a class! A classroom is probably *the* best place to become acquainted with members of the opposite sex!

Service organizations, too, provide a fertile field for seeds of introduction to grow and flourish. When you work side by side with someone for a charitable cause, it makes relationship development as easy as 1-2-3.

While you're at it, don't discount the possibility of going to your place of worship! People you meet here are often more sincere about seeking a permanent and lasting relationship than those you might meet in other settings. One young man in the armed forces discovered that the best place to meet women was *in church!* It seemed that his most stable and enjoyable relationships began in such settings! (Additionally, the girls' parents would usually invite him over for Sunday dinner!)

Don't assume that you need special skills or must meet rigid requirements in order to get involved in any of the above-named groups or associations. A simple phone call asking for information and expressing an interest in getting involved is usually all it takes. Most people will be happy to help you out.

REFERRALS THROUGH FRIENDS

No matter how you decide to improve your social circulation, there is one method you must not miss out on. Rely on your already existing network of friends! This is often one of the safest ways to proceed, even though you may not know ahead of time who you're going to be "fixed up" with. But because your friend is screening your date before you meet him or her, you can be assured that the person is relatively "safe!"

And you can be creative! One young man had a married couple he knew bring their single girlfriends to social or athletic events where, unknown to her, he occupied the fourth seat. Because none of them ever let on to the girl that he was part of their group, the "pressure" was off! It was easy for them to get to know each other.

THE SINGLES SCENE

The problem with bars is that they are largely associated with temporary alliances. Many people refuse to go to bars because they consider them "pickup joints" where the best you can hope for is a "one-night stand." Deep down we are really looking for a lasting, permanent relationship. Therefore, we don't want to have to settle for table scraps when we could be feasting at the banquet of true love.

Dances don't have such a negative reputation. But it may be difficult to meet someone at a dance because you first have to go up to a person you don't know and break the ice. On the other hand, once you overcome this fear, you may find this an especially effective (and enjoyable) way to spend your time.

Dating services and singles clubs can be another fruitful way of meeting people. However, it's usually a good idea to research these organizations before joining them to be sure they're reputable. Singles groups that are affiliated with religious organizations or community centers are usually good bets, but if there is a profit motive involved you have to be a little careful. Be more wary of small, privately-advertised organizations or services that don't have any known affiliations or where you don't know any members.

Personal ads in newspapers and magazines are becoming more and more commonplace. There was a time when this was considered a sleazy approach, but today respectable people from every profession and age group are trying them, often with a great deal of success. If you decide to use this method, make sure you put your ad in a reputable publication. Before placing an ad, review some of the other ads in the publication so you have an idea what to say. The largest and most reputable singles register we know of in the United States is the National Singles Register, published bi-weekly from Norwalk, California. There are numerous success stories of happily-married couples who met through their personal columns. Their address is P.O. Box 567, Norwalk, California, 90650. Write to them for further information.

A WORD (OR TWO) TO THE SHY

We are aware that some of you reading this book may have a very difficult time getting started because of super-shyness. This is nothing to be ashamed of! In fact, being super-shy is actually quite common in this country. Many, many people (more than you realize) are so afraid of encountering others that they keep themselves shut up at home constantly. We understand your dilemma. If you are having a hard time getting started, may we offer a few suggestions?

First, practice dealing with people over the telephone. Call the operator if you have to and try asking for phone numbers. From there, you can practice calling bookstores and asking them what books they have on a particular subject, or calling businesses listed in the yellow pages and asking about the services they offer and their prices. The more relaxed you become, the more creative you can become in the types of questions you ask.

When you feel you are ready to confront people face-to-face, you might try a grocery store, library, restaurant, or other public place. You might begin by asking employees for some help in finding a particular item, or what they have available. Eventually you can work your way up to asking other customers for the time or directions to another location.

Don't be embarrassed if you must resort to such seemingly simple steps to increase your self-confidence. Consider Demosthenes, the great Greek orator, who was initially very uncomfortable with public speaking. He used to practice by himself at the beach by putting pebbles in his mouth and trying to speak clearly above the sound of the waves breaking on the beach. With such persistence and desire you, too, can gain supreme self-confidence!

Eventually, you'll be ready for some dates. When you are, if it's still hard for you to approach someone directly, having a friend set you up on a blind date may be a good idea. Don't be afraid to use this option frequently. Why? The more practice you get, the more self-assured you'll become. If you're afraid you'll run out of things to say, write down possible topics and keep a list in your pocket, as was previously mentioned. If you can't remember what you had written down, excuse yourself for a moment and secretly review your list.

Remember, even shy people can win the one they want! You may have to take small steps in the beginning, but those small steps will help accomplish your goal as surely as the big ones, as long as you keep on practicing. "If at first you don't succeed, try, try, again!" Good luck and happy hunting!

3

Taking the Offensive

Principle: People are like mirrors, always reflecting the same attitudes that they think others have towards them.

The one you want is out there waiting for someone to love! The miracle is that *you can be that person!* All you have to do is take the initiative to act. It's already in the program for them to respond. Human beings have been designed in such a way as to return those feelings of love which they recognize as genuine. The challenge you have is to (1) Make sure your love *is* real and (2) Effectively communicate that love. Both responsibilities require you to take control of the situation from the very beginning, and not leave anything to fate.

Many times it may seem easier to sit back and blame romantic setbacks on your incompatible astrology signs (". . . by the way, what's *your* sign?"), but the real problem is your own inaction. As Shakespeare so wisely put it, "The fault, dear Brutus, is not in our stars, but in ourselves . . ." You, alone, hold the key to your success. You must be determined to turn that key, especially in *this* —the most vital challenge of your entire life.

As the authors of this book, we can reveal the secrets of *what* to do, but only *you* can actually *do* it. Even at this early stage of the book, adopt the motto, "If it's to be, it's up to me!"

LOVE TACTIC #7 Be First To Show Interest In The Other

One of the most helpful facts about human nature is that we most often take notice of, and feel attracted to, people who appear to have a genuine interest in *us*! This is what makes your heart skip a beat, for example, when you catch someone looking at you across a crowded room. *All* of us are susceptible to such kinds of attention. *The best way to favorably impress someone is not by telling them marvelous things about yourself, but by letting them know that you are favorably impressed by them.*

People are reactive creatures, similar to mirrors. Are you aware that many of our attitudes and, indeed, our behaviors toward others are greatly determined by the way others treat us *first*? So the way we feel about others is generally a reflection of the way we think others feel about us!

For example, who do you usually smile at? Yes, those who smile at you first! Also, don't you tend to dislike anyone whom you suspect may secretly dislike you? The most important revelation of all, however, is the realization that you *love* those whom you truly believe *love you!*

The secret, then, to winning someone's love is to first convince him or her of your real, genuine love *for them!* If you want to succeed at love, you'll have to be more than just a mirror. You must *act*, not *react!* You want love to flow *from* you, not merely to be reflected *by* you! This requires patience and self-mastery, which are the ultimate keys to winning someone you want.

Too often in life we sit back and wait for "Mr. or Ms. Right" to come along and show us how much they care, before we are willing to commit ourselves to care back. But there's something we should realize. Everybody does the same thing! Nobody (or very few people, anyway) seems to want to be the one to lead out because of the pain and effort that must be invested.

If you're simply waiting around for your dream person to show up, you could have a very long wait! But it's not necessary to leave your love life to fate. Take advantage of your opportunities! There's a whole world of people out there waiting for you to sweep them off their feet, if you simply have the courage to take the first step.

Showing interest in the other person *first* means being the first to: (1) smile, (2) make eye contact and acknowledge them, (3) extend a vocal greeting, (4) try to engage the other person in conversation, and (5) suggest the possibility of getting together for some sort of date. *Don't give up, even if there is no immediate response.*

Taking a visible interest in the other person is the *first* step to winning their heart. It immediately fills their need for attention (and *everyone* needs attention!), and paves the way for future progress. But, remember, it does not insure a positive response right away. That will come in time. Meanwhile, continue to show interest as you develop your skills in the more advanced techniques.

LOVE TACTIC #8 Go For One Date At A Time

QUESTION: How do you eat an elephant?
ANSWER: One bite at a time.

QUESTION: How do you win someone's heart?
ANSWER: One *date* at a time.

As soon as you have gained someone's attention by showing enough interest, it's time to begin building a relationship. This is done by spending exclusive blocks of time together, commonly known as "dates." A date is simply an opportunity to interact with the one you want on a personal level—one on one.

The first date can be very uncomfortable for both parties. This is because it is generally exploratory. You're getting to know the other person, and learning about their likes, dislikes, idiosyncrasies, or other things that you didn't know before. This can make the first date very interesting. Be yourself, but don't start revealing your faults and self-doubts. We all have these, of course, but you want the other person to leave with a warm feeling of having spent an enjoyable evening with a person who is confident.

Something magical happens when human beings spend time together. They grow on each other. There is a psychologically-binding effect. It appears that magnetic forces between people are more real than is commonly believed!

However, don't betray your anxiousness to tie up the social calendar of the one you want! It's dangerous to ask for more than one date at a time. This can frighten off a potential sweetheart before the binding effect has even begun. At the same time, don't settle for less than a real date. Don't believe that a relationship can grow just by seeing someone every day at class, work, or in some other neutral setting. This won't provide enough electricity to adequately charge the relationship.

So set your sights on that first date. Work for it, and it alone, until you succeed in getting it. No more, no less. Then, *after* completing a date and giving it a little time to be digested, go for another one. Don't push for too much commitment at once. By focusing on one date at a time, you'll actually be building the relationship (at a rate slow enough to keep from chasing away the one you want).

There is a story recounted about an Arab sheik who was once making a journey to a distant city. He had to travel through an extensive desert to get there. While on his way, a terrible windstorm came up and he was forced to set up his small traveling tent for shelter. The wind was furious and the sand beat wildly upon the outer covering of his tent, but he was safe and snug within. Suddenly he heard a pleading voice from outside. It was the voice of his camel.

"Oh please, kind master, " the camel asked, "the wind is so harsh and the beating sand so unrelenting, may I just shelter my mouth and nose from the storm by placing them in the safety of the tent through the tent door?"

The sheik was touched by the humble nature of his faithful camel's request. He thought, "Surely my faithful servant, who carries me so tirelessly and without complaint through scorching desert sand, deserves some respite from these savage winds?" So he permitted him to put his nose and mouth just inside the tent door.

After awhile, the camel said, "Oh master, thank you, kind sir, for the relief you afford me by your goodness and mercy. Is it possible I might also shelter my eyes from the stinging sands . . . ?"

To make a long story short, the sheik eventually found himself out in the violent sandstorm, wondering how he had allowed himself to change places with the camel! The answer: The camel kept his requests for favors surprisingly simple and humble. The smaller the request, the harder it is to deny!

So it is in developing a relationship. You must spend time with the person, *one on one*, to build it properly. This requires many dates, but only ask for one date at a time. Furthermore, if the one you want seems hesitant to grant you time even for a single date, be creative. Think of something you can ask the person to do with you, even if it involves as little as fifteen minutes! For example, you can ask them to let you take them out for a "quickie" ice cream cone later on in the evening, with a promise that you'll have them back home before they know it! Who could be so cold-hearted as to refuse this humble request? Little by little, you'll surely reach your goal.

WHO ASKS WHOM?

A common mistake many people make is to try to get the other person to ask *them* out! One young woman told of meeting a guy at work who really "rang her chimes" like nobody before. He quickly became the one she wanted. She tried to make it obvious she was interested in him. Although he was very nice to her at work, he seemed to ignore the hint and never asked her for a date.

At that point she realized that, in order for the relationship to progress, they needed to go out together. However, she incorrectly concluded that the only way to accomplish this was to entice *him* into taking the first step. So she wrote him a note saying (in effect), "Larry, I've come to appreciate your friendship a great deal and would like to get to know you better." She then signed her name and phone number, obviously hoping that *he* would take the first step and ask *her* out.

That's not the way to do it. Once you decide that this is the person you want, make up your mind to take responsibility for the relationship and risk doing the asking. Trying to shift this responsibility to the other party is *not* the way to succeed. As you might have suspected, "Larry" never even mentioned receiving her note. So she wound up feeling worse than before she sent it!

TAKING THE FIRST STEP . . .

Developing a relationship is kind of like learning to walk. Don't worry about anything other than that first step. If you try to get too far ahead of yourself, you'll trip and fall.

But sometimes, even when you're just concentrating on one step at a time, that one step (the first date) can prove awfully elusive. It doesn't matter! Don't be deterred! You won't get anywhere without the first step. So just make up your mind that you'll work for that first date until you get it. Anyone with a fair amount of dating experience will tell you that things don't always fall into place. Even the most desirable people encounter obstacles. So try not to take it personally.

BE LIKE IKE

Former president Dwight D. Eisenhower experienced the same frustration when trying to get a date with the one he wanted back in his single days. His dream girl told him she was booked up, not only for the *next* weekend, but for the *next three weekends!*

Now the average guy might have taken the hint and given up. But Dwight wasn't your average guy, and he chose to *act* rather than *react!* He was determined to get that one date and waited until Mamie finally said "yes" for the fourth weekend. The rest is history!

STEP BY STEP

Remember that even though the first date is not always easy to get, sometimes it *does* come easily. Then it may be the *follow-up* date that's hard to obtain! Or they may *both* prove elusive! Or . . .whatever! Just keep in mind that the most important date for you to concentrate on getting right now is *the next one!* Eventually, if you keep concentrating on moving one step at a time (all the while applying the other tactics is this book), resistance will melt and the one you want will finally become like putty in your hands! The beginning of any project is always the hardest part. A wise man once said, "That which we persist in doing becomes easier. Not that the nature of the thing has changed, but our ability to *do* has increased!"

LOVE TACTIC #9 Avoid Being Defensive

The most difficult part of being the first person to extend ourselves in a relationship and show interest in the other is that it leaves us extremely vulnerable. If the one we want shows no indication of reciprocating our friendship, it leaves us feeling very foolish.

When this happens, our first impulse is to take quick action. We immediately try to cover up our foolishness and redeem as much of our pride as possible. How do we do this? Generally, we'll withdraw from the contest or, even worse, try to take some punitive action toward the one who has rejected us. For example, we might bitterly snub the person or speak badly of them to others. This kind of defensive behavior only backfires on us, though, and makes the situation worse. What many people never realize is that rejection can almost always be overcome through patience and endurance. This is accomplished by continuing to meet your prospective loved one's basic needs for attention, understanding, acceptance, appreciation, and affection even though they may be neglecting yours. It takes courage and fortitude to be a true and unconditional friend to others, but it pays off in the end!

Lord Melbourne once said, "Neither man nor woman can be worth anything until they have discovered they are fools . . . (and) the sooner the discovery is made the better, as there is more time and power for taking advantage of it." So don't be afraid to look foolish! This fear only paralyzes our ability to reach out to others. And only by reaching out consistently can we maximize the level of trust others will feel for us. There is no shame in rejection! Endure it well! All great human beings have gone through it and, interestingly enough, usually in an amount proportionate to their greatness!

By allowing ourselves to remain open and vulnerable to another human being, even in the face of rejection and feeling foolish, we show our sincerity and true greatness of character. This will persuade others to become similarly open with *us*.

On the other hand, becoming defensive when someone hurts you by not responding to your attention is certainly not the answer. It only reinforces their distant attitude and makes the other person feel justified in their initial standoffishness towards us. By exhibiting a sort of "If-you-don't-want-me-then-I-don't-want-you" type of attitude, we demonstrate very clearly that our ability to be a true friend is shallow. Deep down, the one you want senses their need for someone with *staying power*, someone who will stick with them *in spite of themselves,* and love them even when they act unlovable. So if the other person is resisting, you have a better chance of defusing it with non-defensive behavior. Don't fight fire with fire, or else you might wind up burning down the whole house! Drown resistance with waters of acceptance and love. A few years ago the words of a popular song said, "Love is surrender." What the song is really saying is that sincere caring can only be conveyed after one has surrendered his or her ego and false pride. Make the effort to achieve unconditional friendship and stick with it, even if the going gets tough. Don't get defensive just because the sincerity of the love you extend doesn't seem to sufficiently impress itself upon someone's heart when you first offer it.

RECOVERING FROM REJECTION

No matter who you are, you're going to experience some degree of rejection in trying to win someone's heart. If not in the very beginning, it'll happen at some point down the road. Try not to let this shake you. For heaven's sake, don't resort to negative reactions towards the one you want when you experience any of this rejection! You might comfort your wounded ego a bit, but it'll cost you a good opportunity to build a successful relationship. Great victories in romance are always accompanied by a little pain along the way. No pain, no gain. No war was ever won without losing a few battles along the way, so you mustn't become overly discouraged and give up the fight just because today's struggle seemed to end in defeat. Remember, "You're not beat until you quit!" And, friend, we've got news for you: You're just getting started!

Do you remember our saying that people are like mirrors? It still applies here. Be confident that, eventually, whatever attitudes you send out will come home again. Putting up defensive barriers will only encourage others to maintain them as well. Instead, counter their apathetic response with renewed love, kindness, and attention. Continue to be positive even if they react negatively. Return good for evil, as it says in the

4

Making Time An Ally

Principle: The longer the amount of time a relationship has to grow and mature, the stronger the bonds of emotional attachment two people will feel for each other.

James Thurber once said, "Love is what you've been through with somebody." A little solemn reflection on that statement would soon bring nods of agreement from any thoughtful human being. Of course, we love those with whom we have *shared life itself!* And the more of life we've shared, the deeper the love runs! Can there be any greater bonds of emotional attachment, for example, than those which exist between the remaining members of an old battle-seasoned war battalion? And what exactly knits those families so close together, whose personalities and temperaments would not otherwise so naturally incline the group? It is *shared experience*—the good and the bad! The more they've been through together, the stronger the bond! Ask anyone widowed after 50 years of marriage about this principle and they'll be able to fill you in!

Day by day, little by little, the threads of experience which people share with one another become like strands of a spider's web carefully being spun around them, binding them ever so imperceptibly closer to one another that they don't realize it until they make their first efforts to sever the relationship. Their success in walking away free and clear at that time depends a great deal upon how much experience has been shared between them by then. And of course *that*, in turn, depends upon how much *time* has been allowed for the experience to occur. The more time the relationship has had a chance to grow, generally speaking, the stronger it will be. It was George Washington who said, "Friendship is a plant of *slow* growth."

LOVE TACTIC #10 Take Your Time (Go Slowly)

Marriage experts state that, on the average, the strongest and happiest marriages appear to be those where the couples took at least a year to get to know each other before tying the knot. Consider the example of Theodore Roosevelt (who was known for his strong passions). He took a year and a half to develop a good, strong relationship with his sweetheart. Afterwards, he boasted that his worshipful adoration of her knew almost no limits! And this, in spite of the fact that she held him at bay—practically at arm's length—throughout the whole blossoming relationship!

Had she been too quick to express a willingness to commit herself to him, either by spoken word or through physical affection, his appreciation for her would certainly not have been as great. In fact, it's likely that his anxiousness was the very thing that kept her hesitant, until she finally "broke down" and fell for him.

Theodore Roosevelt understood the frustration of taking it slow in winning the one he wanted. Almost from the moment he met her, he knew she was the girl for him. He vowed in the privacy of his journal "that win her I would, if it were possible." Still, their relationship took a year and a half to grow sufficiently strong for her to return his affection.

Have you ever tried to rush a budding romance along too quickly? This is a very common mistake. Since relationships grow stronger with the passing of time, the trick to succeeding is to try and keep the friendship developing as long as possible at first, *without frightening off a potential lover!* Unfortunately, what most of us do instead is to try to extract some sort of commitment from the one we want at the earliest possible moment. This can seem threatening and ominous. Why? It makes people feel like they're being backed into a corner before they're ready, making them anxious to find an escape. If people are allowed to progress at their own pace, however, the natural course of their emotional growth will lead them to actually feel comfortable about making such a commitment.

Compare winning the one you want to going fishing. When you throw your hook into the water and feel that first nibble, you can't jerk the line too quickly. Sure, it's a temptation to try to pull it in right away! You don't want to take a chance on its swimming away. But if you act *too* quickly, you'll wind up pulling the hook right out of the fish's mouth and losing it completely! This is because the hook needs time to work itself into the mouth and become securely imbedded there. Given enough time, the fish will do most of the work for you, as long as you supply the hook and the bait! So give your lure enough time to work its magic in love, as well! Your human "fish" will bite the bait and become firmly attached to your hook! Do you see the analogy? Make sure the relationship is good and strong before you begin to "reel in" your sweetheart.

FEAR OF COMMITMENTS

Why do people resist getting involved in relationships? Is it love they are running from? Actually, no! People run from making commitments, *not* from being loved! It's only when they start to feel obligated by accepting your love that they'll turn it away. And when we hint that we're including someone in our future plans, the natural human instinct is for them to run as fast and far away as possible!

There was once a young man who fell into a deceptive life of fraud. He had a number of aliases he used as he traveled around the country. During one particular journey he met a girl, and though at first he deceived her and took advantage of her gullibility as he had many others, he soon realized he felt differently about her. He found himself falling in love and felt a strong desire to "go straight" and marry her. Although this would mean completely changing his lifestyle, there was no doubt in his mind that it was what he wanted.

He went to her, made a complete confession, and asked her to marry him. However, it was such a shock to her that instead she called the police! He had no choice but to quickly hop on a plane and get away. He didn't have much time to mourn his loss as he was making his escape.

The Great Realization

Later on in the airplane, though, the young man had an interesting introspective experience. He knew he felt something inside, but couldn't really identify the emotion. Only six hours before, he had wanted to marry this girl more than he had ever wanted anything in his entire life. Now there was no hope of that ever happening. Yet, what was it he was feeling? It wasn't really disappointment. It wasn't anger . . . and then it dawned on him! It was *relief!* For in spite of the fact that he *had* wanted to marry her, the truth was that he was *also very glad now that he didn't have to!* He was relieved that forces beyond his control had emancipated his heart, so that he was no longer bound by any feelings of emotional attachment or obligation. He felt a new appreciation and, indeed, exhilaration for his new-found sense of freedom.

The truth of the matter is, *it's common to feel two conflicting desires at the same time.* One is usually just a little stronger than the other, so that's the one we're most aware of. On the one hand we desire to be free and uncommitted, while on the other hand we yearn to belong to someone. So, while trying to win someone's heart, *you can't ignore their ever-present desire to remain free* (even though at times it may be hidden from view). This points out the wisdom of going slowly. You don't want to scare someone off before he or she is ready for a commitment!

How do you succeed in this? By being slow about revealing your anxiousness to see the one you want all the time. Let the person think that you have only limited intentions of getting together again in the future—possibly one or two dates, but nothing more. This is called "keeping from getting too serious." It doesn't mean that you should stop paying attention to the person. It just means that you should not let the person feel too sure of your long-range intentions.

If a person is going to be comfortable seeing you, you can't threaten their freedom. Everyone has a personal need for emotional breathing space. They must not be given reason to believe that you are expecting them to share their life and future with you. Otherwise, like a person who is choking and fighting for air, the person may desperately seek to escape you.

As long as you keep a person believing that the relationship is merely casual, time will be on your side. Meanwhile, the subconscious process of emotional bonding will continue to bind their heart more closely to yours!

Avoid Impatience

Let's say you're trying to do the right thing. You're trying to take your time in developing the relationship before introducing the element of passion. But then an unexpected turn of events occurs. Someone else starts moving in on your guy or girl! You'll undoubtedly get spooked by this new competition and feel like you've got to hurry. It's natural to feel that if you don't get moving and "sew this one up" for yourself right away, you might lose them permanently!

Don't panic! Remember the story of the tortoise and the hare who decided to have a race? Aesop tells how the hare seemed to have the race won every step of the way. However, the tortoise continued plodding along, never giving up, and never deviating from his proper course. Yes, there must have been times when he thought, "Why bother?," since his rival seemed to have the inside track. But in the end, his relentless, "slow but sure" method turned out to be the quickest and the best! People often spend years unwittingly sabotaging one relationship after another by rushing romance, when they could have exercised patience just once (for, say, only three or four months) by developing a solid friendship *first*, and then been happily married today!

What if rivals do come on the scene? What if they try to quickly introduce romance into their relationship with the one *you* want? Although they may appear to be successful at first, they'll be creating a flaw in the foundation of their relationship which will, in time, become all too evident. They're moving too fast. This can actually work to your advantage if, like the tortoise in Aesop's fable, you keep building your relationship in an unhurried and meaningful way!

Your rivals will experience obstacles. They always do. And when that happens, they'll pay the price of not having built a good solid foundation of pure friendship first. By then, you'll be ready to step in and take over! When the one you want is feeling the need for someone who really cares about them and loves them unconditionally, you'll be there ready to pick up the pieces and carry the person across the finish line!

You'll have your romance, too. But it will occur at the proper time—later—and will be all the more powerful for your having waited!

LOVE TACTIC #11 Be Attentive On A Regular Basis

In *The Little Prince*, by Antoine de Saint-Exupery, the importance of showing regular, almost clock-regulated, attention to someone you'd like to win was clearly demonstrated. In this classic allegorical commentary on love, a lonely but skeptical fox meets a little prince who is out "looking for friends." The fox, realizing that he, too, would like a friend (but also very aware of his own suspicious nature), pleads for the little prince to undertake the task of taming him. But the prince doesn't know how to go about it and asks the fox what steps he should take to accomplish such a feat.

The fox, although bound to obey his instincts, also has a clear understanding of how to get around them. So he explains to the prince that he must expect to exercise great patience in this process. He instructs the prince to sit down at a distance from him in a field of grass, just to observe him for awhile. (He knows that this will gratify his need for attention, while not alarming his sense of freedom.)

Admitting his own apprehensiveness, the fox warns the little prince that even though it may not appear obvious, he will actually be very aware of the prince's presence, ever watching him out of the corner of his eye. However, he further explains that as long as the prince doesn't make any sudden, quick movements in his effort to tame him, and as long as he will return and sit a little closer each day (so as to condition the fox to expect his attentions on a regular basis), the time will come when a relationship will begin to develop. The fox adds that, by coming at the same time each day, the pleasure of his anticipation will be enhanced as the appointed hour draws nigh.

How does this apply to you? In your efforts to "tame" the one you want and win his or her heart, *show attention on a regular basis!* Condition the one you want to expect your presence regularly, even though initially this intrusion into their world may be viewed skeptically "out of the corner of their eye." In time, if you don't make any rash or indiscreet efforts to "capture" the object of your affections, they will find themselves becoming a bit curious towards you and even anticipate your next appearance with some degree of subconscious gladness!

If you begin by making your presence felt in a person's life only once or twice a week, that's fine. But make sure you are regular enough about it so that the person will notice if you don't show up sometime. In time, people develop acceptance of anything that occurs regularly in their lives. So again, take your time in building a relationship, but be *regular!*

BECOME A HABIT

Nothing is quite as powerful as the force of habit in influencing someone's behavior. No tool is more useful in getting someone to do what we want. But can a person actually become conditioned to feel *comfortable* in your presence? The answer is *yes!*

The famous Russian scientist Ivan Pavlov did much to demonstrate the effects of conditioning on living creatures through his "salivating dog" experiments. They came about after noticing that his dog would salivate a great deal more than usual when he was fed. He wondered if the dog could be programmed to produce the same effect, even without the presence of food. So Pavlov began to ring a bell each time food was brought to the dog. This regular pairing of events was continued for quite some time. Then the dog was observed when the bell was rung by itself, without the accompaniment of food. Guess what? The dog salivated with the same anticipatory excitement as if it had just been presented with a juicy steak!

People can have similar experiences, sometimes without even realizing it. (That doesn't mean the one you want will "salivate" at the mere thought of you. Or, who knows, maybe they will!) But if you show attention to the one you want through regular telephone calls, visits, and doing things together, he or she will subconsciously get used to receiving regular attention from you. Where does this lead? The person will become accustomed to feeling good each time they are in your presence, and begin to subconsciously look forward to your next meeting!

LOVE TACTIC #12 Be Persistent

It's not easy to keep showing attention to someone who just seems to want to brush you off. However, don't give up prematurely! Any act of goodness or friendship extended towards another always makes an impression, even if it's not an immediate one. Every such exertion towards the one you want will bring you one step closer to triumph in winning that person's heart.

One of Aesop's more famous stories involves a crow who was dying of thirst. This crow came upon an abandoned pitcher. Once it had been filled with water, but now it was only partially full. The crow put his beak into the pitcher, but found that he couldn't reach down far enough to get to the life-saving liquid. At first he seemed destined to die of dehydration, with water (ironically) only inches away.

But then an idea popped into his head. The crow found a pebble nearby and dropped it into the pitcher. Looking in, the water didn't look any closer, but the situation was desperate, so he resumed the process. He found another pebble and then another. About to die of thirst, he noticed that at last the water was close enough to the top for him to get a drink.

Giving someone attention is like putting pebbles into the pitcher of water. Human beings have an unquenchable thirst for attention. This compelling emotional need must be met continuously, and thus serves as an extremely potent psychological reward. Whether people seem affected by it or not, *they are!*

At first you may not have any visible indication that the attention you are giving is accomplishing something, but rest assured that *it is!* Keep trying. Whatever time and attention you invest in a relationship will ultimately yield a most worthwhile return. If you quit too soon, though, you'll deprive yourself of the ultimate reciprocation of love that would inevitably be yours!

DELAYED REACTION

Another reason why persistence is so important is the *delayed reaction effect*. Realize that you're trying to get the object of your affections to warm up to you. Often, the desired response will come, but not immediately enough to see the direct correlation between your action and the response.

Let's say, for example, that Jim has met Susan, who really strikes his fancy. He'd like to become much better acquainted with her. Imagine what might happen if he showed a great deal of enthusiasm in one of their first encounters:

JIM: "Hello, Susan! Why, what a surprise it is to bump into you here! Do you come here often? I'm here twice a week and don't remember ever seeing you in here before . . ."

Although Susan does remember Jim, she has never really spoken to him before on a familiar basis. Finding herself caught unexpectedly off guard, she has a hard time regaining her composure. She tries to respond without getting herself involved too deeply in a situation she has not yet been able to completely evaluate. So she unintentionally comes across as definitely uninterested.

SUSAN: ". . . er, hi. Uh, no, not usually . . ."

Jim notices Susan's lack of enthusiasm right away. He tries his best to get her interested anyway, with a warm smile and further attempts at conversation.

JIM: "Have you seen Bill Smith or Jan Green lately? I don't think I've talked to them since the night I met you. I've been wondering what they've been up to lately . . ."

But his attempts are in vain. It soon becomes all too apparent to Jim that Susan does not share his interest in becoming better friends.

SUSAN: "No, I haven't seen them, either. Well, I'd better be running along . . ."

JIM: (still smiling and acting enthusiastic, but feeling like a jerk): "Well, it's been real nice running into you! Tell everybody 'hi' for me if you see them before I do. Goodnight!"

SUSAN (feeling relieved that this unexpected encounter is ending quickly enough, but not wanting to risk prolonging it by any show of reciprocated enthusiasm): "Uh, yeah . . . sure . . . Goodnight . . ."

Afterwards, Jim thinks to himself, "Well, it's obvious enough she's not interested in getting to know *me!* I sure made a fool of myself on that one. Now it looks as though I like her and she's just going to give me the cold-shoulder. Well, I sure won't make *that* mistake again. I can tell when I'm not wanted!"

Meanwhile, Susan has now had some time to emotionally digest the experience she's just been through. To her surprise, she finds she even enjoyed it. "My, he was nice!" she thinks to herself. "And what a nice smile! I wonder if he could possibly be interested in *me?* Well, I'm certainly going to have to take advantage of the situation, the next time the opportunity presents itself, and somehow get to know him *better!"*

In most cases, though, Susan's resolution is already too late. The one who was initially interested has already decided to become more cool and distant (and less vulnerable) in any future encounters with the person who failed to respond right away. What happens when Jim and Susan meet again?

SUSAN: "Hello Jim! What a coincidence bumping into you twice in one week!" (Actually, by this time Susan has come here on purpose, hoping for just such a coincidence.) "I guess it's fate, huh?"

JIM (determined not to play the fool again): "Guess so. Well, I better run. See ya . . ."

This time Jim goes away feeling a lot less foolish, but Susan is more convinced than ever that "you can't trust a man. One day he acts interested and the next day he acts like he could care less!" And thus another potentially great relationship goes down the tubes.

All this can be avoided, however. Decide that you'll stick it out and do the right thing, regardless of the lack of apparent reciprocation from the one you want. Have some faith that the tactics you're learning in this book will work if you give them

5

Pacifying Their Fears and Gaining Their Trust

---

*Principle: People have a subconscious need
to stay free and emotionally uncommitted.
Therefore, they will go to great lengths
to avoid circumstances which threaten
to limit that freedom.*

It is extremely important to exercise restraint when sharing your hopes and dreams with the one you want. There are some things you need to keep to yourself! Anytime you start to let on that your future happiness is hinging *on them*, particularly by your verbal intimations of this, they will begin to feel trapped. Sensing the responsibility being placed on them before they've decided they want it, their instinctive reaction will be to get out of the situation before they get in even deeper.

On the other hand, if you keep your intentions to yourself, you can keep the relationship developing while the bonds of attachment grow ever stronger. It may seem silly not to *talk* about something which, in other ways, may appear so obvious, but you'll be surprised how easily the one you want will accommodate your charade. It is the least intimidating approach for *both* of you. People want to *fall* in love of their own volition, and *not be pushed.* We agree with Thomas Hardy's assessment that, "A lover without discretion is no lover at all." Blabbing blows everything. If you can't maintain your own confidences, after all, how could another ever have trust in you to keep *theirs?* Mature persons of wisdom and experience know enough to keep their motives to themselves. It does no good to disclose one's intentions in the delicate early stages of romance, as it has the irrepressible tendency to drive the one you want away from you.

LOVE TACTIC #13   Show You Care, But Don't Say It!

Not long ago a young woman expressed to one of the authors her aversion to any more "game playing" in her life. She said all she ever wanted again from romance was someone who would sincerely care for her and "lay it on the line." She felt that she could emotionally respond to this kind of openness and candor, though she was told that such could not be the case. It was explained that even though she might sincerely believe she could get excited about such a person, human experience indicated that she would feel differently if it actually came to pass.

A few weeks after this conversation the principle was clearly demonstrated to her. A very eligible young bachelor came knocking at her door and pretty much swept her off her feet—for a few days. She soon had to admit that her new suitor was treating her exactly as she had said she wanted to be treated. However, his openness in talking about their future together was scaring her to death!

The relationship was much too stressful for her. Within a few days after realizing that she wasn't feeling the way she had hoped she would, she terminated the relationship (and, unfortunately, broke an innocent man's heart). Although she felt guilty about hurting such a wonderful guy, the relief she experienced upon breaking off the relationship only reinforced her belief that it was not "right."

Could this relationship have worked out? It very well might have, if the young bachelor had only been wise enough to realize the importance of holding back any talk of "them" and "their future." Such conversation contains too many implied expectations of commitment. Instead of creating stress for the young woman, her hopeful suitor would have been better off playing it cool in the beginning. As long as stress is present in a relationship, communication will be inhibited. This makes it difficult for a relationship to grow. What reasonable way is there to keep a relationship as non-threatening as possible? *Avoid talk that implies commitment to one another!*

Let's be candid here. We all know you have serious intentions, or you wouldn't be reading this book in the first place! *But don't go talking about them!* It's o.k. to *show you care through your actions, but show a little inconsistency when it comes to expressing it!* Don't say it! Don't wear your heart on your sleeve! Whatever you do, don't let your conversation indicate that your present or future happiness depends on the person's reciprocation of your feelings. Don't let the person know that your future plans are beginning to include him or her. This will scare the person off.

SHOW, DON'T TELL

Don't verbalize your feelings. Hold back, especially in the first few months of active dating. Some things in life are better left unsaid. This is especially true in romance. It's o.k. to show that you care. It's o.k. for the one you want to even become a bit *suspicious* that you *might* care. *But no confirmations, please!* Don't *say* it at this early stage! Don't verbally confirm any suspicions they may have until much, much later on in the relationship. (This goes for written communication as well as the spoken word. Sending little cards, notes, and letters that hint your love will only sabotage your efforts to really win someone's heart. This will be one of the most difficult acts for most readers to refrain from, but will richly reward those with enough self-control to refrain.)

People feel trapped and cornered by premature romantic confessions. However obvious your devotion might otherwise seem, it remains non-threatening until you start talking about it. Once you make a verbal confession of your love, however, any continued cooperation from the one you want would be a subtle acknowledgement of that person's commitment to you. They will be faced, then, with the sad choice of accepting your love and surrendering their freedom, or shutting you out of their life. And there is little question which it will be! They are not about to make any permanent commitments to you until they are good and "hooked!"

Remember, people do not run from your love. *They run from getting committed to something they're not yet sure of.* So unless sufficient time has elapsed to allow the other person's feelings to grow and become very strong, any threat to their freedom will produce psychological barriers and cause the person to start avoiding contact with you.

BECOMING ADDICTED TO LOVE

Many psychologists and counselors have described being in love as a type of addiction. In fact, there is some evidence that the pleasurable physical symptoms accompanying romantic love, such as increased heartbeat, sweaty palms, and a feeling of euphoric infatuation, actually do result from the release of phenylethylamine in the brain when the appropriate psychological and emotional responses are triggered.

With this understanding, then, of how love can affect us in a very real way like an addiction, consider the following analogy: When a drug pusher is trying to get someone hooked, how does he go about it? Does he walk up to a potential client and say, "Hi, wanna get hooked?" Of course not! He must be much more subtle than that! Nobody starts out with the intention of getting themselves hooked. And this is just as true of romantic love! Do people jump at opportunities to surrender their freedom? No, but people do feel drawn to situations that produce pleasurable feelings in them. And it's only when someone becomes *convinced* that the trade-off is worth it that they are willing to give up some of their freedom.

So a pusher must be subtle, and should not talk about the long-term *cost*, but rather the immediate *benefits*. He doesn't say, "How would you like to spend the rest of your life hopelessly dependent on what I have to offer you?" Who would ever accept such a crazy offer? Instead he says, "Hey, wanna feel good? No cost, man. This one's on me!" And so, gradually—step by step—a dependency is developed.

You should go about winning love from another in a similar fashion. If you start talking about how much you care for the one you want, this will automatically be read as your asking for reciprocation, or "payment." You're giving notice indirectly that you'll be expecting payment from the person in the future, and that can be very frightening to them. Instead, just give the one you want consistent, caring *attention*, without any indications of anything out of the ordinary. Later, once your special someone is good and hooked and there's no chance of losing them, there will be plenty of time to start receiving love in return!

6

Being Irresistably Likable

Principle: The more positive and beneficial the experience someone has when interacting with you, the greater will be that person's desire to continue the association.

Can you get someone you want to *like* you? Even though the human mind will not be forced into anything, it most certainly can be led! And if you know and apply the rules, you can coax any person you choose into enjoying and looking forward to the pleasure of your company.

Countless books have been written on this very subject. Persons of great experience and wisdom all agree: The things you do, the way you treat and act towards others, *do* determine how they think of, and act towards, you! So if you want to be well-liked, follow the guidelines in this chapter.

LOVE TACTIC #14 Light Up!

A grandfather was talking proudly about his grandchildren. Although he made it plain he loved them all, he reluctantly admitted that he was partial to one of them in particular. "I try not to be that way," he explained, "but you know how it is!

We tend to respond to the way others act towards us, and the little guy is always so excited to see me whenever I come around that I can't help myself!"

The same tendency exists in all of us. Whenever you notice that someone is particularly happy and excited to see and talk to you, don't you find yourself feeling emotionally rewarded just for having been there with them?

Did you ever wonder why dogs are such popular pets? It is for this very reason. People love coming home to someone who gets excited to see them, even if it's just a lovable, tail-wagging animal who can't talk.

So learn a lesson from "the little guy" and from "man's best friend." When the one you want comes around, or calls, show some excitement. Light up!

LOVE TACTIC #15 Show Those Pearly Whites (Smile)!

One day, two high school boys were discussing their favorite subject—girls—when they stumbled upon a very important truth. They had both agreed that they wanted a girlfriend with a cute face, and were trying to decide what quality determined "cuteness." Suddenly it dawned on them. "Cuteness" was almost invariably related to the amount of smiling a girl did!

Think about it. Aren't the people who you're most attracted to usually the ones who exhibit bright, happy smiles? You'll find that even the ones who you *aren't* particularly interested in become much more attractive when they smile. Why is a smile so powerful? A smile communicates *love*. It radiates acceptance. And making a person feel we accept them is one of the most effective ways we can influence people.

Try an experiment. Walk past a number of people, glancing at them *without* smiling. Keep a mental tally and notice how many of them respond to you. Then try the same experiment with a similar amount of people, *but this time smile and nod as you pass them*. You'll find that you will get a much more positive and gratifying response in the second experiment. (You may even meet somebody special!) By smiling and nodding you're conveying a very positive impression. You are giving others the feeling that they are worthwhile and special.

Can you imagine how many people go through life never realizing that this is *the most effective key* to being attractive to members of the opposite sex? And it's so simple! Even the most ardent opposition melts away, like morning frost before the sunshine, when we're smiled at. It has been said that people can say or do just about *anything*—and get away with it—as long as they smile when they do it!

No matter what the topic of conversation, a smile can make everything right! If you have a warm genuine smile on your face, and make good eye contact, you'll help that person to feel much more at ease. Later, even if they can't remember what you talked about, they *will* remember *the feeling* they had during the conversation. Remember, it's easy to smile! It's such a powerful, positive tool that you can never use it too much!

A smile says many things. It says you're happy. You're confident. You're feeling secure. It says you enjoy talking to the person you're with, and you like being with them. It shows you want that person to feel comfortable, and that you care enough about them to try and relate.

A would-be lover without a smile is like a warrior going into battle without a weapon. It is indispensable! Armed with a smile, no challenge is too formidable. It is a wise person, indeed, who realizes the importance of including a smile in their romantic arsenal to help them win the one they want!

LOVE TACTIC #16 Speak With Enthusiasm!

Enthusiasm is contagious! It breeds excitement in others! Therefore, it is one of the keys to influencing others in a positive way. Few human beings are immune to its infectious powers. When people are enthusiastic it makes those around them feel happier and more alive than they were before. Because this is a positive experience, it contributes to the bonds of friendship that strengthen people's attachments to each other. So when speaking to the one you want, don't just sit there in a lifeless heap. Put some enthusiasm in your voice! Be a little bit dramatic in your verbal communications.

Remember, people get bored easily. Any effort you make to liven up your conversations will be appreciated by others, whether they readily show it or not. Enthusiasm is a subtle way of *showing* you care, and will endear yourself to any with whom you practice it.

Don't be too sober or serious. It's so much better to have a light, positive attitude about life. Have a good sense of humor and don't be afraid to laugh freely. You'll also find that others will respond more readily to you if you smile and exhibit a sense of humor.

Try to radiate happiness as much as possible. If you're trying to interest somebody in spending time with you, an upbeat, happy attitude is essential. Be animated! Enthusiasm will make you an enjoyable companion to the one you want!

LOVE TACTIC #17 Talk Positively

The difference between an optimist and a pessimist is that the optimist sees a glass of water as half full, and the pessimist sees it as half empty. Since, subconsciously, we would all prefer half a glass of *something* to half a glass of *nothing*, it is usually more rewarding to be in the company of the optimist.

No matter where you go in life, or what situations you encounter, you'll have opportunities to judge for yourself how full the glass is. Life is full of plights and predicaments. How you share your view of your circumstances with others will determine the degree to which your company will be enjoyed. If you have a positive outlook, the one you want (not to mention everyone else with whom you come in contact) will subconsciously value your friendship more dearly. It pays to talk positively!

Single college students, when polled about desirable character traits they would like in a future mate, have consistently rated "sense of humor" high on their lists. Yet when pressed for a more precise definition of what this actually means to them, respondents indicate that the term does *not* refer to the ability to tell jokes effectively! Rather, it is the ability to look on the bright side of things—the willingness to laugh at a hopeless situation. People who do this are uplifting to be around and, whether they realize it or not, quietly endear themselves to others. It is emotionally rewarding to be in their presence.

LOVE TACTIC #18 Discuss The Other Person's Interests

It is a fact that most people do not have great confidence in their abilities to carry on a conversation. Yet, communication with others remains a basic human need. So if you want your friendship to be highly valued and sought after, you must learn how to help the one you want to be comfortable talking with you.

Surprisingly, the key is *not* necessarily having an extensive knowledge of many subjects. Rather, it is a willingness to *let the other person do most of the talking*, on any subject *they* are interested in! You can draw out anybody in this fashion by assuming the position of a sincere student willing to learn from a more informed instructor. Normally, conversation is characterized by a subtle kind of tug-of-war. In the usual exchange, each participant merely waits for the other to stop talking so they can shift the topic back to one more along the lines of their own interests! It is a rare and gratifying experience, for *any* person, when someone else encourages them to keep on talking about what interests them.

How can you best encourage this? By using sincere inquiry and quiet listening. Ask about the other person's goals, accomplishments, experiences, or attitudes. In short, ask about anything and everything *relating to that person*. It is the one subject on which *all people* are experts!

Dale Carnegie once reported the case of a celebrated bigamist who had captured the hearts (and bank accounts!) of twenty-three women. When the bigamist was asked how he had gotten so many women to fall in love with him, he responded that it was no problem at all if he just got the woman to talk about herself. Although there is often more to it than just that, there is no question that encouraging the other person to talk about his or her interests will win them over. Thus, conversing in terms of the other person's interests should be a fundamental technique in your strategy to develop a solid friendship with the one you want!

LOVE TACTIC #19 Use Flattery

Flattery will get you *everywhere!* This is a well-known fact. It is an *extremely* effective way for a person to endear themselves to others. But quite often people hesitate to use it for fear that their gestures of praise will be dismissed as insincere. It's true that most people act suspicious and distrustful when others pay them flagrant, outright compliments. But deep down they are gratefully eating it up, in spite of any outward skepticism. As Paul H. Gilbert put it, flattery is "the art of telling another person exactly what he thinks of himself."

So don't be fooled! When people seem disbelieving of, and resistant to, your flattery, realize that it's *just a show on their part*. Actually, they are deeply affected by it—more than they'd like you to know. The human need for appreciation is stronger than any human ability to resist it. Therefore, your compliments and words of praise will go a long way in building relationships. Be liberal in offering it.

A word of caution, though. Flattery is very potent, like fine perfume. A little bit goes a long way. Sprinkle it around and trust it to do its job. Don't feel the need to pour it on unceasingly just because the recipient doesn't seem to be responding to it. *Too much* flattery may cause your praise to appear unduly suspicious and undermine your genuine sincerity. People tend to put up psychological barriers and become more resistant when they have reason to think they're being "set up" and "put on." But having said that, let us repeat: Your compliments and words of praise will go a long way in building and strengthening relationships. Use flattery. It will make you an enjoyable companion and strengthen your relationship with the one you want.

LOVE TACTIC #20 Understay Your Welcome

It is, of course, well-recognized that by hanging around someone for too long in any given situation, a person can wear out their welcome rather easily. But consider this: If you *understay* your welcome when you're with others, you can actually leave them wanting more of you, *even if they weren't that interested in you to begin with!* This simple, but certain, tactic not only eliminates subconscious resistance to developing a friendship with you, but also creates a positive atmosphere for future get-togethers. People will enjoy your company *more*, as a result of having you available *less!*

So be sensitive as to how much time you spend with the one you want. Depart while things are still going good, even though you're having a good time and may want to stay longer. You be the one who cuts the conversations, the phone calls, the dates, or other encounters a little bit shorter than expected. Just say, "It's time to go . . . ," or, "I've got to get in early . . . ," or just a plain "Goodnight!," but be sure you're the one to initiate it!

Seek out the other person's company, but then also be the first to take leave of them. If you allow the other person to tell you when it's time to go, you will be inadvertently surrendering much of the potential influence of this tactic.

LOVE TACTIC #21 Be Graceful When You're (Temporarily) Rejected

One of the great classic musicals of all time is *The Music Man*, starring Robert Preston and Shirley Jones. In the movie, Preston (as travelling flimflam salesman "Harold Hill") comes to gullible River City, Iowa, with the clear intent (clear to the audience, not so clear to the residents of River City) of swindling the naive townspeople out of their hard-earned money. The scheme necessitates his masquerading as a music professor (hence the film's title). Promising to organize a boys' band, he makes his money by selling band instruments and then skipping town without completing his agreement. In order to pull everything off smoothly, though, the plan requires him to first win the confidence of the townspeople by romancing their local librarian (and part-time music teacher), Marian.

But, as is true of every good love story, there's a hitch. Marian is very suspicious of "Professor" Hill and is not easily romanced. Time after time, he approaches her on the street and cheerfully doffs his hat in an effort to introduce himself to her, but she always gives him the cold-shoulder and walks on by. Still, he remains undaunted.

Most people, when stiffed like that, would respond negatively and defensively. But not the positive-thinking Professor Hill! His vast amount of salesmanship experience had apparently taught him that a positive attitude and smile would ultimately tear down the walls separating the two of them. He responded to her temporary rejection of him with an even bigger smile and a pleasant comeback. And, sure enough, in the end, she succumbed to his charm and was finally won over by him.

Real life is like that, too. Those who are willing to lose some small battles gracefully will wind up winning big wars impressively!

DEALING WITH THE SKIDS

One of the most important things taught in a driver's education class is how to regain control of your vehicle when it starts to slide out of control. "Turn *into* the slide!" students are instructed again and again. So it is with relationships.

Let's say you have a clear idea where you want the relationship to go, but you can feel the person slip-sliding away.

That's not the time to turn towards your goal with even more determination, in hopes the one you want will follow. It won't happen! Instead, you'll throw your whole relationship into a real spin-out! It's better to temporarily "go with the flow," and not seem to resist their efforts to slide off the road. If a person doesn't seem ready to accept the degree of involvement that *you* want, then it's better for you to appear willing to accept the degree *that he or she wants*. In reality, that doesn't mean that you're willing to give up your original plans for the relationship (any more than the driver of a vehicle is willing to slide into a ditch). But sometimes you have to turn in that direction long enough to regain control and gently guide the one you want back to you!

When you get turned down in your request for a date, or brushed off in a conversation, don't turn *off* your charm. Turn it on stronger! *Smile even bigger!* Be willing to bow out temporarily with parting words of kindness and good will. It is this kind of behavior on your part that will convince others that the friendship you offer is genuine, sincere, and worth having. People can't help but love and admire someone who is gracious in the face of apparent defeat. Losing gracefully will subconsciously induce others to be trusting of you in the future. And, remember, love is based on trust!

7

Exhibiting
Self-Mastery and
Leadership Ability

Principle: People respect, and are subconsciously drawn towards, those who exhibit qualities of aloofness and independence. They are repulsed by those who manifest tendencies to cling.

Obviously, it's important in romance to exhibit very positive and accepting attitudes towards those whom you desire. But you mustn't ever let it appear as though your feelings for them are affecting your decision-making abilities or independence! Remember this: *It's practically impossible for a human being to experience romantic feelings for someone they can manipulate like a puppet!* Thus, if you want to be loved *romantically*, it is of paramount importance that you demonstrate to others that you are an independent, self-respecting person whose wrath they will incur if your goodness is ever taken for granted! Without this element of fear (yes, *fear!*) in a relationship, true romantic love can never fully develop.

If a person feels they can walk on your feelings disrespectfully *and get away with it*, human experience has clearly shown that they will not be stirred up with romantic desire for you. Here, then, are a number of ways to establish your independence and command the respect that is so essential to romantic love.

LOVE TACTIC #22 Plan Out Dates Ahead Of Time

This may be the easiest way to exhibit leadership and demonstrate emotional independence to the one you want. When it comes to dates, *have a plan!* Never give the mistaken impression that you are content to just let things happen to you. Know ahead of time most (if not all) of the details regarding where you're going, what you'll be doing, and how long it will take. Don't leave these things to chance, or it will appear that you're not in control. Have definite objectives and goals in mind for each date, which you have had an active part in outlining. This will demonstrate your ability to act as an independent agent and will earn you the respect of others.

This doesn't mean you should be *selfish!* Always consult with the other person in the planning process. Ask the other person what *they* would like to do. If he or she wants to do something other than what you have in mind, don't be stubborn! You can still demonstrate your active role in the planning by offering options, or at least hearing their ideas and communicating your agreement.

If you're not the person initiating the date, don't remain passive. You still have some say in the outline of events through your power of consent! You may assertively agree or disagree with the events as they've been presented to you. But at least insist on being informed. Remember, showing leadership qualities doesn't necessarily mean you must initiate *everything.* But it does mean that you are made aware of the plan for the date. This insistence will command respect from those you date!

LOVE TACTIC #23 Demonstrate Independent Thinking

What people are actually seeking from romance, whether they

consciously realize it or not, is someone to lean on and draw strength from during life's frightening and distressing moments. Because of this, people are instinctively attracted to those persons who appear emotionally strong themselves, because they'd be most capable of providing such companionship.

Think of a situation where you would need someone to talk to. Maybe you're upset about something, or you're just feeling lonely. Who would you rather talk to? Would you prefer someone who's independent, clear-thinking, and level-headed? Or would you prefer someone anxious to have you make their decisions and do their thinking for them? Be honest, now. Most people are repulsed by such insecurity. Most people are attracted to those who they sense are strong! In short, most people want *to lean*, not *be leaned on!* So it follows that if you want to attract others to you in a long-term relationship, you must demonstrate an ability to do your own thinking and make your own decisions in your associations with others. How can you do this? There are several ways.

SHOWING DECISIVENESS

Be decisive when given choices. When your date asks you what you'd like for dinner, or what movie you'd like to see, respond with some definitiveness (even when such matters appear trivial and you really don't care!). Such opportunities to assert your decision-making abilities mustn't be overlooked!

In dating relationships, many people innocently defer judgment in small matters back to their date. They don't realize that they'd command greater respect, and thus become more desirable, by simply making their own choices.

BENEFITS OF CONTRARINESS

Be contrary, sometimes. Don't always go along with everything your date wants and suggests. You won't be adequately respected if you do. The person mustn't be allowed to receive the mistaken impression that you could be easily led around by them, as if you had a *ring through your nose!*

Make some suggestions of your own at times, even if you'd be perfectly content to let your partner have his or her way all the time. And even if the two of you wind up not doing what you've suggested, it will stick in the other person's mind that you're not just blindly following their every whim. This will automatically enhance your desirability.

GIVING OPINIONS

Speak your mind! There's nothing wrong with offering opinions in a discussion. You may not want your views to seem too outlandish or offending, but at the same time you don't want to come across as an easily-intimidated, browbeaten person with no opinions of your own! The main idea is to speak your mind without concern for whether people will think you are boring or wrong because of it. The "points" you make by exhibiting such an independent attitude will more than compensate for any potential mistakes you might make.

Don't feel that your opinions have to agree with others'. *Be your own person!* Be comfortable saying what you think, even when it is contrary to prevailing thought. Don't be afraid to stand alone! Nothing is more attractive than someone who has the courage to stand up for their convictions.

This does *not* mean, however, that you have to be unpleasant in doing so. It is certainly possible to pleasantly disagree. Never try to force someone else to accept your ideas.

Be honest, open, and forthright. Don't be afraid to manifest independent thinking. It is one of the keys to fulfilling romance!

LOVE TACTIC #24 Communicate Your Personal Destiny

A young man who was having a hard time winning the girl of his dreams sat down after a particularly uninspiring date. "What am I doing wrong?" he wondered. He couldn't quite put his finger on it, but finally concluded that he couldn't go on any longer centering his life around *her*. He decided that, no matter what happened, he was going to maintain the attitude that he still had a special goal in life to accomplish, whether she loved him back or not. If she wanted to accompany him on that mission, she could be part of it. If not, that was fine, too, because he would go on to fulfill it *without her!*

Although his determination was mostly a final attempt to salvage as much of his self-esteem as possible, an amazing turn of events resulted. What happened? His attitude of "I'm going somewhere in life, with or without you!" inadvertently demonstrated his emotional independence to the girl of his dreams and won her love! It's much easier to fall in love with someone who is going somewhere in life regardless of what you do, than it is with someone who you know is basing their entire future on you.

Joan of Arc won the unwavering love and devotion of the battle-smitten armies of fifteenth-century France by exhibiting this very attitude. She once declared to one of her generals, "I will lead the men over the wall." His response was, "Not a man will follow you." But Joan, naturally possessing those same qualities of independence and self-determination that we've been discussing, merely said, "I will not look back to see whether anyone is following or not!"

In your quest for love and devotion, then, be like Joan of Arc! Communicate your intentions to accomplish something worthwhile in life to the one you want, and convey your intention to do it alone, if necessary. Such an attitude will inspire the one you want with desires to follow and be with you!

LOVE TACTIC #25 Be Unpredictable

A prominent psychologist, speaking to an assembly of college students some years ago, remarked that one of the things people need most in their lives to be happy is a little variety. Variety is, indeed, the "spice of life." It provides mental stimulation and keeps us interested in continuing on with life's wearisome struggle. Without it, life becomes dull and uninteresting, and people find themselves easily bored.

Sometimes we fail to realize just how prone human beings are to becoming bored, and thus how easily drawn they will be to someone who shows promise of keeping life interesting. So do the unexpected from time to time! You can hold others' interest simply by never letting them be sure of your next move. This doesn't mean that you won't behave dependably most of the time. It just means that, every once in a while, you will surprise people by doing something a little different from what they are anticipating.

An example? Surprise your special someone with a gift *when they least expect it!* When they think they've got you hooked, *ignore them!* And then, just when they start believing you've stopped caring about them, *drop by for a visit!* Do the unexpected! Be unpredictable! Be nice to them when they're cruel to you, and when they treat you nice, don't be afraid to act a little indifferent. Your ability to keep 'em guessing will be one of your most effective weapons in maintaining their respect for you and winning their love.

How often do you hear people in relationships exclaim, "I just can't figure him (or her) out!"? Isn't it interesting, though, how in every case the one saying this is usually the person in the relationship who is *most hooked?!*

LOVE TACTIC #26 Act Indifferent To Their Opinion Of You

A number of years ago a young man and woman had been seeing each other for awhile and a potential romance was in the offering. The young man had been particularly intrigued by the young woman and the independent attitudes she exhibited. One night, however, she lost much of her appeal when she inadvertently let him know that she was concerned about his opinion of her. It happened rather innocently, really. They had been talking about some trivial matter when she suddenly came out with a rather bold statement of the way she viewed a particular issue. The young man disagreed with her and it must have shown on his face. However, less evident to her observations, he felt himself extremely attracted by the strength of character and the independent aloofness she was showing. At last, he thought, he had found a girl who was his equal in every way!

His sudden fascination was short-lived, however. When the young woman realized that she had said something contrary to the way her suitor believed, she quickly backed down and admitted feeling badly about having expressed herself in such a forthright manner. *Most damaging of all, though, she admitted her concern that the young man might now think less of her for having been so bold!*

Can you see the irony in this? Only a moment before, the young man had begun respecting her more because of her courageous ability to express her feelings without any apparent regard for what he might think of her. But then she became apologetic and blew everything! If she had only continued acting indifferent to his opinion of her, the young man most certainly would have respected her more for it. But when she exhibited a willingness to back down and compromise her independence, *simply to please him,* she lost esteem in his eyes. He couldn't help feeling this way. Respect towards another person is cultivated by one's perception of how independent and aloof they are.

So in your associations with others, *act indifferent to what they appear to think of you (even though you may actually care a great deal)!* Don't admit to them that their opinions of you matter! A recent song asked, "Why did you have to be a heart-breaker, when I was being what you want me to be?" The answer to that question is this: Because you can't have romantic feelings for someone you don't respect, *and you can't respect someone who you know is willing to sacrifice their individuality to suit your opinions.* Romance can only flourish when you manifest a carefree attitude of indifference about the other person's opinion of you. This is a fundamental principle of human behavior!

LOVE TACTIC #27 Don't Fish For Feedback

When caught up in the agonies of romantic pursuit, it's only natural to want to find out where you stand with the one you want. What do they think of you? At times, the urge to seek some sign of reciprocation will become almost too strong to resist. *You mustn't yield, however, to this temptation! Fishing for feedback is definitely detrimental to your romantic health!*

There are two fundamental problems with sending up trial balloons to try to get a reading on someone's romantic feelings about you. First, any feedback you get is, at best, an unreliable indicator of a person's true feelings. Most people don't even know their own minds when it comes to love, so anything they tell you wouldn't necessarily be an accurate indicator of what the person subconsciously feels. It's very possible that a person is *growing* to love you but is not yet consciously aware of it. The transition from a subconscious to a conscious state of love is possible and will inevitably occur if you don't become discouraged and give up prematurely.

Second, probing for emotional attitudes is a hint that you're hoping for reciprocation from the one you want. This, in turn, exposes your emotional fragility. It signals that you're vulnerable to rejection by them and, consequently, are at their mercy! This will diminish their feelings of dutiful respect toward you and undermine the strength of your otherwise growing romance.

Never ask someone, or act concerned about, how they feel towards you, *until you're sure you've already won 'em over!* Seeking for assurances of affection only communicates emotional insecurity on your part and destroys the kind of respect necessary if others are to truly burn with romantic desire for you later on. Ironically, the more aloof you can *appear* about the other person's attitude towards you (at the same time extending yourself to them in true friendship), the more you'll earn their respect and, ultimately, their love!

LOVE TACTIC #28 Express Anger Verbally When The Right Moment Arrives

If you've ever been dumped by someone you wanted and can't remember ever having chastised them somewhere along the way, then you probably lost them unnecessarily! Does this sound strange? Well, it's true, nonetheless! *Showing anger towards the one you want is sometimes necessary for a happy relationship.* Although it's usually best to be agreeable and pleasant when trying to build a relationship, there are times when a sociable complacence is *not* the proper course to pursue. In order to elevate the relationship beyond the level of being "just friends," you need to demonstrate your ability to get angry with the person (even if you have to fake it a little bit)! A good, verbal chewing out is sometimes the only way to show the one you want that you are, after all, independent-minded and worth respecting!

Can you imagine a child growing up without the need for occasional chastisement? Of course not! Having someone on hand to enforce behavioral limits is, in fact, a necessary part of a happy and secure childhood. Well, the same applies to adults. They're just kids themselves, after all, in grown-up bodies. And adults, too, should be put in their proper place from time to time! A future mate will be much happier knowing that you're not afraid to show anger when they get out of line!

Listen to Lee's explanation concerning the difference between Karen, the girl he couldn't live without, and all the previous girls in his life who were incapable of stirring him to that same, high level of devotion: "She's the first girl in my life," he said, "who's ever stood up to me!"

This ability to stand up to the one you want and occasionally tell them off when they abuse your feelings or otherwise take you for granted is an essential key to romantic love. Nobody can really get excited about you if they're not secretly just a little bit afraid of crossing you! This is one of the best-kept secrets of romantic love. Make a note to remember it!

So stand up for your rights and get angry with the one you want, if you really want them to love you! Follow these guidelines, though:

1. Don't scold prematurely. In other words, make sure you have patiently laid a foundation of sufficient selflessness and "long suffering" on your part to justify your right to be angry.

2. Don't get side-tracked fighting about petty, irrelevant issues. The only thing you ever really need to show anger over is any basic disrespect, or lack of regard, for your feelings. (This is the only charge you really ever have any right to bring against them, anyway. You have no right to make yourself their judge on other matters!) Express disappointment in them. Say something like, "Hey, I've taken just about all the lack of consideration I'm going to take! I've given unselfishly and you've just taken it for granted. Well, I refuse to put up with that kind of treatment from *anybody—even you!*"

3. Don't stick around to let the person try and fight with you. Don't argue. State your case, show anger while doing it, *and then depart!* Leave them to their conscience and let your words sink in. Being sucked into a verbal ping-pong match will only weaken the otherwise very powerful effect this tactic can have. You'll be surprised at its power. Remember, *reason* doesn't motivate human beings—*emotion* does! Once you get the emotional pendulum moving, it will eventually swing your way. By employing this tactic, you will incalculably strengthen your sphere of influence with the one you want!

(*Caution:* This tactic will backfire unless strictly used in conjunction with Love Tactic #29: "Show Forgiveness After Expressing Anger.")

LOVE TACTIC #29 Show Forgiveness After Expressing Anger

Yes, you *can* gain a person's respect by being able to stand up to and chastise them when they deserve it! But it's *absolutely essential* that you be the first to demonstrate kind and charitable feelings for them afterwards, if you don't want to destroy the foundation of friendship you've previously established. Human beings are extremely sensitive to chastisement, and the one you want is *no exception.* If you don't take steps to reassure the one you've stood up to that you're still friends, it won't be long before they'll despise you as an enemy! This would be as fatal romantically as to never have been respected in the first place!

Therefore, as soon as your angry words have had a chance to sink in, take steps to show the rebuked person that, although your reaction was strong, you're still loyal. You still care. Don't apologize or act as though your anger wasn't justified. (It most certainly *was!*) This is not the time to back down and start acting like your anger was a mistake. Just seek out the person's company and resume the relationship, completely putting the incident behind you.

The other person will undoubtedly act a bit standoffish at first, even if he or she knows that your anger was justified. Their pride will still be smarting. (After all, the truth can *hurt!*) *But don't you be discouraged!* Just be persistent in renewing the friendship. Soon, amiable feelings will return on their part. It'll become evident that your friendship is unconditional and that you intend to be their *true friend* in spite of any standoffishness they may exhibit. When this happens, your relationship with the one you want will take one of its biggest steps toward romantic fulfillment. It is the same principle by which two kids in junior high become best friends after clearing the air with an after-school fist fight!

8

Inducing Emotional Dependence

---

*Principle: People become emotionally ''hooked''
on those persons who can truly satisfy their
never-ending need for human understanding.*

There is a big difference between *loving* and being *in love*. If
you *love* someone, you're still in control of your emotional
feelings—you still have a choice regarding how you'll allow
yourself to feel about, and react towards, that individual. If
you've fallen *in love*, however, you're no longer calling the
shots. You become hopelessly dependent upon (and at the
mercy of) whomever you have allowed yourself to fall for.
Remember: The key to winning the one you want is to first
get that person to become emotionally dependent *on you*—not
the other way around!

Have you ever wondered why it is so common for clients to
fall in love with their psychotherapists? It's because there is a
very real tendency for people to fall in love with those who
satisfy their emotional needs. In an effective counseling session, the client finds that his or her emotional needs for compassionate understanding are being met, perhaps for the first
time. They find themselves becoming willingly dependent on
their counselor for a continued satisfaction of those needs.
They become "hooked" on their therapist.

Likewise, as you learn to satisfy a person's deep-rooted emotional need for understanding, you will in time find them becoming emotionally dependent on *you*. Being successful at love sometimes requires playing the role (to a small degree) of a psychotherapist (and a good one at that!). The better you become at this, the deeper the love that will be felt for you by the one you want. The following tactics will help you to assume that role.

LOVE TACTIC #30 Be There (In Person!)

When Sir Edmund Hillary was asked what compelled him to climb mountains, he responded, "because they're there!" This same principle may be applied to love. The (unromantic, but true) fact is that a person's availability plays a large role in having someone fall in love with them.

The first requirement that must be satisfied, then, is for you to make yourself available to the one you want. You must make your presence *known* and *felt*. This will not always be easy. You mustn't be afraid, though, of "intruding" to some degree into his or her life. Sometimes the greatest love is found, not because we went out and actively sought it, but because somebody pushed it on us at a time when we thought we weren't yet interested. When people buy, it is always from the salesman who was there to sell to them. And when people are ready to fall in love (mark these words very carefully!), *it will always be with someone who is relatively close at hand!*

One enterprising young college student made use of this principle while courting his wife-to-be. He said that even when she wasn't around when he called, he would always leave a message with her roommates so as to keep her constantly aware of his proximity. (Still, he never let her think she had him all sewed up, either! Later, when she'd return his call, he'd be out on a date with someone else!)

So be there for the one you want—even when they don't seem to need or want you! The time will come when they *will* need someone—and you'll be there to step in! Like the patient who has come to depend on his therapist in a time of crisis, the one you want will turn to *you* in their hour of need.

Remember, the underlying message of all advertising is: "If you're in a buying mood, I've got something to sell!" Whether it is an unexpected visit, a quick phone call, or just a note letting the person know you're thinking about them, such small acts of kindness will eventually result in their emotional dependence on you.

The necessity of actually being there in person in order to win the one you want cannot be overemphasized. *Personal, face-to-face contact is vital.* Too often, people try to develop relationships subtly (through the mail, for example) and wonder why it doesn't seem to work. Well, that's the chicken's way out! Building a relationship is no easy task and cannot be accomplished from a distance.

Sure, there are stories of people who met and corresponded by mail at one point in their courtship and are happily married today. But this is only part of the picture. In order for someone to fall in love with you, they've got to get to know you first. Remember, "to know you is to love you," and *getting to know you requires personal, face-to-face contact.*

Why do you think there is such a high incidence of office romances? It's because *work throws people into situations where they have to be together!* This lays the groundwork for further relationship development. You don't have to work with someone before they'll fall in love with you, but you do have to personally spend time with them!

LOVE TACTIC #31 Listen Reflectively

People want someone they can confide in. They really do! They are happiest and function best when there's at least one other person who really knows and understands what they're going through.

And yet, despite this fact, many people seem to have a hard time revealing their true thoughts and feelings to others. How often have you heard a frustrated but caring partner in a rocky relationship lament, "I beg him [her] to tell me what's wrong, but he [she] just clams up and keeps it inside!" Many people find it difficult to open up, even to this kind of sincere prodding.

What can you do to win someone's trust and break down the communication barriers? Start using a method known as *reflective listening*. This technique can be one of the most successful ways to strengthen your relationships with others. Although entire books have been devoted to the particulars of this technique, here we will simply outline the essential keys to listening reflectively. Commit them to memory. Practice them in your relationships with others. You'll immeasurably increase your influence with people in general—and especially with the one you want!

1. *Remain silent while the other person is speaking.* Don't try to interrupt. Let the person talk as long as they want. The more willingness you exhibit to let the other person express himself or herself fully, the more completely you'll help satisfy their emotional need to be understood. This also encourages the person's honesty and openness.

2. *Keep your body still.* Fidgeting conveys impatience and disinterest on your part. You know how important body language is, right? Well, fidgeting can prevent the speaker from revealing what's really on their mind and in their heart.

3. *When the speaker pauses for some acknowledgment that you're really listening and understanding, just nod your head. Restrict your comments to such things as "Mm-hmm" or "Yes, go on . . ."* As one man explained it, "I don't want sympathy or criticism. I just want a listening ear."

4. *Keep your eyes focused on the speaker while he or she is talking.* Not looking at the person implies that you're really not interested in what they're saying. (Think about it. What's the first thing *you* do when you wish a person would shut

up and quit talking?) You can't really expect people to open up to you if they see that you're not truly interested, now can you?

5. *Occasionally, when the person pauses for some response from you, briefly sum up (in your own words, if possible) what you feel they are trying to say.* Try to describe their feelings *even more accurately than they themselves have.* This process will help the speaker to more clearly identify his or her own feelings, while experiencing a sense of unity with you.

How about an example?

TIM: "You know, I've had it with the people at my office!"

TINA: "Go on . . ."

TIM: "All they ever do anymore is pick, pick, pick on everything I try to do!"

TINA: "Sounds as if you're upset because the people at work are overly critical."

TIM: "You got it! They're anxious to jump down my throat for practically nothing, but they never notice anything good that I do."

TINA: "Kind of like they're quick to criticize you for trivial, unimportant things, while totally overlooking your positive accomplishments?"

TIM: "That's exactly the way it is!"

Once you can get the person to respond positively to your summation of their feelings, you can be sure that you're on the right track. You'll be surprised at how anxious people will be to continue opening up to you when you make them feel understood. Believe it or not, this simple technique can keep people talking about themselves and their feelings for hours! It even works with those people who are normally withdrawn and incapable of such communication!

6. *Don't provide any evaluations or opinions regarding the person's expressed attitudes or feelings.* This takes a lot of practice and self-discipline, but don't you sit in judgment!

Don't criticize! But, then, don't sympathize, either! Just try to be objective. Any opinions from you at all (either negative *or* positive) may cause the person to regret having opened up to you. The doors of communication will then close again.

But why not show sympathy, you might wonder? Even sympathy is a type of judgment. It tells a person that you've stopped listening and started to evaluate—before they've had a chance to completely present their case. It casts doubts on your objectivity, even if it *is* a bias in their favor. After all, if you're not completely fair *this* time, how can they have confidence that *next* time, *after they've opened up their soul to you,* they won't find themselves on the opposite side of your good graces? That's emotionally frightening, and will prevent a person from revealing on a deeper level, where you could have even greater influence.

7. *Let the other person reveal himself or herself to you at their own pace.* Don't push. If they seem to wander illogically in their conversation, let them! Don't try to direct any thoughts back to where *you* believe they should go. Just try to understand the main gist of the conversation from moment to moment. If they want to stop talking altogether, fine! Be willing to accept that. Don't try to dig for information the person may not yet be ready to reveal. By providing a non-threatening atmosphere in which they can express themselves *at will*, without fear of criticism or judgment, you'll soon be *sought out* by *them* "just to talk." This kind of patient listening is rare indeed, and they'll soon recognize that being with you satisfies a life-long thirst they've always had. It is doubtful whether anyone else will ever be able to give them such a deep sense of being *understood.*

The more understanding you provide for the one you want, the greater influence you'll have with that person. In addition, that person will become more strongly attached to you. The importance of reflective listening as a tool in your arsenal to win love cannot be emphasized too much. It is perhaps *the most essential tactic of all* to include in your overall strategy for successful romance. Practice and use it!

LOVE TACTIC #32 Avoid Being Critical

Although certain practices are essential for success in love, there are others that must be *avoided*. What's one of the biggest no-no's? *Giving criticism!* Although people invariably try to justify this action by claiming that they're merely trying to help the person "improve," the sad fact is that it very rarely has this effect.

Experience has shown that the only predictable result of criticism is the weakening of trust in human relationships. It's true that occasionally a person will take a critical, judgmental remark to heart and make some beneficial changes because of it. But it *still* makes them less willing to open up and be vulnerable to the person who criticized them. And if you're trying to win someone's love, this loss of trust is completely self-defeating. If they really need to have their faults pointed out, fine. *Let someone else do it!*

Consider your own feelings in this matter. Think about the last time someone offered you some so-called "constructive criticism." How did you react? (Be honest, now!) Not too well, right? Even if the critical observations were true, they were undoubtedly painful! What happened afterwards? Did the experience increase your feelings of *fondness* for that particular individual? Of course not! Even those who don't show their hurt still *feel* it! *And they won't be anxious to repeat such an experience,* so it will only be a matter of time before they'll start avoiding their critic. *Don't let that critic be you!*

You can often be critical without even realizing it. Although you may guard against it in most cases by first asking yourself, "How would I feel if someone were to say this to me?," there are still a few subtle types of criticism that we may not even be aware of:

1. *Using the word "why?."* If you want to really set someone on edge, try using this single-word interrogative about five times in a row in casual conversation. But do so at your own risk! If you end up in the hospital, we'll have to assume that you underestimated the maddening effect this little word can have on people. But don't say we didn't warn you! The word "why?" creates an automatic defensive response. By using it, we unintentionally demand others to justify themselves to us, or to justify their perceptions of things.

   Think about it. Perhaps this is the reason why it becomes so exasperating to an adult when a little child asks "why a thing is so." The adult gives his best answer and the child asks "why?" again. Although the adult may not be aware of the cause of his irritation, it's because the adult's whole value system is put on trial each time that word is used. In some ingenious way that the adult is helpless to understand, the child has made himself the judge, and the grown-up the defendant. That can be exasperating!

   If you sincerely want to understand someone's reasons for doing a certain thing, or believing a certain way, without any intention of passing judgment on their motives, try to soften your interrogation so that it shows you simply want *to understand*, not *judge*. Generally, you can do this by simply saying, "Could you help me to understand some of the reasons why it seems to be so?," or "Could you help me to understand why that course of action seems best?" This will show your willingness to assume good faith on the other person's part, and a desire to understand rather than to judge. And this will be very effective in helping the one you want to feel less criticized.

2. *Giving advice.* As the proverb goes, "Don't give advice. Wise men don't need it, and fools won't heed it." But, you must be informed, they *will* resent it! All advice says, in effect, "You know what you oughta do? Well, let me tell you . . . !" It implies that the person being given the advice is unable to figure out for himself what direction his own life should take. That can be extremely demeaning.

   But people will try to trick you into it, nonetheless! They'll come to you asking, "What should I do?" *But don't fall for that old trick!* What they really need is someone who will reflectively listen to them. If you don't believe this, just think about how many people in your own life have already ignored your advice—even when they came begging for it in the first place! This is because people *already know, in the back of their minds, what they should do.* Knowing *what* to do has never been the problem. They're just experiencing some sort of subconscious conflict about actually *doing it! That's* the problem! And your telling them again what they should do, when they don't really *want to do it*, only enhances their sense of *conflict, guilt,* and consequently, *resentment towards you* for tormenting them further. So save your breath—and advice. What people really want when they ask for advice is *a listening ear.*

3. *Criticizing while claiming you don't intend to.* This can be the worst form of criticism. It feigns friendship, but proves disloyalty. It goes like this, "I don't mean this to be critical, *but.* . . ." It's hard to avoid a tightening of your stomach muscles when you hear these words addressed to you. Often the person doing the criticizing thinks that qualifying his statements in this way somehow makes them less offensive. Wrong! We often feel *more* hurt by someone who pretends to be a friend and then criticizes us, than by a proven enemy who has been openly hostile all along.

   These few subtle forms of criticism that you may unintentionally use in your relationship are by no means exhaustive. They are just examples of the many ways in which you may unwittingly be critical. Be constantly on guard against using them.

The moral of the story? If you want to be loved, *don't criticize!* The less you indulge in criticism, the easier it will be for others, including the one you want, to love you. It's a good tactic to remember. *Avoid being critical!*

LOVE TACTIC #33 Express Genuine Admiration And Praise

Over the years, marital therapists have learned some great lessons about behavior through their first-hand observations of human relationships. For example, it has been noticed that *the intensity of love feelings one person will experience towards another in a relationship occurs in direct proportion to how important and worthwhile they believe they are in the eyes of that other person.* In other words, the more important a person feels that he or she really is to you, the stronger and deeper will be their reciprocated feelings of love, dependence, and attachment for you.

THE VALUE OF FEELING VALUABLE

There is a good reason for this. One of the most important human needs, next to feeling unconditional acceptance, is to feel valuable. Don't *you* need to feel important? Don't *you* need to feel that you have real worth? Well, others have these needs, too! People not only need to feel accepted in spite of their faults, but also need to be recognized and appreciated *for their positive qualities.*

This type of emotional need can only be satisfied by others. Effectual praise and recognition *cannot be self-administered!* Self-praise is just too shallow. No matter how much a person tells himself "I'm great!," another voice deep inside echoes back "Who do you think you're kidding? Can't you see that your credibility is flawed—your motive is suspect?"

Objectivity is the first requirement of a credible judgment. And deep down, all of us intuitively realize that it is impossible to be emotionally detached and objective about ourselves. Just as nature has decreed that no human being can ever actually see their own face, so has it denied them the ability to objectively view their own character. *We need others!* It is only through others that we can comprehend our own existence. Like blind men, we depend on others to describe to us what we "look" like and to tell us if we possess any beauty. If there is anything admirable or praiseworthy in our character, it must first be described to us by someone else willing to be our "eyes." *We just can't trust our own judgment in such matters.*

Now how does all this tie in with winning the one you want? In this way: The one you want is a human being with a need for admiration and praise, which *they are helpless to satisfy alone. If you are aware of this and make a conscious effort to satisfy their hunger in this respect, they will develop a deeper dependence on you.*

THE REASSURANCE OF BEING REASSURED

Most people are literally starving for such emotional reassurance! That's why your effective expressions of genuine admiration for another person will go far in cultivating that person's love for you. In spite of popular teachings to the contrary, the truth is that *the opinions of others always have more effect on what we think of ourselves than all the self-affirmation we can muster.* Patting yourself on the back all day long will not make you even one fraction as confident as a single pat from another person who says, "Well done, John!" or "Good job, Sue!" Thus, recognition of our positive virtues *must* come from another person if it is really going to mean anything to us. By expressing genuine admiration and praise to the one you want, you'll be meeting an emotional need that they are incapable of satisfying for themselves.

ADMIRING ADMIRINGLY

Now that you're aware of the importance of admiring the one you want, you need to be aware of three points in order to express genuine admiration effectively.

First, you must convince the person you're admiring that your appraisal of them has real merit. You must persuade them that your judgments are cautiously discerning and, therefore, accurate—that you are not praising out of a mere sense of loyalty to them. How can you do this? *Spend time getting to know the person. Listen first, in order to understand.*

Earlier in the book you read about the use of flattery to enhance your likability. Although flattery can (and *should be*) sincere, it may be regarded as a *premature evaluation* (perhaps rightly so). Herein lies its true deficiency. Both the giver *and* receiver usually recognize such compliments as superficial observations made *in passing*. Flattery alone, therefore, won't satisfy a person's deeper emotional needs. How can you penetrate more deeply? *By investing the time to really understand the person.* If you really want to get your praise across, you must first spend time getting to know the *real* person behind the mask through reflective, non-judgmental listening.

Second, after you've made the effort to get to know the real person, consciously note that person's good qualities. Every person has traits worthy of admiration. *Every* coin has two sides, and even negative behavior is usually just a distorted form of some positive, but frustrated, trait. A marital counselor once pointed out to the wife of an alcoholic husband that his sneakiness was just a twisted form of creativity, while his tendency to indulge in self-pity was evidence of undeveloped compassionate abilities. She then admitted that his job did require much creativity. And she had always noticed how quick he was to show concern for others. Everyone has good qualities waiting to be discovered. Find them!

Third, having found those qualities worthy of admiration, tell the person what you have discovered and observed! Praise their virtues. Tell them how much you benefit from their association. This will show the person how important they are to you. By so doing, you'll encourage that person to be willing to depend on you for a greater sense of worth. And this, in turn, will draw you one step closer to a fulfilling love relationship!

LOVE TACTIC #34 Supply Sympathy

Everyone needs some sympathy from time to time. Sometimes people try to act like they're above this need, but they usually turn out to be the ones who need it most. By giving sympathy to the one you want in a time of need, you can greatly relieve their emotional burdens and strengthen the bonds of attachment that they feel for you. It is a law of human nature that people gravitate towards those who help them through emotionally-difficult times.

Since sympathy is a form of personal judgment (although admittedly a positive one), the same rules apply for its use as for giving meaningful praise: *Do not give it prematurely!* The Bible says, "He that answereth a matter before he heareth it, it is folly and shame unto him." Spend time trying to understand how the person really feels before offering words of intended comfort. Otherwise, the sympathy you give will appear shallow and won't have the lasting impact you want it to. Sympathy should only be given *after* a deeper level of mutual understanding has been reached through empathic, nonjudgmental listening. What does that mean? *Listen reflectively first!* Then, after your sincere effort to try to *understand them without judging them* has been firmly impressed in the person's mind, offer your sympathy. He or she will be much more receptive to, and appreciative of, the sympathy you offer.

The word *sympathy* means "together in feeling." People need to know they're not alone in how they think and feel about things. All you need to express, therefore, is something along the lines of, "You know, I don't blame you a bit for feeling that way. I'd feel the same way under similar circumstances."

Easy, isn't it? Whether it's fear, anger, or just plain emotional pain that is burdening the one you want, reassuring statements of sympathy will work wonders in restoring them to a happier state of mind. This can't help but make the person more emotionally dependent on you. Don't neglect opportunities to supply sympathy. It's another key to winning the one you want!

9

Shaking Their Confidence

Principle: The more insecure a person feels about where he or she stands with you, the more vulnerable they will be to your romantic advances, and the more intensely they will desire you.

People can never fully appreciate someone's love if they are allowed to take that love for granted. There must be some ongoing apprehension that the love so freely given could be lost at any time. Always remember this: *While people disrespect that which they have in the palm of their hand, and are attracted to that which they can't get, they become absolutely frantic with desire over that which they already possess but are in danger of losing!*

Therefore, in order to successfully stir up someone's romantic passions for you, you must create some uncertainty on their part regarding your feelings for them. It becomes necessary to create a gnawing fear in their mind that, in spite of your general appearances of devotion, you're still constantly on the verge of changing your mind about them. They must be led to believe that, at any given moment, they could lose you forever! When you do this, you've set the stage for romantic passion and love to really blossom.

Insecurity is the mother of infatuation. Doubt is the key to unleashing another's potential for experiencing romantic passion towards you. In the midst of the garden of love and friendship that you cultivate and freely offer to someone, plant some seeds of doubt. This will keep them wondering if they really *do* have you, after all. The following tactics suggest ways of doing this.

LOVE TACTIC #35 Use Silence

What do you think would happen if you unexpectedly stopped talking to your partner in the middle of a date and suddenly became very silent during the remainder of your time together? This simple technique can be one of your most subtle and effective ways to tune up a relationship. It will get the person you're with to start doubting their influence over you and wondering if they're losing your interest. It will motivate them to become more attentive to your needs to try and maintain their hold on you. But this tactic requires fixed determination. Why? Because the unsettling effects of silence on a relationship can disturb *you* as much as *them!* The temptation for you to say something and get the conversation going again can become almost overpowering. Wise is that person, however, who exercises self-discipline and resists this temptation, allowing the power of *silence* to work its disquieting miracle on the one they want. Those who learn to use this tactic appropriately will ultimately reap rich rewards from such an exercise of patience.

The nice thing about silence is that it leaves *everything* to the imagination of the one you're with. And when you're dealing with people's insecurities and self-doubts, imagination is always your best tool. *Telling* a person that they're in danger of losing you is not nearly as effective as *letting them wonder!*

One young man, whose story is not at all uncommon, used this tactic with the girl he later married. He appropriately made use of it at a time in the relationship when she had begun to take his constant attention and tokens of affection for granted. Her appreciation of him was at a low, so one night when they were out together he turned on the silent treatment as he was driving her home. This was quite a change from his normal, outgoing self and, of course, she noticed it right away. As they drove along and the silence continued to build, the quiet completely undid her, emotionally, and shook her confidence. (That's what you have to do: *Shake their confidence!*) For the first time in a long while she felt him slipping away, got quite humbled by it, and asked him to pull the car over. When he did so, she told him with tears in her eyes that she had a feeling she was losing him, and asked if anything was wrong. She was ready to start making amends!

This sort of reaction is not unusual, folks! It worked for one aspiring lover, and it will work for you, as well. Use this tactic to your advantage. Even if the one you want doesn't outwardly appear to be concerned about losing you, you can rest assured that this technique *will* cause them to secretly worry and wonder if such is the case.

Another hopeful suitor, motivated by the above example, reported his attempts to use this tactic on a pretty and popular girl who had previously acted somewhat aloof towards him. Even though she finally agreed to go out with him, she didn't show too much enthusiasm. In fact, all evening long she acted kind of bored and didn't contribute much to the conversation at all. It was as though she were thinking, "Ho-hum, let's get this over with. I can't wait until he takes me home and drops me off!"

Meanwhile, her date forced himself to exude enthusiasm by remaining very talkative and friendly throughout the evening. He acted as though he wasn't even aware of her mood. It was obvious that she felt she had him wrapped around her finger, so her behavior remained like that of a spoiled child.

Then, about ten minutes before dropping her off, he decided to stop paying attention to her. He stopped smiling at her. He even stopped looking at her. And he *completely* stopped talking to her. He just kept his hands on the steering wheel and his eyes on the road ahead. It seemed as though his thoughts were suddenly a million miles away, and he acted totally preoccupied and aloof!

He knew *exactly* what he was doing, but she had *no idea!* This was certainly a stark contrast to the attentiveness he had exhibited throughout the earlier part of the evening. After a few minutes the thought obviously crossed her mind that, uh-oh, she might have offended him. (In fact, that's exactly what she had been unconsciously trying to do—brush him off without making herself appear like the bad guy.)

Even though she had previously wanted to discourage him, she certainly didn't want him to be *mad* at her. So for the first time that night, *she* tried to pick up the conversation herself, while he responded with short, preoccupied answers, as though it was too late. He was polite, but that's about it. He made no efforts to really enliven the conversation, as he had previously. In short, he was *giving her back some of what she had been giving him all evening, and it was beginning to unnerve her.*

His original plan was to just drop her off without any further conversation at all. He wanted to leave her wondering what had happened—wondering if he had suddenly stopped liking her, or what! But then the most amazing thing occurred! She absolutely came *alive* in her efforts to revitalize his interest in her. She not only began making enthusiastic efforts to get him reinvolved in the conversation, but started throwing all sorts of compliments his way and commenting about what a wonderful evening she had been having. And then, when he still didn't seem to be won over, she went to great efforts to convince him to come in for a while. Being condescendingly nice, he went in for a few minutes. However, he didn't stay long.

This is an instance where, with a very simple method, the tables of desire were quickly turned. The girl's attitude toward her date from then on was much more appreciative and respectful.

Don't be afraid to use the silent treatment when appropriate. If you don't pull in your welcome mat once in a while, eventually you'll be completely taken for granted. And that would be *fatal* to your hopes of inducing romantic interest in you by the one you want!

So, occasionally turn on the silence! Yes, let it get good and loud! If you have the courage to let the one you want go home at night with the echo of silence still ringing in his or her ears, it will, ironically, stimulate passion and stoke their fires of emotional desire for you!

LOVE TACTIC #36 Drop 'Em Cold!

Nothing—absolutely nothing—can turn a person's disinterested, uncaring attitude around and make them burn with feverish romantic desire for you like being dumped! Marital therapists have long been aware of this typical, predictable reaction in human relationships. A person's apathetic feelings will immediately turn into passionate longing when they realize that a possession which had previously been taken for granted is in danger of being permanently lost.

A classic illustration of this can be seen in the relationship between Rhett Butler and Scarlet O'Hara in the classic motion picture, *Gone With The Wind*. Throughout almost the entire story, Rhett Butler remains selflessly devoted to Scarlet in his attempts to win her love. Only when he walks out on her in the end with his famous line, "Frankly, my dear, I don't give a damn," does she finally realize that she can't live without him!

This type of situation is more true to life than most people realize. Take a similar incident that happened to a young college woman. A particular young man, whom she had no interest in whatsoever, took a deep romantic interest in her and began courting her with a passion. He showered her with phone calls, drop-in visits, and other bits of attention. She says that, at the time, she just felt kind of annoyed and irritated by it all. In spite of the many brush-offs she gave him, though, he persistently hung in there and showed he cared.

Finally, she got her wish—or, at least, what she *thought* was her wish. He gave up on her! He abruptly stopped coming around and calling. And would you like to guess what happened? "I actually started missing him!," she admitted.

You see, unknown to either of them, the attention and selfless love he had been showing her all along had been developing a subconscious bond of affection inside her for him. It was *only when he dropped her,* however, that she recognized her own hidden feelings and became aware of the fondness that she had developed.

This type of reaction is not uncommon. *It is the rule!* In many cases, though, this unforeseen advantage to the suitor is lost. Why? Because the "dumper" never returns to the "dumpee" to pick up where they left off. By making such a second effort, the dumper would find a much more responsive and appreciative dumpee eagerly waiting for a second chance!

Every salesman knows that, in order to get a customer to buy, there has to ultimately be some sort of urgency element in the decision-making process. Never a message of "whenever you get around to it, it'll be here waiting for you . . ." but "if you don't buy today, you may not have the opportunity tomorrow!" The psychology of selling is especially operative in romance, because the exchange of vows made in marriage is the most important sales transaction a human being can ever make! The message you have to convey is "It's now or never!," and you have to reinforce the impact of this message by letting the person experience a little bit of what life without you can be like.

One girl who had been taken for granted for years by her boyfriend's non-committal attitude finally informed him that she was taking a job offer in another city and moving away. Not thinking that she had the intestinal fortitude to ever leave him, he asked her how she could even think of doing such a thing. She responded, "I love you, Monty, but I can do fine without you." Well, that completely undid him, just as he deserved to be undone, and he proposed one week later! But if she hadn't shown her ability to drop him cold and go her own merry way, they'd probably still be hanging out there in limbo to this very day! Just remember—most addictions are not realized until the source is cut off. If you never let the one you want experience the pain of withdrawal by losing you for a while, they may never become fully aware of how hooked they really are on you!

Wouldn't it be a shame to spend your entire life always being taken for granted by the one you want? Often, one good demonstration of emotional muscle-flexing is all that is needed! Just showing how painful life can be without you will forever keep the one you want appreciative and respectful of you.

Some people claim that such tactics are exploitive and immoral. Not true! Yes, whenever you strive to enhance your own situation through the impairment of someone else's, you are being exploitive. But when you attempt to improve someone else's position, *along with* your own, then that is *good business!* (This is generally referred to as the "Win/Win Philosophy.") Ideally, *both* parties in any human exchange or transaction should benefit, and that is certainly the aim of this book.

Knowing this, be bold and courageous! After you've been persistently selfless in a relationship, don't be afraid to drop 'em cold. Let them know what it's like to live without you for a while! Then magnanimously return to the one you want and give them another chance. You'll be surprised at the effectiveness of this tactic!

LOVE TACTIC #37 Create Competition

Would you like to stir up the latent passions of the person you want and get them to actually *crave* your affections? Then create a challenge for them! Give your special someone something to be jealous of. Don't let them think they're the only show in town! Have many friends of the opposite sex. Go out and spend time with them socially. Don't be afraid to flirt a little, either! It will absolutely amaze you how much a little rivalry can stir up a person's hot-blooded romantic desires for you!

One young man had been dating a girl somewhat casually for four years, until he found out that she had begun dating someone else. Upon hearing this he immediately began to experience passionate feelings that he didn't think he was capable of. Both his appreciation and affection for her were elevated to new heights!

Similarly, the one you want is a latent bomb of passionate feelings just waiting to be set off. All you have to do is light the fuse! Ann Landers once defined love as "friendship that has caught fire!" If this is so, then the key to love (once you have established a good, solid friendship) is to somehow take that particular relationship and create some combustion!

The tactic of creating competition, of course, is as old as romance itself. In fact, browsing through a used bookstore recently, someone came across a copy of *Ovid's Love Books*, written almost two thousand years ago for the citizens of ancient Rome. (It seems that *nobody*, not even the originators of romantic love themselves, has ever been immune to the frustrations brought on by affairs of the heart!) The reader was surprised to find that as long ago as *that*, Ovid was strongly recommending the use of a *rival* to stir up the reciprocated affections of one you want!

But in spite of people's awareness of how well this technique works, many refrain from ever using it! Their reasoning is simple: They've narrowed down their interests to one person, so why waste their time on others? There are two very good reasons to keep yourself in circulation, though. First, if you're to be fully appreciated by the one you want, *then they have to feel lucky to get you.* It is therefore necessary to create the illusion that your affections could be lost *to someone else.* As the one you want becomes convinced of this possibility, their appreciation of you will soar. Second, as you interact with others (dating, just being friends, flirting, or whatever), your own emotional need for companionship will be somewhat satisfied. This will make you a stronger and more self-confident person in other aspects of your life, *including your relationship with the one you want!* This, in turn, will help you to

radiate a spirit of confidence and independence, further challenging your special person to new emotional heights. So
don't become a hermit! Play the field! *It's good for you and for
the one you want!*

LOVE TACTIC #38 Break A Date!

Although breaking a date with someone runs the risk of getting them angry at you, this is precisely why it can be such an
effective tool in winning their love! It shows a person that
you're not intimidated by their opinion of you or what you
do. It's a subtle way of reasserting yourself in a relationship at
a time when the other person is beginning to think that he or
she is "in control!" By breaking a date, you cause the person
to doubt their ability to dominate you, which will in turn fan
the flames of their romantic passion for you. Remember: People crave the unobtainable. They *most* desire to conquer that
which appears invincible. Breaking a date can re-establish the
challenge for the one you want and create heightened interest
and longing for you!

One young man found this out only after a number of failures with previous romances. He stated that he always tried
to be open and honest with the ones he wanted, but found
that his openness only drove them away. Time after time they
would lose interest in him, always leaving him shortly after he
confessed to them how much he cared.

Finally, his instincts began to tell him that it was this very
openness that was destroying all these good possibilities. So
he tried a new tactic. Instead of confessing devotion when a
new relationship began to warm up, he called the girl on the
phone and broke an approaching date.

Afterwards, he says, he spent the night worrying (even *cry-
ing!*), thinking he had perhaps blown one of the best things to
ever come along in his life. *But he didn't blow it!* Where others
had deserted him at this particular stage in previous relationships, this girl fell madly in love with him! You see, he had

10

Keeping Them Interested and Hoping

Principle: In order to keep a person's romantic passions stirred up, they must be given some spark of hope that you could still reciprocate their feelings. Without this hope, interest in you will ultimately die.

Romantic infatuation is a delicately-balanced human response. It thrives on *uncertainty.* On the one hand, too much self-confidence in a person will kill excitement. On the other hand, no confidence at all *will starve it to death.* So while keeping the one you want from any certainty that you're hooked on them, you must still provide them with some glimmers of hope *that you might become so!* How do you do this? Read on.

LOVE TACTIC #39 Resume Contact (After Temporary Lull In The Relationship)

Once you have established some basis for the other person to think you are losing interest, you are ready to proceed. Surprise the person by once again calling them up on the telephone. Start dropping by to see them anew. Most importantly, start asking them to *go* places with you and *do* things together again!

Have you realized yet that part of the overall strategy of this book is to keep the one you want somewhat confused and off balance? You don't want the person to know quite what to expect from you next! This requires that your interest *appear to shift from hot to cold, and then back to hot again!* (You may have heard of this before as *"blowing hot and cold."* Well, it works like *magic* in mesmerizing the one you want!) Any seasoned lover knows the importance of varying the approach while developing a relationship. This type of unpredictability is as essential to romantic survival as *changing colors at will* is to the continued existence of a chameleon.

As a general rule, people are more prone to respond when given a second chance to maintain their affiliation with you. This is because they are much more motivated! They won't always be able to fully appreciate the blessing of your affection until they've experienced the void that comes in its absence. Thus, when an opportunity to regain it comes along, there will be much greater appreciation and passionate desire. So after letting the one you want stew in the prospects of having lost you for a while, resume contact and *give them that second chance!*

Just because the going gets tough does not mean that the relationship is over. It's not over until you quit. So don't be afraid to take a tough stand from time to time, to scold if necessary, or even to break off contact with the one you want. *But don't fail to resume contact and pick up where you left off after the smoke clears. You'll be surprised at how positive the results will be!*

LOVE TACTIC #40 Send Mementos

After you've created some uncertainty on the part of the one you want about your feelings toward them, send a small memento of your affection to revive their hopes. Whether by a short note or a small gift, any message you communicate should remain vague and non-committal. Keep actual words in any written communications at a minimum. The very fact that you are taking the time to send *anything at all* intrinsically gets the message across that you care.

A word of caution, though. Beware that you do not send mementos too early in a relationship, or at a time when the other person is already over-confident as to your feelings for them. If this happens, such additional evidence of your love will only be taken for granted. The very person you hope to win may end up disrespecting (and even despising) you! Yet this is a common mistake of naive lovers. Don't feed an already oversized ego! Remember that passion thrives on insecurity! Before you make a person's day by sending them a token of your affection, make sure that they are experiencing intense doubts about your fondness.

LOVE TACTIC #41 Awaken Physical Attraction

The exhilarating experience of "falling in love" is unquestionably a sex-linked phenomenon. Whether you're consciously aware of it or not, the mainspring of all romantic activities is the instinctive sexual drive of the human species. Its constancy and strength is what keeps husbands and wives and, consequently, families together in the first place. Without it, few people would ever be sufficiently motivated to commit their entire lives to another individual in such an exclusive arrangement as that of marriage.

For this reason, then, it is futile to expect to win someone's heart completely and fully without being able to stir up some physical desire for you. And that, dear friend, is why *kissing* was invented! Serving as much to stir up passions as to gratify them, kissing is an invaluable tool for helping to bond couples emotionally and prepare them for marriage. It provides a subtle incentive for increased physical closeness. It is a tool (much like fire) with a similar potential for good or bad, through proper or improper use. If used wisely, the fires that are awakened can motivate people to make the commitments necessary for permanent relationships. But if allowed to burn out of control, they can destroy any possible hope of permanency in a relationship.

"That's just fine," you might say, "if you can get the person to kiss you in the first place! But how do you get over *that* hurdle?"

No problem. The underlying philosophy of *Love Tactics* is that a person must *act*, not *react*, in order to succeed at romance. So when the other person shows no inclination to initiate affection, *you* be the aggressive one. It doesn't matter if you're male or female, as long as you've already established a firm foundation of friendship and respect before making your move. It doesn't matter who takes the initiative, as long as *somebody* takes this step. In fact, marriage counselors often find that their male clients actually *want* the woman to be the aggressive one in the relationship!

Make sure the one you want is comfortable with your physical closeness by engaging in non-sexual touching first. Everyone desires the warmth of physical affection and human touch. Sometimes, however, the person you have designs on may be uncomfortable either expressing *or* receiving physical affection. Why? Often it is because the person is just not accustomed to close physical contact. In such cases, you may gradually "condition" a person to being touched by you. How? By proceeding very patiently. Begin by touching the person you are with in a non-sexual way, briefly, and from time to time whenever you are engaged in conversation. In time, gradually increase the duration of contact, as well as the frequency. A person's back, shoulders, and arms are generally safe, nonthreatening parts of the body that can be touched with little risk of a traumatic emotional response.

Eventually, however, you must move on to the real thing. When you finally *do* kiss, don't act like you intend to "test the waters" first, one toe at a time, carefully watching every reaction. Just go for it! Act as though you've made an independent decision about what you want to do. Act as if it's irrelevant to you whether the person has any desire to kiss you back or not. Make it seem almost as though it's just a game to you—a lark or a challenge—and that it's no big deal if the person's not interested in kissing you back. (By the way, the first kisses are probably better being short and sweet. A long, passionate, suffocated kiss right away may result in a short, unpassionate, suffocated relationship! Make it a *fun* thing, rather than a *serious* event.)

What happens when the one you want does *not*, in fact, want to kiss you back? That's no big problem either! It's o.k.! Don't let it throw you! Haven't you ever heard of *stealing a kiss!? Trying* to kiss the person is *part of the process of warming them up and instilling the desire!*

Remember—success in romance (or in any other project in life, for that matter) is dependent on your willingness to *act* independently of other people's opinions, and not merely to *react*. *Love Tactics* is not merely a system of guidelines to analyze people and figure out whether their whim of the moment is to *like* you or not. Rather, it's an active system of principles to help you *win their love*, whether they like you at first or not!

What happens if the one you want turns away from your initial kissing overtures? Just carry on with normal conversation as if nothing happened. Ignore any rebuff as if it's no big deal. Later, in the quiet hours of reflective contemplation *after* the date, the seeds of desire will begin to grow. The one you want will begin to fantasize about what it might have been like *if . . .* and the next time they will!

When your kiss is returned, kiss with enthusiasm, but not for *too* long! *You* be the one to end the kiss. Don't make it too long. It's better to leave the person hungering for more, rather than bored by too much! Why? Because if you continue so long that the other person feels the need to terminate the experience, you'll diminish your influence in the future. Remember: *You* be the one to initiate and *you* be the one to say when enough is enough. Keep control of the relationship. It will drive the one you want wild!

As to the more passionate physical intimacies commonly sought and indulged in, you'll find them contrary to the focus of this book. It is strongly advised to avoid them altogether until you are married! This may not be what you want to hear, but past experience only confirms the wisdom of this counsel. Historically speaking, people in nations with strict codes of morality and chastity have been happier. The more intimate physical privileges traditionally reserved for marriage are, in fact, the very *enticements* of marriage itself! To engage in them prematurely and, in effect, *give away your bargaining chips for nothing*, only cheapens your own worth to the other person. It can destroy any chances of developing a real sense of commitment in the relationship. *Somebody* is going to be used, and there will not be enough respect to cultivate the full and complete romantic love necessary to the happiness of both parties. Frequently, however, couples indulge in such mutual exploitation without realizing the damage they are doing to the relationship.

And make no mistake about it—the ultimate goal of *Love Tactics* all along has been to convince the one you want that they should marry you! The most rewarding love of all is that which exists *in the institution of marriage!* But if you surrender your body and soul in full measure to another person prematurely, without requiring them to marry you first, you will unwittingly sabotage your efforts to attain this objective!

Sure, premarital sex is highly prevalent in today's modern society. But look around you! Isn't *unfulfilled love* just as prevalent? You see, it's not that premarital sex is harmful because it's disapproved. Rather, it's disapproved because it's harmful! It spells the difference between a temporary relationship and a *lasting* one.

We will, however, stand by our recommendation to use kissing to enhance a relationship, remembering to maintain control at all times. Prudently engaged in, kissing will help you to secure a commitment and win lasting love from the one you want!

11

Confronting Diplomatically

Principle: When the one you want feels completely
understood and accepted by you,
their ability to resist loving you will go
right out the window. They'll find themselves
falling in love with you in spite of all contrary
logic and their best efforts to resist.

One of the most challenging obstacles you will ever encounter in your pursuit of the one you want is their tentative assessment that you can't handle the truth. They'll figure it would hurt you too much to tell you straight and simple, for example, that they don't want you (other than just as a friend). So, trying to be kind, they'll look for some other way out of the relationship without disclosing their real reasons why.

However,, if you allow them to get away with this avoidance of confronting you with the truth, *that* will actually be the fatal factor and coup de grace to the relationship. You must prove to the one you want that you not only can face the truth, even if it means your being rejected by them, but that you can accept it without being shattered. The more crucial issue here is not really one of their not *loving* you, as their not believing you love *them*.

If they feel that deep down you don't really understand their doubts and fears, then they must conclude you really don't know and accept *them*, as the person they truly are. If they believe that you would be crushed and embittered towards them if you knew how they really felt about you, then they must conclude that your love for them is shallow and *conditional*, based upon some fantasy version of the person you merely *think* they are.

Miraculously, though, as soon as you can demonstrate to them that you can not only sense their true feelings, but *accept them*, even in the face of your own personal rejection, their very doubts and previous objections will become unimportant to them. When being faced with the realization that, "My goodness! Here's a person who *really* cares about me, in spite of myself!," their other reasons for hesitation towards you will pale in comparison with the prospect of being truly loved for *who they are!* And when a person feels truly understood, accepted, and, yes, loved, somehow all the other prior concerns which seemed so important to them before suddenly don't mean so much anymore. They'll find themselves falling in love with you, in spite of all the reasons they can think of why they shouldn't. In the final analysis, after all, love is truly a language of the emotions—not logic!

LOVE TACTIC #42 Confront Resistant Behavior

As you attempt to develop a relationship with someone you want, quite often they will begin to experience doubts about what they are getting into. They will begin to have a number of extremely logical, personally convincing, *secret* reasons why the relationship is all wrong and will, in their hesitation to get in any deeper, begin to show distinct signs of resistant behavior towards you. This will manifest itself in symptoms of moody behavior, guarded and unresponsive communication, disrespect towards you, and, finally, outright avoidance of you.

Such behavior needs to be confronted. If the feelings underlying this type of behavior remain buried, they will ultimately destroy the relationship altogether. But through unselfish and caring confrontation on your part, such resistance may be defused and rendered powerless. Such a method is outlined below. Think of it as a way to show you CARE: Confront, Ask, Reassure, and Empathize.

Confront the person's uncooperative behavior. "Maybe I'm mistaken, but I sense that something's wrong . . ." One of the most exhilarating experiences a person can have in life is the feeling of being understood. We don't want to have to *tell* others when we are feeling distraught. We want them to sense it on their own. *We want them to read our minds!* As one disgusted wife tried to explain to her imperceptive husband as she was in the process of divorcing him, what every spouse wants in a companion is "someone who can read them like a book!"

What people don't often realize is that they subconsciously give clues as to what they're thinking by the way they act. Being sensitive to such unspoken acts and confronting the one you want will go a long way in satisfying their need for understanding. This, in turn, will eliminate emotional obstacles to their becoming committed to—and loving—you.

Ask for a confirmation or denial of your observations. "Am I reading you right? *Is* something actually bothering you? . . ." By informing the one you want of the message that their behavior communicates to you, and then asking for a validation of your interpretation, they will be impelled to come to grips with the actual meaning they intended to convey. "Hmm . . . I *have* been acting rather cold and distant . . . Now, what exactly have I meant by this? What have I been trying to communicate here?"

The important thing is to make the person consciously aware of their own motives in their actions toward you. Indeed, they have already been intimating something all along which, subconsciously, they would like to be able to say to you. All you're doing is calling their bluff and inviting them to say what's on their minds. In order to do that, though, they have to first decide exactly what *is* on their minds, and if it's worth mentioning or not. That requires a little bit of thinking on their part. By inviting them to put their feelings into words, you are forcing them to *crystalize their feelings into defined terms that can be dealt with.*

People often behave in a certain way without really knowing why. Until *they* know exactly how they feel, *you won't be able to help them.* The first step in changing someone's attitude is to get them to recognize *for themselves* what that attitude is.

At this point it doesn't really matter if they're ready to come clean and openly admit their newly-discovered feelings or not. The mere realization that you have *already* been listening to them *with your heart,* and are willing to listen more, will go a long way in stripping the one you want of their power of resistance. In the long run, logic cannot withstand the force of emotion. The sense of fulfillment that the one you want will experience from feeling understood and accepted by you will ultimately override any hesitation they may have about surrendering their heart to you.

Don't push the person for more details than he or she is ready to give. *You don't need to.* You've already brought them to a crossroads in the relationship—to a point where they must make a choice between honesty and repentance. Both are good, and either will strengthen the relationship. Either they must admit what's been troubling them to explain their behavior, or they must *change* their behavior to be consistent with their denial that anything is wrong!

Reassure the person of your intention to merely understand (not judge) on the basis of what is admitted, especially if there seems to be a little hesitancy for them to express their feelings. ". . . Because I'm willing to just listen, if you're willing to talk. I just care how you feel . . ." The biggest reason for breakdowns in communication is the fear of being judged. Human experience has shown that our honest feelings will not always be accepted by others without comment or criticism. Some encouragement from you will be necessary to assure the other person that they will not be thought less of because of their personal fears or concerns.

Finally, **empathize**. Be understanding. Once the person does start to open up a little bit, don't blow it! Just listen, like you promised you would. Don't criticize. Don't try to change the person's mind or show how their reasoning is wrong. If you do, you'll regret it, because it will be a long, *long* time before the person will ever open up to you again.

Let the person proceed at his or her own pace. If you're not yet too competent at reflective listening, just nod your head and say "Mm-hmm . . . Yes, go on . . ." But *don't* pronounce judgment on what is being said.

The acid test, of course, is when the one you want admits to having doubts about the relationship. Don't panic when he or she states that the two of you are not right for each other! Remain calm, no matter how much of a personal rejection their words may become! *You are still going to win out!*

The only way to defuse such sentiments, though, is to allow the person to get them out in the open and have you be *completely accepting of them*. Showing that you disagree with these feelings will only reinforce them in the individual. (Of course this doesn't seem to make sense, but it's really how it works!) Be totally accepting at the time of the discussion, but reinitiate contact with the individual several days later, without warning, and show your intentions to maintain this friendship—even without romance. *You may rest assured that romance will come along in due time.*

Your willingness to let the one you want open up to you at a pace comfortable to them, coupled with your obvious sensitivity that something was bothering them in the first place, will encourage them to rely more and more upon you. This method of understanding is one of the finest ways to communicate love and overcome any obstacles that may be blocking romantic progress with the one you want!!

12

Demonstrating Commitment

---

*Principle: The more convinced a person
is of his or her personal importance to you,
the more intense will be their feelings
of love for you.*

After all is said and done, the ever-present question being
asked by both participants in a relationship is, "How important am I to you, *really?*" All other questions are mere off-
shoots of this one. The more valued each feels to the other,
the greater will be the feelings of love they will have in return
for their partner. The following tactics discuss ways of demonstrating how much you value the one you want.

LOVE TACTIC #43 Hang In There!

Occasionally, after all is said and done, it will appear that the
one you want is completely unmoved by your efforts to win
them over. *But don't be fooled by such deceptive appearances!* This
seeming ability to resist you indefinitely is simply *nature's way
of shaking out those pursuers who are less sincere—and less committed.* The challenge you face is to prove through your endurance that your love is *true.*

In your frustration, though, you may find yourself asking, "What am I doing wrong . . . ?" If you've faithfully done your best to apply the tactics in this book, the answer is, "Nothing." You are on the right track. You just need to keep using *Love Tactics* a bit longer, and more skillfully, as you learn from your mistakes and improve with practice. In due time, reciprocation will come.

You're allowed to make mistakes, too, by the way! It's o.k. if your voice shakes occasionally, or if you fall flat on your face every now and then! You're only human, and people will still love you in spite of these things—maybe even *because* of them. Just keep getting back up and trying again. The only permanent mistake you can really make is to *quit.*

If you have had a handful of dates with a particular person and still feel like you're not making any progress towards winning them over, don't be discouraged! Not too long ago an article was written by Dr. Joyce Brothers that should encourage every hopeful but frustrated lover. Commenting on a survey of married couples, she disclosed that *over half* of the women said they didn't feel that they were in love with their husbands-to-be until *after at least twenty dates!* In other words, you really can *grow* to love someone. Human experience indicates, similarly, that men are likely to grow to love those women who patiently continue to interact with them.

THE VALLEY OF THE SHADOW OF APATHY

How well can you hang in there? This depends on your ability to persevere *even when you occasionally lose all feelings of desire.* In other words, expect that there will come a point when all the excitement you first felt for this special person will temporarily dissipate. You may find yourself thinking, "Wow! Before, all the pain seemed worth it. But now I feel like I don't even care anymore! Before, it seemed like the one I wanted was worth *any* price. But now I'm not even sure I'd want them if they came begging!"

But "this, too, shall pass." You're actually closer than ever to your goal. *Now* is the time when your true ability to love will be tried. This is because love, in its ultimate form, is a commitment of pure will power—with no gratification attached.

This doesn't mean that you don't deserve happiness and emotional fulfillment anymore. You *do*, and it will still happen. But first you must walk through *the valley of the shadow of apathy* to claim your prize! Be forewarned that this experience is inevitable in any developing, worthwhile relationship.

Is it reasonable to ask you to hang in there forever, with no desire or hope of gratification ever again? Of course not! But the truth is: *If you hang in there for a while, in spite of your temporary loss of interest, your feelings of desire will eventually return.*

If you're truly committed to endure to the end, there is no heart that you won't be able to win over. To quote a well-known maxim, "The race is not to the swift, not the battle to the strong, but to him that endureth to the end."

Sometimes it may seem awfully frustrating and you may not know all the answers. But rest assured, *there are answers. There are solutions. There is a way.* It's just a matter of persisting until you find out what that way is. *You can do it!!*

LOVE TACTIC #44 Say "I Love You"

Although earlier in this book we stated that you shouldn't wear your heart on your sleeve, there does come a time in a relationship when it is wise to say "I love you." But that time comes only after you have consistently proven your love—not with *words*, but with *actions*. Words are cheap, and people know it. Remember: "What you do screams so loudly in my ears, I can't hear a single word you say!"

The main thing to remember in expressing your love is that *people run from commitments.* If someone suspects by your words that what you are really saying is, "I want a commitment from you," it may inadvertently drive them away. Use the words "I love you," but try to do it in the context and intonation of, "It doesn't matter to me whether you return my affections or not. My desire for your happiness stands, regardless!" The degree to which the one you want actually believes this will determine your success in winning their love. Your words must somehow convey the message that your love is an unconditional commitment to their happiness, with no strings attached. It mustn't come across as an attempt to back them into a corner where they'll feel obligated to say "I love you" in return. People will *not* allow themselves to be trapped this way! Expect much, gain little. Expect little, gain much!

Remember, though, that these three little words can lose their potency if your actions contradict them. Think of the words "I love you" as the bullet, and your actions as the gunpowder. If you put a bullet in your musket without having packed in a good supply of gunpowder first, then upon firing your weapon your bullet will fall harmlessly to the ground. On the other hand, if you forget to load the bullet, even though you have packed in a good supply of gunpowder, your firearm will not accomplish its purpose, either.

When America first came into being, the nation's position was a fragile one. American armies didn't have the expertise or strength of the Royal British Forces. Nor did America possess the financial resources of England. Colonel William Prescott, who led the American troops at the Battle of Bunker Hill, realized the precariousness of his untrained army's position against much better armed forces. As they observed the enemy advancing up the hill, he advised them, "Don't shoot until you see the whites of their eyes!" He knew they might not get a second chance, so every shot had to count.

Likewise, when you're trying to win the one you want, realize that there will only be so many opportunities to effectively say, "I love you." But don't say it too soon, or the words may seem as though they have no real force behind them.

Patiently prove your love first. Keep watching the one you want advance steadily "up the hill to the slaughter." Then, when you can see "the whites of their eyes" and sense that the words will have the proper impact, *fire away!* If you imagine that you've got only one shot and have to make it count, you'll intuitively be more capable of choosing the right moment to say, "I love you!"

13

Removing Final Barriers

Principle: By backing off from a relationship that you have been aggressively pursuing for some time, the other person will automatically let down his or her emotional guard and, thus, become more vulnerable to your renewed advances in the future.

Often, when a person continues to resist you, it is because they think you haven't gotten the message yet. Oh, yes, perhaps they realize that you are aware of their *declared intentions* to stay uninvolved and uncommitted to you. But they just think you haven't yet realized how *serious* they are about it.

Backing off from the relationship for awhile can take care of all that! The real issue at this point is to convince them that you really understand that they mean business in their determination not to get involved with you. This is the only effective way to convince them that you understand, and in the final analysis you're going to have to demonstrate your ability to communicate with them if you're ever going to win their heart over. If you can succeed at communication, it is only a matter of time until you can turn the tables on their rejecting attitude towards you. Once you've shown your ability to understand, you'll be on much more sure ground to stage your comeback.

LOVE TACTIC #45 Strategically Withdraw

Among the famous legends of ancient Greece is the story of the Trojan Horse. For ten long, frustrating years the Greeks had assaulted the city of Troy in an unsuccessful attempt to win back their beautiful queen, Helen. The walls of the city were impenetrable, though, and the Greeks found it impossible to get inside. Direct confrontation appeared hopeless. Finally, in desperation, they resorted to a much more *subtle (and effective!)* strategy.

The Greeks built a large wooden horse, hiding some of their soldiers inside. They left it standing outside the walls of Troy. Then the rest of the army boarded their ships and sailed away, making it appear as though they had abandoned their cause and given up.

When the Trojans first found the horse, they were fascinated by it. *No longer feeling threatened by a direct confrontation with the Greek army, the Trojans let down their guard.* They not only opened their gates, but *brought the monumental horse into the heart of the city,* as a memento of their unexpected "victory."

That night, while the Trojans slept, the Greek soldiers inside the horse disembarked and again opened the gates from the inside—this time to their waiting comrades who had sailed back in the dark of night. The city was destroyed and Helen was saved. Strategic withdrawal had accomplished in a single day what ten years of direct encounter had failed to achieve!

Likewise, after aggressively pursuing the one you want and finding the stony walls around their heart to be unyielding to your love, employ the Trojan Horse strategy! Make a strategic withdrawal! The sense of relief that most people will experience when they can finally let down their emotional guard will be great, and upon a fresh new encounter with you, they will not be willing—or able—to resist.

The great lesson of the Trojan Horse is that those things that cannot be accomplished by pure force can often be accomplished through strategy. Love is not something that can be forced. But by using strategies of persuasion based on behavioral psychology principles, it *can* be induced!

LOVE TACTIC #46 Enjoy Being With The One You Want!

After all is said and done, love ends where it begins. In a word: *Commitment!* The desired object of love is to have someone who is truly committed to you and to your happiness, but it begins with your commitment *to them!*

The reason why so many love affairs don't work out is because neither person in the relationship was ever truly committed to the other person's unconditional acceptance and happiness. Each one expected the *other* to demonstrate commitment *first*. But when someone becomes clearly aware that you are truly committed to love them *unconditionally*, it is guaranteed that he or she will then love you back. As Ralph Waldo Emerson once said, "Love, and you shall be loved."

When you have accomplished all that you've set out to do and finally win the one you want, enjoy! Nothing material can compare with being happily in love, so take the time to stop and appreciate what you have! Realize that love is worth more than all the treasures on earth. So be aware of this fact, and quietly give thanks to divine providence. Good luck, and enjoy being with the one you want!

Conclusion

There you have it! The formula of the ages! Practice these principles and they will enrich your life immeasurably. It is the authors' fondest wish that you may have a happier life through their application.

The overall philosophy of *Love Tactics* can best be summed up in the poetic words of Emmet Fox:

Love*

There is no difficulty that enough love
will not conquer; no disease that enough
love will not heal; no door that enough
love will not open; no gulf that enough
love will not bridge; no wall that enough
love will not throw down; no sin that
enough love will not redeem.

It makes no difference how deeply seated
may be the trouble, how hopeless the outlook,
how muddled the tangle, how great the mistake; a sufficient realization of love will
dissolve it all. If only you could love
enough you would be the happiest and most
powerful being in the world.

*Dr. Emmet Fox, "Love Card" (DeVorss & Co.: Marina Del Rey, California). Reprinted with permission by Blanche Wolhorn and Hedda Lark.

Good luck with *Love Tactics!* As you apply these principles in your life, you'll become increasingly convinced—as we are—of their effectiveness in winning the one you want.

If you have any questions or a particular problem that you'd like some additional guidance on, please feel free to write to us in care of the publisher. We'd be happy to hear from you! Please share your successes with us, as well! The greatest reward any author can receive is knowing how much their book has helped someone!

MORE
LOVE
TACTICS

Contents

Preface

After the publication of *Love Tactics: How to Win the One You Want*, it soon became apparent that our little guidebook had struck a resonant chord in the hearts of tens of thousands of aspiring lovers all across America. The avalanche of mail we received in response to the book reaffirmed our initial belief: Winning the love of the one you want is, indeed, a most universally shared aspiration!

Many people wrote to us for additional counsel after reading *Love Tactics*. However, most people wrote about problems that were already covered in the book. This was very comforting to us, for it proved how very comprehensive *Love Tactics* actually was. Some readers, however, didn't realize this. They wrote because they failed to recognize the very solutions that were outlined in the pages of the book!

SO WHY THIS BOOK?

More Love Tactics is intended to reinforce the basic lessons of the first book, as well as provide scores of new examples and strategies to enhance your effort in winning the one you want. Yes, it's hard to see straight while in the midst of the painful throes of romantic heartache. *More Love Tactics* provides additional insights, ideas, and understanding to help you accomplish your love goal.

As you read this book, try to shake yourself free from the notion that your situation is unique and different from the rest of human experience. Yes, you may be strongly tempted to believe your situation is exceptional. But your particular love story—or frustration—has been told thousands of times before, and will be told thousands of times in the years ahead. That may not seem very romantic, but it should give you some comfort in realizing that you are not alone.

We have seen the same tales of woe in letter after letter, almost always prefaced with the introduction, "Dear Mr. McKnight and Dr. Phillips, forgive me for writing to ask your advice, but my particular situation is different from any other . . ."

One of the first steps in resolving your romantic difficulties is to accept the reality that your relationship problem most probably does *not* fall into the category of the exception. Rather, it falls in with the rule. Once you reconcile yourself to this fact, you will be positioned to make rapid progress in the application of the love strategies outlined herein.

The interesting thing is, the problems we hear are generally the same. And the mistakes that bring those problems on are usually the same as well. What many people who write to us fail to see, though, is that the very solutions to their problems are found in the tactics that they are discarding. These formulas are found in the book, but many readers do not apply them because they feel their situation is unique. We have not come across a case yet where we haven't been able to say, "The answer to your special problem can be found by applying Tactic #5 or #18 or #25." It does, however, take courage and commitment to do the right thing rather than the easy thing.

Ultimately, the best teacher is experience. For this reason, don't be afraid of failure. Use the lessons from this book, together with the lessons you learn from life, to guide you. This book gives you the keys for success. But just like any skill, it takes practice to be able to implement the tactics well. Practice consists of trying and failing, trying again and failing a little less, trying still another time and starting to get the hang of it, and at last succeeding on a consistent basis. But none of this will happen unless you get out there, do your best, and then accept the consequences.

Don't be afraid of failure in winning the one you want. You won't be beaten until you have quit trying. What happens if you get better at applying the principles found in *Love Tactics* and *More Love Tactics* but discover that the one you want has gotten married to someone else before you've perfected your skills? Realize that, bitter as this disappointment is, you will now be improved enough to go on and win someone even better!

Many people write to us about broken relationships (including broken marriages). They wonder if the Love Tactics philosophy applies in these situations. *Absolutely!* The only difference is that it may take a little longer to win back the one you want. Why? You may have to undo months or years of damage. Sometimes, it may be easier to start out fresh with someone new. But only you can make that decision. To respond to the many questions about damaged or broken relationships, *More Love Tactics* includes an entire section on "Winning Back the One You Have Lost."

AN INSTRUCTION MANUAL IN BASIC LOVE

You can use this book as your main guide to love. Consider it an instruction manual in winning the heart of the one you want! Written in a simple and straightforward manner, *More Love Tactics* is intended to be of practical use to anyone who is trying desperately to win the love of another but may be unschooled in the psychology of romantic love. (Or inexperienced in the school of hard knocks!)

It is easy to make mistakes as a naive, inexperienced suitor. You'll learn techniques in this guide that, along with the experience you'll gain with practice, will help you do *the right thing* to gain or save a relationship. You'll also learn many of the things to avoid that can cause unsuccessful romantic results.

LOVE TACTICS ARE MORAL!

Some people think that there is something immoral about using "tactics" or "strategies" to win the one you want. But think about this objectively. Romantic strategies simply make fair use of the basic rules of psychology.

Like any successful formula in life, the philosophy we offer has its critics. We never realized how controversial the subject of love and romance was until the first edition of *Love Tactics* came out! Some people were offended by the suggestion that one should take control of his/her own romantic destiny.

One female reader wrote to us and said she thought we needed professional counseling for recommending the things we did in *Love Tactics*. We also heard that a group was being organized for the express purpose of suppressing our book! Be that as it may, our philosophy has always been that truth is truth, and will surface eventually anyway. If the tactics we suggest are properly used, they will help you achieve the successful results from love that you have always hoped for.

It is not, as some may think, immoral to take a hand in one's own destiny. There is nothing wrong with using tactics in the pursuit of love. You must put that notion out of your mind. After all, you've been using tactics all your life, even if you haven't been calling them that. And don't forget what the savviest of the savvy know when it comes to romance: *"All's fair in love and war."*

No one is going to take your place in helping you win at love. You sink or swim on your own. Oh sure, it would be nice if the one you want would just tell you what you're doing that's wrong. But that's not going to happen! The determination to do what it takes to win the one you want must come from within.

Holding the door for and being polite to a complete stranger are actually attempts on your part to make a nice impression on someone and get them to think well of you. Striving to say the right things in an employment interview is an attempt to convince a prospective employer to hire you. Efforts to look good and smell nice on a date are subtle attempts to manipulate the way a person feels about you. Are these so wrong?

Most rational people would agree that these simple tactics are fair play in the game of life. Well, the same thing applies in using psychological interactive methods in your efforts to win love. There is nothing wrong with smiling at someone. You know that people are more attracted to a smiling face than a sour one. And if, by some quirk of fate, you discover some irresistible combination of alluring one-liners that have the person you're interested in eating out of your hand, then more power to you! As long as you're honest and care about the other person's happiness, you are morally on the right path.

THE GOAL OF *MORE LOVE TACTICS*: EVERYBODY WINS!

Have you ever gone on a date and not tried to make the very best impression possible? Of course not! You dress up and fix your hair because you want your date's impression of you to be a favorable one. When you go out to eat, don't you tend to use better table manners than you might use at home? When it comes to conversation, don't you try to say those things that you feel are going to be a positive reflection of your intellect, wit, or some other quality? Well, of course you do!

Then doesn't it make sense to use sound principles of psychology that will motivate a person to trust you more, feel more bonded to you, and be emotionally stimulated by your very presence? The answer is very clear. Sure it does!

The science of psychology is the study of how the mind works. Its principles play a definite part in developing a strategy to win someone's heart. As to the criticism that *Love Tactics* teaches game playing, our response is, "What's wrong with that?" Should you take love so seriously that you can't smile and enjoy the challenges it presents? If so, you're destined to live the rest of your life at a disadvantage when compared to those who have developed an ability to "grin and bear it."

Remember, chess is a game, too, but that doesn't mean only immature or immoral people play it! Nor does anyone accuse chess players of being dishonest just because they don't wear their next move on their sleeve. In fact, any chess player who did such a thing would not be very challenging or fun to play with, and would soon find him or herself without any willing partners.

Well, romance is more like a game of chess than you may be willing to believe. And contrary to what you already *do* believe, unpredictability in the courting process is a winning move time after time! Theory may suggest that unpredictability can hurt a relationship and inhibit healthy interpersonal growth, but actual experience and practice in life show the contrary to be true.

The purpose of using love tactics is to provide beneficial results to everyone, both the suitor and the pursued. And that, we assure you, is the intent of the strategies described in this book. We not only want *you* to win, but we want the *one you want* to win, also. Both parties in any human exchange or interaction should always benefit. *More Love Tactics* emphasizes a win/win philosophy—everyone benefits!

We did not make the rules of love; they were established at the dawn of time. As authors, we have done our best to write down these laws as we have seen them in actual use. We've tried to systematize and explain them, so you can best use them to win the one you want.

We believe that forcing someone to do or feel something *against his/her will* is wrong and will ultimately backfire. But what if you can give them a good reason to *want* to do the very thing you want them to do? Wouldn't that be to their benefit as well as yours? Sure. So, this tactical approach can be upheld as moral. That is what the philosophy of this book is all about.

KNOWLEDGE BRINGS POWER AND CERTAINTY, BUT CERTAINTY REDUCES THRILL

As with most things, there is both good and bad news about applying the principles in this book. The good news is that your certainty of success will improve. The bad news is that the thrill associated with chance will diminish.

In everything in life there is a trade-off. Using this book is no exception. Yes, there is a sacrifice you make by using this book. You will exchange some of the thrill of gambling for the increased likelihood of success. However, we believe the trade-off to be worth it!

Some people feel that they may lose respect for someone who responds to tactics. There is some truth to this. After all, how can you outsmart a god or a goddess? (And isn't that the way we want to perceive the one we want?) If you realized that you had the ability to melt someone you had previously thought of as being above you, wouldn't that take away at least some of your perception of that person as an object of worship? Yes.

But look at it this way. You can have your choice. Either throw yourself to the fates completely and have no say-so in the direction of your love life, or take your destiny into your own hands, and use of your love life, or take your destiny into your own hands and use proven principles of success in your romantic affairs. To win, maybe not necessarily a god or goddess after all, but certainly the one you want! Besides, since no person knows everything, there will always remain *some* risk. And, thankfully, *some* thrill.

Introduction

If you're reading this book, you have probably experienced frustration in a love relationship. You may have had past difficulties finding and winning the one you want, or you may be experiencing problems with an existing relationship. Whatever the case, it's our guess that you're not happy with the way things are. It's our hope that this book will help bring you happiness.

YOU ARE GOING TO SUCCEED!

The first thing you must get through your head as you read this book is that *you are going to succeed in winning the one you want!* It's a matter of principle! The insight gained by reading this book will give you an unfailing edge in creating the rewarding romantic relationship that each human being craves and hungers for.

Relationships are not really that hard to maintain, as long as you stick to a few basics. Once you know them, it's simply a matter of practice. As you will learn by experience, from this day forward, so long as you continue to apply what you learn here, your relationships will get better and better!

DON'T FEAR MISTAKES

Consider the following conversation between two friends:

Chris: Say, Terry, how come you always know the right thing to
        do in every situation?
Terry: Well, I guess I just have what you call good judgment!
Chris: Yeah. But where did you get such good judgment?
Terry: Experience, Chris, experience.
Chris: Yeah, but where does *experience* come from?
Terry: Bad judgment, Chris, *bad judgment.*

Just accept the fact that you learn from mistakes and failures,
whether you want to or not. Each effort will make you a better, more
skilled person in the art of love.

LOVE IS BOTH ART AND SCIENCE

People need to be in a committed, loving relationship but often don't
know how to get there. And yet, getting another person to fall in love
with you need not be such a difficult process if you just understand
the psychological principles upon which relationships are based.

What this book does is explain these principles in a fundamental,
scientific way. Some people have claimed that in so doing we have
lost some of the spontaneity and creativity of the love process, as
well as the naturalness of it all. But you have to learn to walk before
you can run. You have to know the fundamentals before you can
become advanced in *any* skill.

Being skilled at loving relationships is really an advanced art
form. In fact, love is both art and science. Can people really go out
and create masterpiece relationships without a fundamental knowledge of what makes relationships work? Probably not! This lack of
knowledge, though, is a basic reason that there is so much romantic
frustration in the world. Many people try to run before they have
even learned to walk.

People have, in effect, been handed the assignment of making a
masterpiece love relationship in their own life. Many not only lack
the skills but also the fundamental knowledge of how to begin! It's
important to master the basics first, in order to apply them effectively. That is how this book is designed to help you. Once armed
with this basic knowledge, it will be your responsibility to get out
there and practice, practice, practice, until you are truly able to
achieve your goals.

KNOWLEDGE IS THE KEY TO
WINNING SOMEONE'S HEART

Choose the most attractive, intelligent, charming, and elusive person you know or ever hoped to know. How would you like it if, within a reasonable period of time, that person became so absolutely wild and crazy about you that, when you finally gave the go-ahead, he/she would willingly and gratefully make any sacrifice necessary for the privilege of marrying you?

Well, you can accomplish just that! What does it take? You'll need an understanding of the behavioral patterns and psychological laws relating to the phenomenon of romance. Then, armed with this understanding, you can learn to design a strategy to overcome the natural human aversion to commitment. Work on this step by step. You can lead the one you want down the primrose path to romantic love fulfillment.

LOVE TACTICS REFLECT REALITY

Whether we like it or not, the Love Tactics philosophy, as expressed here and in our previous book, reflects reality! We want to reassure our readers that we take the recommended tactics and strategies found in these pages very seriously.

Like many of you, we may not always like the way things are, but then our feelings about the way the universe *should* be have no relevance to the way things really are. People will not fall in love with you unless you have given them a reason to. You have to give them sufficient cause, or it just plain won't happen. Knowing what you can do to create this motivation will give you power.

Make up your mind to trust and apply the tactics recommended in this book! You have to learn to stand alone in the application of these strategies.

THE FUNDAMENTALS OF LOVE:
FRIENDSHIP, RESPECT, AND PASSION

This book is to be used as an instruction manual on how to get the one person you want to love you back. It does this in two ways.

First, it explains and defines the three components of romantic love and describes how each one works. And second, it provides many suggestions, which are designed to cultivate each of the parts.

In the art of love, the three primary components are *friendship*, *respect*, and *passion*. Almost every human relationship in existence consists of some mixture of these three elements. The ideal romantic relationship must contain all three, though. Remember, for the relationship to continue permanently, *both* people need to experience all three feelings toward each other.

Relationships having fewer than all three components may be satisfactory but won't be very fulfilling. This is kind of like watching a television show when one of the three primary color emitters inside the set isn't doing its job! Of course, if *none* of the elements is present, you'll have a blank screen.

If you keep improving your skills and use these components as your constant guideline, you can expect to meet and marry the person of your dreams. Love is not that difficult to cultivate if you face reality, take the bull by the horns, and do the right things to nurture love's development.

LET'S GET GOING

You can't change people. This book can tell you only how to win another's heart. You're on your own when it comes to finding a person capable of capturing *your* heart, so choose wisely.

The first part of *More Love Tactics* focuses on you—strategies are given to help you improve the person you already are. In addition, this section deals with the kind of person you're looking for. It will help you become aware of the kind of person you want, and where you can look for your potential dream lover. The second part of the book presents dozens of techniques that are designed to help you in the most exciting search-and-succeed activities of your life. The final section of this book will help those who feel they've already found their love, but have lost or are in danger of losing that person. How to win back another person's love is the theme of this section.

Not all of the strategies found in *More Love Tactics* may be suitable for each person. Some may work better than others, some are more effective with certain people rather than others, some may even seem contradictory to your goal. But sometimes it's the very contradictory nature of this philosophy that will help you succeed in the highly emotional concept of love!

Remember, you must nurture *friendship, respect,* and *passion* in order to win the heart of the one you want. This fundamental understanding is the bedrock foundation of the Love Tactics strategy. Don't depend on the responsiveness of your partner while you are still in the process of winning them over. You must ignore what they say and do while you act out your part on faith. This is the way to ultimately win. Trust that if you cultivate the relationship properly, you will ultimately reap a magnificent harvest!

Part I

BEING AND FINDING THE RIGHT PERSON

The first part of *More Love Tactics* focuses on self-exploration. You might wonder why, in this quest, it is important to be the right person. The answer is that you need to understand yourself in order to become better prepared in the search for the one you want.

The goal of love is the union or merging of two beings into a greater whole. If you're less than whole yourself, you may bring problems and imperfections into the relationship. Subconsciously, everyone seeks the very best person to unify with, but it is important that you, too, are as perfect as you can be in order for your relationship to be happy and fulfilling.

Marriage itself will not bring you fulfillment and happiness. Nor will you be fulfilled if you alone are happy. In order to have the best of both worlds, you'll need to choose the person who has the qualities you most desire, and you must bring the best "you" into the relationship.

1
Looking at Your Character

So you want to win the one you want. That's fine. Primarily, that's what this book is going to teach you. You'll learn how to influence and get the best possible response from the person you desire.

But a relationship does not simply involve the other person. You're involved, too (good thinking)! Why is this so important? Well, if you have problems, the relationship will have problems. You know the saying, "A chain is only as strong as its weakest link." Sure, it's important that you select a partner who provides a strong link, but it is just as important for you to be a strong link as well! You should bring the best possible person you can to the relationship.

In trying to get the one you want to fall in love with you, you must remove as many potential obstacles as you can. For example, the one you want may desire somebody who is good-looking, has a lot of money, or has a certain kind of education. These can be potential obstacles. Regardless of whether or not you can satisfy those "demands," being of good character is paramount. Character can win out over superficial qualities. It may just be harder and may take a little longer to win.

Character can actually overcome the necessity of having a good visual appearance. However, because human beings tend to judge others initially on physical appearance, this can create another obstacle you may have to overcome with your character.

LOVE TACTIC # 1   Make the Most of Yourself

Every person is an embryonic god within him/herself. When people go into therapy, they explore their deeper subconscious thoughts and are able to find the divinity within themselves. They discover that there is good within every person. So the more time you take to honestly evaluate your strengths, as well as your weaknesses, the better you'll feel about yourself.

Even if you're afraid that your core is negative, don't despair. We promise you that it is not. The deeper you go within yourself, the more positive qualities you'll find. This will reinforce your self-esteem, which will reflect in your appearance and come across in your character. Others will notice.

Your feeling of positive self-esteem will attract others to you. People want others to lean on, and they are more inclined to lean on those who feel good about themselves. The more time you spend on introspection, the more vibrant and desirable you'll be.

LOVE TACTIC # 2   Inventory Your Strengths

It's time you get to know more about yourself. Take a piece of paper and write down your strengths and weaknesses. Begin with your strengths. Include things that you've accomplished, ways in which you feel good about yourself, and things that are potentially good about you.

If you have a problem, something that you can change and make better, include it. It's helpful to know your negatives and realize that you're not locked into them! You may not be able to change everything, but just coming face to face with your own limitations is, paradoxically, a strength in itself. It's not so much what you have, but how you face what you have and what you are that makes you a strong person.

You may want to divide your list into categories. Include physical appearance, intelligence, personality, vocational qualities, social qualities, and so on. By looking at the categories, it will probably be easier for you to figure out what your strong points are, as well as weaknesses that you may want to improve. As you feel more confident and become more aware of your strengths, you will be better able to use these strengths to gain the respect and desire of the one you want.

Part of this evaluation process is to determine the factors that make you unique. Each and every person has special qualities that can help make them more desirable to others. By pinpointing these strengths clearly, you will be in a better position to attract the one you want.

Modesty is a virtue when trying to present yourself to somebody else. But modesty is not a virtue when trying to evaluate your own strong points. Be as clear as you can be in knowing your good qualities. Do not restrict yourself from correct self-analysis by being concerned about being too modest. Remember, this is important information that you're not going to be sharing with anybody else. Run with it!

WHAT ELSE SHOULD YOU INCLUDE?

There are a number of things to include in your strength inventory. Identify your positive achievements. When and how were they accomplished? Why are they important to you? How might these achievements be of interest to the one you want? As you analyze your achievements, you may find a pattern in the kinds of things that are important to you. This pattern may help you further identify those qualities about yourself that you value most.

Further evaluate your strengths by using positive adjectives to describe yourself in specific areas. For example, how do you perceive yourself when dealing with emotions? Describe your aesthetic or creative strengths, intelligence, personality, practical qualities, mechanical or productive features, physical appearance, sexuality, and any other areas you can think of.

For additional information, ask yourself how others might perceive you. Consider asking family members (who are more often biased in your favor than any other group of people) what they think of you. Ask colleagues and friends as well. Go to a friend or relative and say, "Could you tell me a couple of things that you find good about me?" Don't be embarrassed. It can really help in the quest to know yourself better.

Strive to build a portrait of yourself that you can be solidly comfortable with, one that gives you the inner strength that can help you win the one you want.

THE IMPORTANCE OF WRITING

Why is it helpful to write down your strengths? By committing these factors to paper, you will gain additional strength in knowing what your strong points are. Not only will you think about these qualities, you'll *see* them in black and white. In addition, a list can point out glaring weaknesses, which you may want to target for improvement.

During those times when you doubt yourself, if you have a written list of your strengths, read them. It will remind you of the positive aspects of your personality. You'll have a reservoir to draw from, and it can be very helpful to review from time to time. Sit down and review, "What kind of person am I?" "Where have I gone with my life?" "Where can I go from here?"

Experts say the best way to get involved in any kind of self-improvement program is to begin by writing out your goals. It provides a structure and can serve as an ongoing incentive to accomplish the things you want to. By taking a written inventory of your strengths, you are giving yourself an incentive to work in an ongoing self-improvement program.

Awareness of your strong points will put you in a better position to know what you can offer the one you want. This will help guide you in your approach to that person.

LOVE TACTIC #3   Be Real

The more real you are as a person, the easier it is for others to relate to you and become emotionally attached to you. Being real means being honest about your frailties and weaknesses. (Although we're not suggesting that you go trumpeting them through the streets!)

Get to know the real you. You are a wonderful human being. Concentrate on that. The real person within you is always easy for others to love. That's where the expression "To know me is to love me" came from. The more a person gets to know the real you, the more he/she will feel attracted to you.

But this self-analysis may be hard for you. What can you do? Focus on the real strengths that you possess (and *everyone* has real strengths). Next, explore those areas that you'd really like to improve, and determine strategies for doing so. You'll start feeling better almost instantly. In fact, you won't even have to accomplish all of your goals to feel like a better, more lovable person. You'll begin feeling this way as soon as you *start* getting a grip on your life! Really!

LOVE TACTIC #4   Believe in Yourself

As a human being, you have undreamed of power. The tale is told by the Hindus of how, in the beginning of the world, men shared godhood with Brahma and the other gods. However, man became lifted up in pride and Brahma decided to take man's godhood away.

Brahma consulted with the lesser gods and asked where to put godhood so it would be safely out of man's reach.

"Let us put it on top of the highest mountain," some suggested, "then man would have a most difficult time redeeming it!"

"No," said Brahma, "someday man will climb even the highest of mountains. That isn't good enough."

"Let us put it at the bottom of the deepest oceans," others suggested.

"No," said Brahma, "eventually man will someday redeem his godhood if we put it there."

Brahma went on, "There is only one place to put godhood, and that is deep within man himself. It is the last place he will ever think to look, and only when he finally comes to that realization will it then be fitting for him to have it back!"

What's the point of this little story? You have great power within, if only you can believe in yourself. The only thing that will prevent you from accomplishing things is your own unwillingness to trust your power. Like Dorothy's lesson in *The Wizard of Oz*, you really don't have to look further than your own back yard to find the essentials necessary for a happy life.

Basically, you can accomplish anything you set your mind to. As far as winning the one you want, don't allow yourself to become disheartened by some illusionary obstacle, or some unfounded fear of competition. Also, don't waste time comparing yourself to others. You are, basically, no better or worse than any other person. Only false perceptions may make you think otherwise. The differences are in image only, not in substance. Therefore, as long as you plod along doing right, you cannot fail.

LOVE TACTIC #5   Improve Your Self-Esteem

Some people believe that they don't have a lot to offer in a relationship. But every human being has infinitely more than he/she can imagine. In fact, the problem is not in what you are but in what you *think* you are or (more accurately) what you *are not*. So many people think of themselves as being unworthy and unlovable. Do you?

Like it or not, you are a product of how people have treated you all your life. How happy and loving were the people who surrounded you as you were being raised? It is human nature to feel lovable if you received a lot of love in your life. But you may feel there is something wrong with you (and thus believe you are unlovable) if you happened to grow up in an environment where you were not loved, or minimally loved, or even emotionally or physically abused.

Here's the truth: Every person is very lovable. Everyone thrives on love and needs it to be happy. However, the love you have received in the past has virtually nothing to do with your worthiness to receive it in the present or the future.

Let's take this a step further. When somebody smiles at you while you are walking down the street, doesn't it make you feel good inside? It makes you feel like that person has recognized something special in you, right? On the other hand, if somebody makes an obscene gesture towards you or yells at you for driving too slow, don't you feel bad? But as strange as it may seem, in both of these instances, your inner goodness or badness had little to do with the way you were treated.

Imagine that you could somehow become invisible and follow the person who first smiled at you. As you followed this person down the street you'd soon realize that he smiled at a hundred other people. He didn't pause to distinguish who was worthy of being smiled at and who was not. And consequently, if you followed the person who screamed obscenities at you, you would soon see that this is how that person commonly treated others.

Our point? People do not love you because you are good. They love you because *they* are good!

So if you are experiencing much rejection in your life, 90 percent of it can be traced to the mentality of the crowd you are associating with! Truly loving people will love you in spite of yourself.

Of course, there are exceptions to this rule. Sure, some people may have a harder time than others when it comes to inviting good feelings toward themselves. You might even occasionally fall into this "difficult to love" category. But, the good news is that when this happens, you don't have to remain this way. You can become easier to love, even by those who would love you anyway. For this reason you should concentrate on getting your act together. It doesn't matter what depths you may have sunk to in your life. You can always ascend to a higher plane by beginning where you are and starting anew. Always remember: "Today is the first day of the rest of your life!"

WORK TO BUILD CONFIDENCE IN YOURSELF

As you build confidence in yourself, you'll be better able to correct deficiencies and problems that arise in your relationships. One thing you may notice as you read this book is that, from time to time, your confidence will increase. After reading a tactic, you may say to yourself, "I know that's true. It's so clear and obvious. If I just do this or that, then I'll have the person I want eating out of my hand."

Knowledge *is* power! And it's so much easier to take action when you understand the forces you're so caught up in. Learn the forces that control a situation, and develop a plan of action in accordance with those forces. Then watch your confidence grow!

Let's talk more about this. What is the real source of lack of confidence and feelings of powerlessness that abound in most faltering love relationships? It comes from a lack of understanding of the forces at play. Let's say that you feel rejection in your love relationship but can't figure out why or how to correct the problem. Ask yourself if you've failed to nurture a trusting *friendship*. Or if you have lessened your efforts to command the other's *respect*. Have you cooled the *passionate desire* in the other person by being too easy to get? Whatever the reason, the setback should be easier to endure because you know it is correctable.

LOVE TACTIC #6   Be Sincere

There is only one thing that can keep you from utilizing your tremendous power, and that is not being your true self! When you were young, were you ever deceived into thinking that being some- one other than the real you would be better? If so, you may have taken on qualities and characteristics in order to become someone other than who you truly are.

You might also deny some of your true nature because you have been told that a good person doesn't have such feelings. It is essential that you don't shy away from the way you truly feel. As one wise saying goes, "Don't let your feelings tell you what to think, and don't let your thoughts tell you what to feel."

Here's something interesting. The word "sincere" comes from the Latin *sincerus*, which means "without wax." Originally, the expression found meaning with the great Italian sculptors of the Renaissance. The truly classic works stood as they were made, while the lesser works were touched up with wax to cover flaws and imperfections.

Don't try to cover your flaws or your imperfections. Let people see you as you truly are, "without wax." The paradox is that you're actually better when you strive to be who you are, nothing more, nothing less.

That isn't to say you shouldn't strive to grow each day, but you should feel good about who you are already. That person who is at peace with the way he/she is, regardless of how unimpressive that may be by the superficial standards of others, is truly beautiful.

Down deep, everyone really wants to be sincere. All you can do is try. Each step closer to accepting yourself and your feelings is like peeling an onion, layer by layer. The more layers you peel, the more attractive and beautiful a person you become. (And yes, there may be a few tears in the process!)

As you strive for sincerity, there may be times when you may wonder if this is really you or just a show you're putting on. Don't worry. Try your best. Don't fear making mistakes. Simply reveal yourself day by day to the best of your ability. Eventually, the insincerities will peel away, and you'll reach a deeper understanding of your true identity.

Now, how can this principle fit in with a strategy to win the one you want? You must strip away any superficial motives. By doing this (at least in your own mind) it will increase your confidence in the rightness of what you are doing. And one of the first things that will help you to be sincere is to understand that what you are attempting to do is pure, right, and good, not only for you, but for the one you want, as well. The tactics will help you make that person happy at the same time he/she is bringing you joy. The power of sincerity works best when your philosophy is *win/win*. It works against you when you consider your own happiness to be a greater good than your joint happiness together.

LOVE TACTIC #7 Learn from Experience

Do you want to know another nice thing about human beings? They have the capacity to grow and change, and to learn from experience. As we do so, we become more and more enhanced. But we must be willing to change as we learn these new lessons of life. Change, however, is a very difficult thing. Most people are resistant to change and, as a result, do not grow as well as they could. You need to learn from then let go of the person you have been, in order to become somebody better. As you do this, you will grow, mature, and progress. That sounds pretty good, doesn't it?

You can constantly change for the better, if you so choose. No matter how bad you feel you have become, no matter how low you may have sunk, if you try to do things differently, presto, your negative impressions can be swept into the past. You have only your future to face. For that reason, don't regret the past. Learn from it!

LOVE TACTIC #8 Start Again (and Again, and Again ...)

Did you ever wish you could start over again, fresh? There is a thought-provoking scene in the movie *Bonnie and Clyde*. One night, gangstress Bonnie Parker turns to Clyde Barrow after having become career bank-robbers with a stream of killings behind them, and says, "Clyde, what would you do if somehow we could wake up tomorrow morning and find out it was all just a dream, if some way we could start all over again—clean?"

Well, your chances of starting over are more realistic than those of Bonnie and Clyde! In a very real way, you can be "born again"! Just start adjusting your attitude. Work to stop making the mistakes you've been so accustomed to making in your life, but don't expect the changes to occur overnight! And anticipate the occasional setbacks that may come from an effort to improve yourself. Just pick yourself up and start again (and again and again . . .).

LOVE TACTIC #9   Be Patient and Persistent

What should you do if it appears that you're not getting the desired results in winning the one you want? Be persistent in the right actions, because they will ultimately bear more fruit than you can use. "Patience is bitter," said French philosopher Jean Jacques Rousseau, "but her fruit is sweet."

An old Korean fable tells of a young married woman whose husband came home after being away at war for several years. After his return, he seemed detached from life and from her. When she spoke he would ignore her, and when he spoke to her it was always with roughness in his voice. He threw tantrums when the food she prepared wasn't exactly to his liking. Often, she caught him looking off listlessly and sorrowfully into the distance.

The woman approached a wise old sage for help. She asked if there was a potion that would restore her husband to the loving man he used to be. The wise old man told her that it would first be necessary for her to obtain the whisker of a living tiger, the prime ingredient for such a potion. The young woman was terribly frightened at the prospect of trying to get a whisker from a tiger. But her love for her husband and her desire for their relationship to be the way it used to be drove her to obtain the necessary ingredient.

At night, when her husband was asleep and unaware of her activities, she left her bed and walked to a nearby mountain where a tiger was known to make its habitat. There, with a bowl of rice and meat sauce as her only protection, she held out the food and tearfully called out to the tiger, beckoning him to come and eat. At first, the tiger simply ignored her calls. But the woman persisted, night after night doing exactly the same thing, approaching a few steps closer on each occasion.

Finally, one night, they were only a few feet away from each other. They stood staring into each other's eyes, neither one knowing what the next moment might bring. At last, the brave young woman took her leave of the tiger. It was the very next night that the tiger finally ate from her hand. The young woman was jubilant but cautious. Each night for the next few months, she did nothing more than stretch forth her hand upon each visit and let the tiger eat his fill.

At long last, one night, the young woman looked deep into the tiger's eyes as he fed from her hand and said, "Oh, please, precious animal, do not kill me for what I am about to do!" Then she quickly pulled a whisker from the tiger's face.

She ran down the trail and went directly to the dwelling of the sage, relieved that the tiger had allowed her to leave freely. When she arrived, breathless and excited, the wise old man examined the whisker carefully to see if it was real. When he was satisfied, he turned and tossed the whisker into the fire, in front of the horrified young woman.

"What are you doing?" she screamed.

The wise old sage gently responded, "Young woman, is a man more vicious than a tiger? You have seen that through patience, kindness, and understanding even a wild, savage beast can be tamed. Surely you can accomplish the same things with your husband."

The lesson, of course, is clear. You can produce all the effects you might desire from a "magic potion" by the way you behave and act towards the one you want. It may require patience, persistence, and determination, but with these three ingredients, you can produce miraculous results.

THE IMPATIENT LOVE TACTICIAN

It is natural to be impatient. You may have the ability to grow and seek better ways of accomplishing things in your life. But, at the same time, don't abandon your efforts before they have been given a chance to produce effective results.

This impatience has often been exhibited to us in letters that read something like the following:

Dear Mr. McKnight and Dr. Phillips,

Thank you so much for writing *Love Tactics*. I have read your book at least three times and have been faithfully practicing the tactics. However, my current relationship seems to be a special case. It doesn't seem to be progressing fast enough. I know you recommend taking your time, but I was wondering if you know of a really fast way that I can win the one I want. I really hate wasting time, so if you could tell me how to sew this one up quickly, I would be most obliged.

Sincerely,
A true believer

We understand this desire to accomplish as much as possible in as little time as possible, but folks, *love takes time*. Once you reconcile yourself to this fact, you will be better able to take advantage of the hidden powers within you. Going too fast is like building a house on a cement foundation that is still wet!

2
Looking at Your Looks

Physical appearance has always been, and always will be, an important factor in attracting others. If you're honest with yourself, you'll admit that everyone (even you) makes superficial judgments about others. Therefore, the one you want is undoubtedly going to make superficial judgments about you that are based on your appearance.

Do the best you can with what you have. Showing pride in your appearance conveys a sense of independence and self-confidence, which is very impressive in itself.

LOVE TACTIC #10 Make a Good Appearance—Always!

Why is it important to make a good appearance? How should you go about doing it?

People tend to judge others in many different ways. Ironically, those things that are most important (how you treat others in a relationship, for example) are the last things that most people tend to notice. The first thing people notice about others is their appearance! Often, someone will judge you on your appearance, and won't give you much of an opportunity to show anything else about yourself. This makes it very difficult for you to show your true character.

There are some things that you can control about your appearance and some things you can't. You know, for example, that there are certain ways that you are genetically made up that give you a certain appearance. Fortunately, however, those things that are most appealing are the things that you can control.

So how can you make a good appearance? Your physical appearance depends mainly on two things: how you groom your body and how you wear your clothes.

Make sure you are well-groomed. Keep your body scrubbed and clean. Make sure your nails are trimmed and your hair is neat and well-styled. Make sure there aren't any hairs sticking out of your nose! Your teeth should always be sparkling clean.

With regard to clothing, wear apparel that flatters your appearance. Be attractive but not too flashy. Accentuate the strengths of your body and minimize the weaknesses. If you have any doubts, consult individuals whose opinions you respect. Get constructive suggestions on ways you can enhance your appearance. Don't simply accept somebody saying, "You look great!" The statement may be more out of politeness than anything else.

When you go into a store to purchase something, aren't you generally attracted by the product that is packaged best? Of course, you are not a commodity that is on sale in a store or supermarket, but you *are* trying to package yourself to look best for the one you want. Keep that in mind when getting yourself ready to go out and meet people.

Remember, the way you look and the way you carry yourself say a lot about the kind of person you are. Make sure you dress in a way that will communicate these messages to the one you want.

If you continue to have questions about the best ways to present yourself, consider consulting an expert. There are fashion consultants available in practically every city and town. These individuals objectively and constructively will help you.

Yes, it's true that beauty is only skin deep, but in so many cases your first appearance can enhance or diminish the potential for follow-up. Get into the habit of always looking presentable. Be neat, clean, and well-groomed before you go anywhere. Be ready for any unforeseen opportunity. You never can tell when you might meet somebody who may turn out to be the one you want. So it's important to pay attention to your appearance at all times. Every person can look better. There is always room for improvement!

LOVE TACTIC #11 Use Reverse Psychology to Overcome Physical Shortcomings

A person's perceptions of the physical world are influenced by psychological forces. Yes, you can improve your appearance by using makeup and dressing nicely, but these methods are not nearly as effective in securing a committed love relationship as strategically employed psychological tactics.

Everyone has heard of reverse psychology, but few people really understand how it works. Reverse psychology is based on the principle that human beings don't like being told what to do. They tend to resist being directed in their decision-making process. For example, have you ever been told that you couldn't do a certain thing? Didn't you notice that, from somewhere deep inside yourself, you found the motivation and strength to do that thing? (Or at least *tried* to do it?)

Here's another example. A person has mixed feelings for you. On one hand, he/she may love you as a friend but secretly struggles with the fact that there is no romantic attraction to you (no matter how hard this person tries). Do you want to know a great way to get someone like this to become attracted to you? Look that person in the eye and say (in a teasing but understanding way) something like, "It's not easy to endure my beastly looks, is it?"

This statement shows your insight into the other person's hesitancy. It also shows your acceptance of his/her negative perceptions. In other words, you'll be taking the wind out of secret defensive sails!

You'll be amazed at how well this tactic works. When that person's lack of attraction towards you was a secret, it would have been impossible to look at you with complete, uninhibited desire. But once you have openly acknowledged your awareness of this fact, and even given emotional support to the person without condemnation, don't be surprised if a sudden, unexplained, genuine attraction begins to develop towards you.

GOOD LOOKS ARE NOT NECESSARY

Do you feel locked in, as far as your looks are concerned, by what nature has dished out to you? This shouldn't be a problem. Look around you! Everywhere in society there are what you might consider average-looking or even unattractive individuals who are married to extremely good-looking people. There is an important principle at work here: People fall in love, ultimately, based on factors other than looks. These factors have the ability to direct emotions more so than visual appearance alone.

You've heard that "love is blind." This means that looks are relevant up until the magic moment when a person falls in love with you. At that point, you will suddenly become very good-looking to your love. It will be as if someone had cast a magic spell on that person.

What does this ultimately mean to you? Don't feel limited by insufficient looks or even ugliness! At least, not once you get the person to fall in love with you. Up to that point, you might encounter resistance; however, that can and will change if you do the *other* things necessary to get that person to fall in love with you. It can and does happen every day, all over the world. This kind of achieved love often turns out to be stronger in the long run than "love at first sight."

Billy Joel, who has been admired and envied by a countless number of guys across America for marrying beautiful model Christie Brinkley, was asked about the lessons he had learned from his relationship with her.

"One hell of a lot," he was quoted in a *Parade* magazine article. "For example, I understand now that guys don't have to be matinee idols. Guys think that to get the beautiful girl, they've got to be model-handsome, but women are a lot smarter. They look for character, humor, personality, sexuality, power, money—the whole package."

Let's summarize this misconception. Yes, it's true that in order to win the one you want, that person needs to be physically attracted to you. But, if you use the right psychological approach, this will not be an insurmountable obstacle. You can *become* physically attractive to the one you want!

LOVE TACTIC #12 Overcome the Superficial-Looks Factor

If you don't have a high opinion of your own looks, it's important not to be discouraged. The fact is, you can still win the one you want. But what if you're depending on your looks to do the job, and they don't happen to be your strongest point? Reality dictates you're going to have to be aware of this. In this way, you can put your real strengths to work for you. (As long as you practice the principles in this book, you will have *every* other advantage necessary!)

Some hearts can be soft and vulnerable. In these cases, it's not that difficult to *become* handsome or beautiful in the eyes of the one you want in a relatively short period of time. Just follow the strategies outlined in this book.

On the other hand, what if you're trying to win someone who is a little bit more difficult to reach on an emotional level, which is where love is found? Don't be discouraged. *It can be done!* If you cultivate love by using your understanding of the tactics outlined in this book and work to perfect your relationship with diligence, you *will become beautiful* in your beloved's eyes.

It takes faith to believe this. But in the long run, the one you want will ultimately fall in love with you, based on how you interact with that person. Looks, over the long run, are not nearly as important as actions.

3
Finding the Right Person

There are two major factors that determine how happy your relationship will be. They are *being the right person* and *finding the right person*. In the beginning of Part I, we discussed some of the skills that you need to develop in yourself in order to make any relationship succeed. Now, we are going to discuss the tactics that can be helpful to you in *finding* the right person.

Remember, one factor over which you have very little control is the character development and emotional maturity level your spouse has already attained in his/her own life. Be careful in choosing the person you're trying to win over. Once you've won 'em, you're stuck with 'em! Don't plan on changing the person's basic character, because it simply can't be done! You can't knock down Hoover Dam using your skill as a sledgehammer (what you will get is one heck of a headache trying).

A relationship is made up of two persons. Two individuals. Two minds. No matter how determined you are in doing your part to make a relationship successful, if the other person refuses to cooperate, it can make your life *hell*! If you doubt this, talk to someone you know who has gone through a divorce. In other words, even after you do everything you can to cultivate a happy, productive relationship, your total "success" is still dependent on the whims of the person you've chosen as your counterpart. Even though you may be the most perfect person in the world, if the one you have won as your "forever-partner" decides to behave like a rogue or a shrew, you are going to have a miserable relationship. And a miserable life.

"There's just no justice in the world!" we can hear you thinking. Well, that's right. No matter how much effort you put into the relationship, if your partner refuses to be cooperative, you can't make it work by yourself.

So, what's the answer? What can you do to give your relationship a better chance for success? Even though you can't *control* how the one you want is going to interact with you, you can at least maximize the odds that he/she will be a pleasant companion by *choosing well to begin with*! Exercise utmost powers of discretion! Remember the wise man who said, "Before marriage keep your eyes wide open, but after marriage keep them half-shut!" Now is the time to give maximum consideration to the kind of person with whom you *really* want to spend the rest of your life.

We're not saying that you can absolutely ensure that the one you want won't ever go sour on you. Even your most objective, in-depth evaluations cannot predict the future. One's best laid plans can still go awry. And even after reading this book and doing the most meticulous planning possible, you may still wake up several years from now married to a demoness or a cad!

But do realize that human personalities, for the most part, are pretty consistent through the years. If you watch carefully for signs of trouble, you can be tipped off, in most cases, ahead of time. More times than not, we've heard unhappy divorced people say unequivocally that the indications of incompatibility and incongeniality, which eventually became too great to bear, had been there from the very beginning. They just hadn't realized how significant the early indications were. So, do yourself a favor. Face up to potential problems *now* while there is still time!

Instead of feeling sorry for yourself because you are alone, be thankful that you still have the opportunity to choose wisely. Remember, *choosing well* when selecting who you will be spending the rest of your life with is a major part of the secret of your future happiness. Finding someone who is agreeable to you is at least as important as finding someone who turns you on. The Love Tactics philosophy, of course, advocates going after someone who qualifies on both counts. As spiritual leader James E. Faust once said, "It's not near so important to find the right person as it is to avoid the many who are bad. . . ."

Remember that even though you have the power to win 'em, *you can't change 'em*, so make sure this person is someone you really want. Over the coming years, you're going to be investing your very soul in a relationship with this person.

4

Thinking About the One You Want

It's very important to spend a little extra time thinking about the qualities you're looking for in another person. Think of those words of wisdom, "An ounce of prevention is worth a pound of cure" or "To be forewarned is to be forearmed." We could go on and on with our efforts to caution you. But we are quite aware that human beings are emotionally vulnerable to falling in love. And, as we've pointed out before, to be in love is to be out of control.

It's essential that you select the kind of person you want to be in love with while you still have some control! And that's *early* in the stages of the relationship, *before* you let yourself get involved in a situation where you're not thinking clearly.

LOVE TACTIC #13 Inventory Desirable Qualities in Others

Start writing a list of the qualities in others that are important to you. You'll probably want someone you find physically attractive. Include specific talents and interests that are compatible with your own. Focus on the person's character. Is it important for the person you desire to be honest? Should he/she have an awareness of their own deeper feelings? Do you desire maturity, level-headedness, humility, or pride in your future partner? Should he/she be loving? Consider these and any other qualities that may be important to you.

Writing them down will give you a clearer picture of the kind of person you're looking for.

Your list will probably develop and change over a period of time. Things that were once important to you may no longer be. That's okay. It reflects growth. When you see the words in writing, and you consciously acknowledge your current desires and wants, it's much easier to make the transition and let go of things that are not important to you anymore.

Back in Chapter 1 we discussed pinpointing your own strengths and weaknesses. This is very important. But it's less important to precisely specify the unique qualities you seek in the one you want. Yes, it can be helpful to know what you're looking for in a potential partner. But don't let this limit you in getting to know *many* people and making *many* friends. While it's true that you may be a bit more restrictive in your selection of a mate than of your friends, it is actually to your benefit to suspend early judgment lest you misjudge a potentially worthy candidate and thereby miss a good opportunity altogether!

Sure, there's nothing wrong with identifying those general qualities that you're looking for, such as friendliness, attractiveness, and a warm personality, but to be as specific as you were when you inventoried your own strengths may be inappropriately restrictive. Feelings may change. Your priorities may change. Certain qualities that initially may not have been important often grow to become more important to you as you develop a relationship with somebody.

Most people might say that they are looking for their "dream person." How can you really know if you have met your dream person until you get to know that person thoroughly? The only reason this thought occurs to us is because so many happily married couples have told us that they were swept off their feet by someone who they initially never thought had the capacity to do it!

If you feel that you've met your dream person based simply on your first encounter, you're obviously reacting primarily to that person's physical appearance. In order to know if you've really met your dream person, you must get to know his/her soul. You must know that person deeply and completely. So don't be too restrictive when you inventory the qualities you are looking for in the one you want.

LOVE TACTIC #14 Be Careful in Your Selection Process

There are two kinds of love that everyone needs: unconditional and conditional love. That about covers it! The one you want also has those same needs. Therefore, to meet another person's need for unconditional love, you must be a mature person who has the ability to love *first*. You'll need to recognize the importance of reaching out to someone without necessarily getting anything in return.

When you commit yourself to another, which is the ultimate act of love, it's for better or for worse. In the beginning, you must love first without reciprocation. This fulfills the unconditional aspect of love that others need so desperately yet are powerless to obtain on their own. This doesn't mean that you must always love without being loved in return. But, there *is* a necessity for you to love unconditionally at times and bring happiness to others (particularly the person who will be your "other half"). Through your example of nurturing another by fulfilling their need to feel unconditional love, they will be inspired to love you back. You will be loved, in essence, because you loved that person first. You will have won that aspect of their love that is conditional.

"Shouldn't romantic love be *un*conditional?" you may ask. Good question. True love *is* unconditional. But when it comes to narrowing down the field to determine the one you're going to marry, it's certainly necessary to draw some limits.

Although we stress the importance of loving others unconditionally, we do so with the explanation that some love in life *has to be* conditional. For example, marriage, because of its exclusive nature, necessitates some conditions attached to the love involved. Marriage is selective by nature. It involves a process that includes making discriminating choices about the one you want to marry. It is not wrong to be selective in choosing someone to spend the rest of your life with. In fact, it is essential.

Since you obviously can't marry *everybody*, you're going to have to be selective. This process implies placing limitations and conditions on the person you love.

This is a paradox, in a way. It really is possible to both love someone conditionally *and* unconditionally at the same time. The whole process of courtship and marriage involves expectations and conditions. Falling in love is both a selective process (choosing someone you want to marry) and an exclusive process (eliminating all the others) at the same time.

So, what does this mean? It means that if you're going to choose one person to spend the rest of your life with, to some degree your love (and romantic love in general) is conditional. On the other hand, you must love that person unconditionally. Finally, you must hope that your love is returned unconditionally.

Unfortunately, you're not always going to be treated the way you want. Much of how a person behaves towards you depends on their own upbringing and individual experience. These are things that you have had very little or nothing to do with, things that you can't change. Even the best-intentioned people are unwitting slaves to their past. You shouldn't blame anyone for his/her imperfections. The best you can do is be alert to problem traits before getting too deeply involved in the relationship. Then make a conscious decision as to whether or not you are willing and/or able to live with these difficulties. Once you make your decision, you must be willing to live with it, for better or worse.

A wise man, Joseph Wilson, once told us, "The way to avoid resenting someone for not repaying money that they owe you is to forgive them *before* you lend the money. If you can't forgive the person beforehand, then don't lend the money at all." This good advice can be applied toward acceptance of another person. Decide early in the relationship whether or not you can accept the other person "just the way they are." If you cannot, then our advice is to move on to someone new (or reconcile yourself to misery ahead). But don't blame the other person. Blame yourself, because you have been forewarned.

WHY SOME PEOPLE DON'T GO AFTER THEIR FIRST CHOICE

Many people settle on their second, third, or even tenth choice for a marriage partner. Why? Generally, this is the result of insecurities. Often, people don't feel confident that they can win the one they *really* want, and they would rather be rejected by one whose opinion doesn't matter as much! There's nothing wrong with feeling this way, except that it deprives you of your true desire.

Make up your mind to be faithful to your true inner feelings. If you *never* go after the one you really want, then you're either destined to go through life alone or with someone with whom you're not completely satisfied.

LOVE TACTIC # 15 Aim High

Too many of us tend to compromise what we are looking for in a mate. We tend to settle for less because true romantic attraction is always accompanied by feelings of intimidation. To avoid these insecure feelings, we often defer the opportunity until the time when our heart won't be beating so hard (not realizing that a pounding heart and romantic desire cannot be separated).

For example, two sports jocks were in a health spa, discussing the romantic frustrations that one of them was encountering.

"Listen," one was counseling the other, "you've *got to quit thinking of her as being better than you!*"

His advice was good but easier said than done. *You can't be fully excited about someone you're not a little bit intimidated by.* Think about this. If you look upon the one you want as being inferior or equal to you, much of that excited feeling toward them will be lost.

A 25-year-old male we know fell head over heels for a girl and began to exhibit the typical symptoms of sweating palms, twisted tongue, and thundering heartbeat. The frustration of not being able to maintain control over these physical reactions was very disturbing to him. He felt a truly mature person would not have these reactions.

That same person told us of an experience he had a few years later. One evening, he needed a date on the spur of the moment and called up a girl with whom he was friendly. After securing the date, it crossed his mind how calmly and coolly he had arranged things. It occurred to him that maybe he had finally reached the elusive pinnacle of maturity where he was no longer intimidated by the opposite sex.

But then the awful reality began to sink in. The truth was that there had been very little pleasure or joy in this pursuit. It had been almost a mechanical action. Without a little bit of fear or worry about being rejected, there was no real fulfillment. Reconcile yourself to being a little afraid when going after the one you want. Make up your mind to accept that bit of fear, and keep in mind the words of the Roman poet/philosopher Ovid, who wrote, "Let every lover be pale; that is the color that suits him."

LOVE TACTIC # 16 Act in Spite of Fear

Don't be ashamed of being intimidated by the one you want. This is a sign that you're not compromising. Being intimidated is not a sign of cowardice (you can only be intimidated if you are attempting to face your fears). *Do* be ashamed, though, if you let your fears turn you away from *trying* for the one you want. Don't avoid the challenge. Don't restrict your attentions to the ones with whom you're able to maintain perfect control.

"But," you may ask, "how can I get enough control of myself not to blow my chances of winning? What should I do if I get tongue-tied and have butterflies in my stomach all the time?" Practice, friend, practice! And don't be concerned with blowing your chances just because the one you want may notice your fear. Courage is a virtue. Although he/she may be amused at first, if you continue to act in spite of your fears, you will eventually command respect!

It is *not* your excitement over another that will cause that person to lose respect for you. The attention will be flattering. It is seeing you *ruled* by your fears, rather than acting *in spite of them*, that will cause a loss of respect.

This, then, is the answer. Feel your fears, but continue to act *in spite of them*. Your level of anxiety can't help but flatter the one you want. And your level of courage in the face of your fears cannot help but command respect.

As a side comment here, though you may not believe it, know that the one you want is *not* really better than you. It is simply an illusion. Nonetheless, it remains as intimidating *as if it were the truth*. Such illusory perceptions are part of the human condition, which all of us are subject to. So we might as well accept this illusion, realize it for what it is, and then act in spite of our fears.

You've got to feel like you are somewhat lucky (which implies powerlessness) before you can fully appreciate winning another. And this can only be the result of going after someone you weren't quite sure you could get! Therefore, it is important for you not to shrink from scared feelings, but to deal with them. As we have said, if you're choosing your love object correctly, not settling for less than you should, then those feelings of anxiety will unavoidably come. (Actually, the feelings will come the very moment you consider the possibility of going for that person.)

One young friend of ours named Steve frankly shared his frustration (similar to many of yours, no doubt) when he said, "I've given up. I'm just tired of that knotted-up feeling in my stomach that comes with trying to win the girl of my dreams. It's just easier to quit trying."

Our advice to Steve and anyone else with the same feelings is to accept those feelings as an indication of being on the right track! If other people don't experience this same degree of anxiety, it may be because they've settled for less. Your reward will be greater.

Our guess is that most marriages are lackluster due to unnecessary compromise. But don't let this happen to you! Today, marriage surveys show a relatively high level of dissatisfaction. Part of the reason for this may be that many people marry the convenient person, rather than making a go for someone that really rings their chimes.

We realize it may be tough to act in spite of your fears, but look at it this way. Being single, you are still free to keep from making a mistake that could lock you into an unhappy relationship. There is a reason that destiny has delayed your fulfillment in love until now, and it may be so you can read this book and know that you still have a chance to do it right! This is your chance, now, so don't blow it! Today truly *is* the first day of the rest of your life—one with a bright and glorious future!

No person, no matter how great or celebrated, can be supremely happy with a companion unless some degree of insecurity was felt at some point in their relationship. Insecurity is merely the springboard to an exalted love relationship.

LOVE TACTIC # 17 The Best Won't Come Easy

Have you ever felt that you are the kind of person who is attracted only to people who don't want you in return? Don't panic! You aren't the only one! Everyone has experienced this feeling to some degree.

There is a very good reason for this. Most people have a sort of internal screening mechanism that prevents them from wanting someone who would love them back too easily. If you ever attempt to somehow short-circuit this "automatic pilot system" and force yourself to settle for someone who provides very little challenge, you may find yourself experiencing an emotional letdown. This can undermine your determination in continuing to pursue the relationship. In other words, you'll probably get bored with the person, and a superhuman effort will be required to find enough motivation to hang on. The best internal motivation comes from challenge. That's why we tend to be attracted to people who are "hard to get."

It is human nature, though, to want what you can't have. So it is only natural to be attracted to those with a certain degree of aloofness and disinterest in long-term commitments.

Now don't be too hard on yourself for possessing this seemingly "go-nowhere" inclination! There is actually a very good reason for being this way. Things that are most worthwhile always require the greatest effort. But this doesn't mean they're impossible to achieve. There are three possible choices in love and romance:

1. Settle for somebody who wants you from the start, but whose initial and undying enthusiasm completely douses your initial flames of desire and kills your interest.

2. Endure the ongoing frustration of wanting someone you believe is so much better than you are that you could never have that person, and so, consequently, you never try.

3. Accept the fact that you *can* win the one you want, but you're going to have to do just that—*win that person*. In the initial stages of pursuit, you may experience some resistance. However, that initial struggle is going to make the victory all the sweeter when you finally do triumph!

Obviously, the best choice is number three. Go after the person who may be a bit elusive at first—okay, maybe a lot elusive—but whose love will be the most rewarding once won. (And, just think, your subconscious has known this fact all along! That is why we tend to sit and fantasize about the ones who are "hard to get.")

You must also have the insight to realize that there is no other way to obtain the rewarding kind of love you truly seek. This insight will give you the courage to go after the elusive love. How can anyone be fully happy with someone they have never been infatuated with? Yes, it is possible to be happy without the infatuation/passion side of love. But it's not possible to be *as* happy, and certainly not possible, in any case, to be *completely* happy.

Psychologist Robert J. Sternberg of Yale University has pointed out that the most fulfilling "consummate" love between two individuals *must* include feelings of infatuation on the part of both lovers, or else the relationship will be lacking in its completeness.

Yes, "companionate love," as he calls the friendship element, may be better than utter loneliness. But without passionate infatuation, the relationship will lack an important element of loving, which humans instinctively desire. It might be better to go through life single, ever hoping for a complete "consummate" love, than to be locked into a relationship full of regrets and dreams of what might have been.

We do not say this to encourage or justify divorce. If you are already married, identify what is missing and try, with your spouse, to fill the void. If you are still single and looking for a spouse, don't feel bad about your inclination to want the potential mates who are elusive. But take our word for it: They *can* be won. Get in there and do it!

LOVE TACTIC #18 Aim for a Proper Balance

The best relationship is one involving a companion who is willing to please you, and who expects to be pleased, as well. The ideal partner is one who is relatively kind and good to most people but not necessarily a pushover. He/she won't treat you unkindly when you initiate pursuit but will still present a challenge. In other words, the ideal person to pursue may well be the one who tells you that he/she likes you as a friend but feels nothing more than that! This is the one who is willing to be your friend but is not willing to commit him/herself to you. When you finally win that person, he/she may turn out to be the most committed of all! This is the perfect challenge.

The wrong kind of challenge is one where the person you want is rude or dishonest in the beginning. In all likelihood, if such negative behavior is shown to you *before* you have won over that person, you will be in for more of the same later on!

You very well may win the one you want, only to find that the relationship isn't what you'd hoped it would be! A person who mistreats another displays a lack of respect. This type of person will also disrespect *you*, if you ever let your guard down. And that's no way to maintain a relationship.

So look for a person who indicates a willingness to reciprocate your friendship within a reasonable amount of time. What's reasonable? You have to decide that for yourself, but you should probably see some positive signs within three months.

Don't be discouraged if that person doesn't fall in love with you right away. But do give it a second thought if he/she wouldn't even make a decent friend!

5

Knowing Where to Look

There are places to look and there are places to look. In this all-important quest for the one you want, one thing is certain: You are not going to find anyone by sitting at home and doing nothing. You have to get out there. Because there are only a limited number of hours in the day, you should go to the places where you are most likely to meet the kind of person you're interested in. People often spend much of their time meeting people with whom they are incompatible. Why? They may be looking in places where their true interests do not exist.

Most people are interested in developing a permanent relationship. Bars, however, are not usually conducive places to meet people for long-term relationships. And yet, people, out of desperation (or because of not knowing where else to look), often go to bars.

It is amazing the number of people who know intuitively that the kind of person they really want won't be found hanging around in bars, looking for some one-night stands. But time after time, that is where so many begin and end their search.

But what should *you* do? Begin by asking yourself what kind of interests the person you hope to spend the rest of your life with might have. That can help you to figure out where to look.

If that's in a bar, fine. But we're willing to bet that that's the least likely place you'd want to look for a partner in a lasting relationship. More likely, the kind of person who you'd look up to and respect will be working to progress and develop his or her own life, rather than becoming stagnant, sitting around on a bar stool, waiting for something to happen.

LOVE TACTIC #19 Select Desirable People/Places

If you really want to go out and meet people, there are certain places that are better to look than others. Realize that birds of a feather flock together. The people you want to meet, the ones with similar interests to yours, are going to congregate with others of a similar mind. (If you want to hunt ducks, don't go out in the desert!) You've got to go where that type of person would go.

The best places are those that deal with the mind and the spirit. Go to places that are conducive to meeting people, people with whom you hope to develop a deep, meaningful relationship. You can find such places in your neighborhood, at work, or in school. Social gatherings and charitable organizations are other great places for meeting people. In order to determine where you are going to look, you must have a clear idea of the kind of person you are looking for.

Put yourself in the place of the kind of person you want. If you were that person, where would you go? What kinds of activities would you be interested in? The answer should give you an idea of where to start.

If you're interested in meeting a woman, consider the kinds of places that women are more likely to be found, such as cooking classes, art galleries, health and exercise clubs, and concerts. If you're looking to meet a man, ask yourself where a man would likely go. Auto shows, conventions, and sporting events are good places to find men. However, you can expand on these places to include virtually any type of gathering where people congregate. Let's discuss some of the best "people places."

INSTITUTIONS OF LEARNING

In the opinion of many, the college campus is the primo place to find a companion. Why? Because people who go to college are developing their minds and their hearts. Many desirable people are there. That's why college is considered the paradise of young single people. It's an ideal place to meet a life's future companion.

A guy we knew in college was very successful socially. Although he was a macho athletic type, surprisingly his major was in clothing and textiles. One day, when walking past one of his classes, we noticed that he was the only guy among thirty female classmates. Talk about an opportunity for meeting members of the opposite sex! Although we're not advising that you build your entire college curriculum around looking for a companion, we do think that you might consider taking a class or two for this purpose. For example, you will probably find more women than men in cooking or home economics classes, and more men in auto-shop classes. Yes, there are more and more signs of "equality of the sexes" these days. But practically speaking, you might consider taking classes that are predominantly attended by members of the sex you want to meet. Your friends may laugh at first, but we promise it will be *you* who gets that last laugh!

INSTITUTES OF RELIGION

People often meet quality, desirable people at a house of worship. Take advantage of the many social opportunities included in any religious environment. If you don't belong to a particular religion, go through the yellow pages or the community announcement pages and look for different churches or religious groups in your area. You might try one to see what it's like.

SERVICE INSTITUTIONS

There are many public-service organizations where people with common interests can meet. Joining a political or civic group, or a charitable organization can be an ideal way to meet people who believe in a particular cause. By getting involved in such an organization and sharing the interests of others, you can easily cultivate friendships.

When you work with community-volunteer organizations, you will be doing something positive while getting to know others under comfortable circumstances. Working together toward a common goal is conducive to developing a good positive relationship.

WORKING THE WORKPLACE

Although the workplace is considered by many to be a good place to meet people, it does have possible disadvantages. You may have to deal with office gossip, resentment from co-workers, and scorn from your superiors. A new set of problems may arise if the relationship doesn't work out.

However, if you are willing to accept the possibility of these consequences, you may find that looking for someone at work is an ideal scenario. Why? Because you are thrown together with people constantly and regularly in a way that makes it easy for friendships to form. These friendships often have potential to grow into more than a friendship if both people are interested.

SINGLING OUT SINGLES EVENTS

Many well-run singles events are ideal settings for meeting people. It's a lot less nerve-wracking to be among people who are all there for the same reason—to meet someone. Well-established singles activities, such as those run by religious organizations, have the potential to help people cultivate meaningful relationships. Just like anything else, there are "lemons" in any area. So you may have to do some research in order to find out what activities exist, where they are held, and what's involved in getting involved. Newspapers, libraries, and "word-of-mouth" are good information sources.

OTHER INTERESTING IDEAS

Almost any public place where people go to shop or browse can be used to get a conversation started with another. For example, if you are in a bookstore and spot someone who looks interesting, consider sliding up next to that person and asking some questions about the books he/she is looking at! Showing interest in what that person is checking out may lead to a more lengthy conversation.

This tactic can work in virtually any store or shopping situation. You'd be amazed to know how many people meet the one they want in a supermarket. In fact, there are certain supermarkets that have set up "shopping-for-singles" hours when the supermarket is closed to all but single individuals.

Some common meeting places, though, can be less than desirable. Bars, lounges, social clubs, and restaurants, for example, are problematic. These types of places, which are conducive to one-time meetings, generally attract people who are not inclined to develop their minds. Rather, these places are geared toward meeting a person's more immediate gratification needs, not their long-term welfare and happiness.

Remember, you can meet new people almost anywhere. When thinking of possible meeting places, let the sky be your limit. The number of desirable "people places" should be limited only by your imagination. Be creative, experiment, and have fun!

LOVE TACTIC #20 Play the Numbers Game

One principle of success, which holds universally true whether it is in sports, business, or romance, is the Numbers-Game Theory. This theory basically says that the more people you meet and interact with, the more likely you will be to meet the "right" someone.

Realize that, yes, even in the game of love, success is statistical. Even if you didn't know a single love tactic, if you had unlimited time to approach enough people, there are those who are capable of sustaining your interest and who would fall in love with you with minimal effort on your part.

But, with a superior understanding of the principles of love and romance, you'll greatly increase the number of those who will favorably respond to you. Still, realize that if you combine the two factors, knowledge and numbers, you can have an even greater harvest of success.

Although quality is what you are really looking for, many people feel that quantity helps lead to quality. You have to pan through a lot of sludge to find one or two gold nuggets. The more people you interface with, the greater the probability of finding the person who is right for you. So, get out there as often as you can, in as many settings as possible, to meet people.

Remember, the more people you meet, the more *quality* people will be among that number. So increase your chances of finding someone simply by meeting more people. Don't sit back and wait for love to come to you.

There is, however, one drawback when playing the numbers game. The more people you take the initiative in getting to know, the more you will experience rejection. Keep in mind that rejection is often a natural part of the early stage in a relationship. What happens for some people, though, is that too many rejections cause them to lose their confidence and the incentive to try. Subsequently, these people wind up decreasing the number of times they go out to meet people. If you find yourself in this situation, what should you do? Look at the numbers game as a salesperson would. The more people who respond negatively, the closer you are to a person who will respond positively!

Plan on going out and having fun. Don't look to meet the person of your dreams the first time out. And remember: When people reject you the first time you meet them, they aren't really rejecting *you*— they don't even know you! With your use of love tactics, they may grow to love you. The main idea of meeting many people is to give you a chance to do some preliminary screening and find the one who most pleases *you*!

Remind yourself that when you go out there looking, there are some people who are not going to interest you, so you shouldn't spend an excessive amount of time with them. Concentrate on filling your life with positive relationships and leave the negative ones behind.

Babe Ruth is well known for the record number of home runs he hit in his lifetime. But did you realize it took him 1,330 strike-outs to achieve those home runs? Once, when he was in a batting slump, he was asked what he did to get out of it. "I just keep goin' up there and keep swingin' at 'em," the Babe answered. "I know the old law of averages will hold good for me the same as it does for anybody else, if I keep havin' my healthy swings. If I strike out two or three times in a game, or fail to get a hit for a week, why should I worry? Let the pitchers worry; they're the guys who're gonna suffer later on . . ."

So, when it comes to your love life, be like the Babe. If you seem to be in a slump, don't stop going to the plate. Keep getting into that batter's box and remember to take healthy swings! A healthy swing means using love tactics to the best of your ability.

Sure, you may strike out a few times. But just remember, you have to hit only one major home run to make your life rich, meaningful, and worthwhile!

LOVE TACTIC #21 Consider Referrals

Meeting people by going out on blind dates that have been set up by friends (the referral system) is probably one of the most unharvested fields of romantic potential. Even if you don't fall in love with your blind date, you may have an opportunity to meet others through him/her.

Are you resistant to the idea of meeting somebody through friends? Many people are. However, there are ways that this type of meeting can be a comfortable experience.

Begin by thinking of all the people you can approach for help in providing referrals. One of the things that you should do early in your search, is let as many people as possible know that you are looking. You may find it embarrassing to approach some people, but there will be plenty of those who will understand and be willing to help. Of course, this doesn't mean that every friend and acquaintance you approach will immediately give you a list of names, addresses, and telephone numbers! But if you let them know what you're looking for, they'll keep your request in mind. You never know when you'll get a phone call from somebody saying, "Hey, I've got someone for you!" People are itching to play matchmaker!

How do you seek out a referral? Be up front. You can say to your friends, "Do you know someone who would be a good person for me to date?" You can also use a more casual approach by mentioning that you're interested in developing your group of friends. Ask if they know of any people who might be fun for you to meet. By emphasizing the casual, fun aspect of potential relationships, you won't sound desperate.

Gerald Ford, former President of the United States, met his wife through the referral method. His friends gave him Betty's name and phone number. He called her up, took her out, and the rest is history.

A WORD OF CAUTION

Try to be as non-judgmental as possible. Don't give your friends a lot of restrictions or qualifications in their search for someone to introduce you to. Keep it simple. Tell them you're looking for someone who might enjoy going out with you. Take your chances. And don't be quick to let your friends know if you are displeased with their selections. This will discourage them from trying again. You never know when that next person just might be the one! Also, don't look upon each date with desperation. Rather, view the meeting as one step closer to a future companion.

If your friend asks what kind of person you're looking for, draw from the list you made (Love Tactic #13) and mention a few (not all) of the qualities that are important to you. And don't be discouraged if the person you are introduced to doesn't live up to those qualities. It's still a step in the right direction toward meeting the one you want.

Remember, there are millions of single people out there sitting home alone night after night, people you would be thrilled to be with (if only you could find them). Imagine that these singles have friends who might be the key to making a love connection.

Are you afraid to meet somebody through friends for fear that you won't be compatible with that person? Many people feel this way, but it really doesn't matter. Why? Because each new person you meet opens up an entire network of possibilities for meeting others. For example, let's say you are set up with somebody who you think is a real jerk. It could turn out that his/her roommate is really great! Maybe that's the one that you're going to be happy with. You never know, right? So don't burn any bridges prematurely. And, friend, if you're still looking for the one you want, then the time is still premature.

Part II

WINNING THE ONE YOU WANT

By now, hopefully, you've done everything you can to make sure you are bringing an emotionally whole person to the relationship. You should be feeling good about yourself and should be eager to develop a great relationship. You have learned the importance of choosing a person who is emotionally stable, and one who meets your criteria for the person you want to spend your life with. You should have a good idea of where to look, and your search should be starting to pick up some momentum.

Now it's time to learn the "tricks of the trade" in cultivating your love object's desire for you. Your goal? To plant in that person the longing for a lifelong partnership. Let's move to the strategies that will help you to achieve this goal.

Succeeding in a relationship is like succeeding in anything else. *Knowledge is power!* The better you understand what makes a relationship tick, the better you can make it work. Remember this: There is always a reason why a relationship succeeds or fails. If you don't understand what has gone wrong in past relationships, then you're still at the mercy of fate. A correct understanding of what went wrong is *vital* to your future success! So the key to romantic success is knowledge. And this book is designed to help you to gain that knowledge.

6
Combining the Right Ingredients

Winning the one you want is not very tough, as long as you know the steps. "When all else fails," as the saying goes, "read the directions!"

It is the same with love relationships. A good relationship is simply the result of combining certain ingredients. So once you have the recipe, it's just a matter of following it! If your love life seems confusing, let's try to simplify it a bit. It's time for a return to the fundamentals of love. Let's go back to the basics!

Romantic Love = Friendship + Respect + Passion

Romantic love is really just the combined feelings of *friendship*, *respect*, and *passion* that two people feel for each other. In order for someone to fall in love with you, first they must have trust in you as their best friend, one who makes them feel good and happy. Second, they must experience some sense of powerlessness in obtaining and holding on to you in the relationship, so that they feel "lucky" and "blessed" to have you.

LOVE TACTIC #22 Proceed on Principles, Not Reactions

Don't be passive in your quest for love. Be aggressive! Get out there and meet people. As you start developing contacts and begin meeting more people, don't waste your time trying to figure out what a person thinks of you. Early attitudes are usually irrelevant because they are still so new and changeable. Invest your time instead in doing the right things to promote love and create good will. In this way, the one you want *will* like you more and more as the two of you continue to interact.

A common mistake people make in their quest for reciprocated love is to spend time trying to figure out if the other person really likes them or not. This defensive position is not a good way to start.

Would you like to know something amazing? Most people never seem to learn that the key to success in relationships does not lie in putting up a never-ending succession of trial balloons to test the winds, but in simply putting on the jacket of courage and braving the elements, whatever they may be. Why hold back from committing yourself to action until the environment is perfectly hospitable? It sounds great, but you'll probably wait forever. There will always be adverse winds to shake your balloons!

In other words, the momentary whims, the passing moods, or the temporary negative feelings shown to you by the one you want *does not a relationship make!* Just make up your mind to ignore what the other person might be thinking about you. Act. Don't react.

Growing feelings in a developing relationship are still very transient. They can be downright misleading and should be ignored when it comes to plotting your love strategies.

Whether the one you want "likes" you today is not really relevant in your quest to permanently win that person's heart. Countless married couples who are very happy with each other today report that initially one (or both) of them disliked the other. There will be many times along the course of winning another's heart when they will, indeed, question whether or not you are the one for them. The course of true love never did run smooth. Ignore their doubts! You are going to win their heart anyway! This is a battle of wills, and you must keep your determination strong.

Whether the one you adore likes you from day to day is as insignificant as whether a child gets moody toward his parents on occasion. No matter what the attitude is today, it's bound to be a little bit different tomorrow. And, as long as you cultivate your fields with the proper nutrients, any changes will be for the better.

And yet, it's a very common reaction to let your whole plan and intention revolve around whether or not the one you want smiled at you today, showed interest, or called you on the phone! Letting your behavior towards the one you want center around such "clues" as what they think of you is almost as naive as deciding a relationship could never work out because "I'm a Gemini and you're a Capricorn!" (Sorry, astrology lovers, but as Shakespeare said, "The fault, dear Brutus, is not in our stars, but in ourselves.")

Love responds and grows according to what you put into it! So quit wasting your time trying to figure out how much progress you've been making during every step of the relationship. Don't sit around wasting valuable time trying to calculate how much the person likes or dislikes you. It's all irrelevant until they're totally in love with you, anyway. That's when you've won the game.

Don't choose your future mate by compromising and settling for someone who likes you easily, without having had to work for it. Instead, decide who would be a great companion (whether he/she seems to be attracted to you from the start or not). Then, by applying the various tactics and strategies you learn, set out to win that person. Every relationship has a future if you just handle it right!

DON'T BE AFRAID OF TEMPORARY SETBACKS

Never be discouraged—you have to win only once to win at all! Dreams of a lifetime can come true in a single day.

Whenever things go wrong in a relationship, there are always very specific and definite reasons why. Relationships don't go sour without a reason. There is always a traceable cause. As you apply the principles in this book, you will be amazed how a "hopeless" situation can turn around and work out after all. That, in itself, will increase your confidence a great deal!

Don't feel discouraged, no matter how many times in your life you may have been rejected. Remember, it takes only one triumph to make it all right forever. As Shakespeare wisely said, "All's well that ends well." That's exactly how it will end for you if you just make up your mind and stick with a winning strategy to achieve your goal!

Realize that having one worthwhile relationship with the person you love will make what the rest of the world thinks of you insignificant by comparison. In a *Parade* magazine interview, TV/movie star Ted Danson was asked what effect losing his hair was having on his self-confidence. He responded, "I have to be sexy for only one person these days—and she thinks I look like a cute monk!"

Freud commented on the effect that being loved has on humans. He said, "It is amazing how bold one becomes when he knows he is loved!" You'll be surprised at how much stronger your self-esteem will be when you find that one person who makes your life complete. Suddenly, what others think of you becomes less important.

Every salesman who survives in the business eventually learns this secret: You can't judge your next sale on the last ten. For just when you think there's nobody in the whole wide world who wants what you've got, somebody will come out of nowhere and ask where you've been hiding. You will win if you don't give up! And once you start winning, the effect on your self-confidence will cause a positive mental attitude that feeds on itself! Nothing succeeds like success.

THE MORE YOU LOSE, THE MORE YOU WIN!

You must realize that one of the keys to winning is not to be overly concerned about losing. It's actually a matter of statistics. The law of averages will always bring you success as long as you hang in there and learn from your mistakes. In life, you win some and you lose some. This has nothing to do with your worth as a person, nor is it a reflection of your intelligence, talents, or attractiveness. Coming out on top has nothing to do with your natural abilities at romantic endeavors.

What does winning have to do with? It has to do with your *developed skills* in the field of love and human relationships, and that comes from *experience*. Experience doesn't save you from making mistakes, it just keeps you from making them as often. That's why you hear the expression, "If at first you don't succeed, try, try again!" Continued effort in the face of failure will eventually lead to success.

Many people, even though they know the right tactics to use, fail to use them for fear that they will not work. Others fear that they won't implement the tactics correctly. Put these fears aside! No matter how badly you think things may turn out, it is always better to apply love tactics (even a bit awkwardly), rather than to do nothing at all! Take setbacks as part of the game plan. At least you'll gain experience. And that experience will increase your winning percentages in the future! Don't let your fear of losing the one you want paralyze your ability to act, even though you may not feel sure you are doing the right thing. In spite of the fact that you'll learn correct principles from this book, it is only experience and practice that will help you steadily improve your abilities to implement them skillfully.

Sure it hurts when things don't seem to go right! But we promise that if you keep trying and don't get down on yourself, then your abilities will keep improving until you are virtually irresistible when it comes to affairs of the heart!

SUCCESS IS JUST A MATTER OF TIME

Don't ever be discouraged and think that you are not going to win the one you want. If you stick with the tactics you *can* have the one you want, though it may take some time to accomplish your objective! You may feel temporarily defeated along the way. But even though instant success is never certain, it is virtually certain that *failure need not be final,* as long as you continue to persist. When you feel beaten, know that the authors of this book are standing behind you all the way, reassuring you that principle will win out in the end!

Of course you've heard how important persistence is to success in life. But this principle is especially important when it comes to developing romantic loving relationships between people. As Calvin Coolidge reportedly put it, "Nothing in the world can take the place of persistence. Talent will not; nothing is more common than unsuccessful men with talent. Genius will not; the world is full of educated derelicts. Persistence and determination alone are omnipotent. The slogan 'press on' has solved and always will solve the problems of the human race."

What we sincerely hope is that, armed with the understanding of what the one you want really needs in a relationship, you'll have the courage to remain *persistent* in your practice of applying these principles and meeting those needs. If you do, you're sure to succeed in your relationship. But if you surrender hope and give up too soon, then there will be no continued attentiveness to and nurturing of the relationship, and it will wither like a flower without water and sunshine.

There is a universal need today for knowledge on how to behave in love relationships. This universal lack of knowledge is matched only by the widespread embarrassment people experience in admitting that they *want* such information! How do we know? One reader of *Love Tactics* wrote to us and confessed that he had read the whole book in the bookstore because he was too embarrassed to take it to the cashier! We don't mind your being discreet when reading this book, just make sure you do *use* the tactics!

LOVE TACTIC #23 Take the Initiative

You can't just sit back and wait for somebody to come to you. You have to go out there and do everything in your power to make your dreams of love come true.

Sure you'd like it if the person who could make you happy for the rest of your life came out of nowhere and swept you off your feet! You may even fantasize that the one you want is going to come and find you.

There are plenty of people out there waiting for somebody to show interest in them. So get to work. Go find them. Show them a lot of attention. Take some initiative, and it'll have a magical effect. It will sweep that person off their feet! And they *want* to be swept off their feet. They really do! It's a universal human desire. Taking the initiative will give you real strength in your attempt to win another's heart.

Not too many people really take the initiative the way we're describing. That's what creates such great opportunity for you. So if you make that attitudinal shift in your mind and say, "I'm going to take the initiative," you'll become a magical person that others will sit up and take notice of.

LOVE TACTIC #24 Be Aware of the Pitfalls of Premarital Sex

In spite of stressing the importance of marriage in this book, we should make it clear here and now that marriage is merely a *means* to an end, and not the end itself. The end you should be seeking is a secure, permanent-companion relationship with someone you're in love with and who is in love with you. Getting married to just anyone is not that hard. But getting the one you love to commit their life to you . . . now, that's a real challenge! And the only way to get someone to make such a commitment is if that person really wants you.

It is human nature to work hardest for something you have yet to receive (as opposed to working off a past obligation). It's easy to put off making sacrifices for something you already possess. Therefore, if you give of yourself sexually before marriage, you run the risk of surrendering much of your mystique. It may also weaken your ability to command emotional respect from the other person.

Often, people justify engaging in premarital sex by stating that there is a chance of sexual incompatibility if one marries without "trying out the goods" first. Famous sex consultant Dr. Ruth Westheimer's response to this philosophy is that "sexual compatibility" comes naturally when a couple truly love and care about other.

Similarly, syndicated writer Jean Marbella stated in a nationally published article that living together before marriage could actually backfire on a couple. Research from the University of Wisconsin showed that a substantially higher divorce rate existed among couples who cohabitated before their marriage. Theoretically, couples who live together before marriage supposedly work out their differences before tying the knot. However, experience has shown this theory is not necessarily true.

In other words, no matter how good it sounds in theory, in real life, playing house before the marriage vows is just not a good idea!

Writer Sue Browder made a point in an article entitled "Is Living Together Such a Good Idea?" which appeared in the June 1988 edition of *New Woman* magazine. She writes, "If you're interested in marriage, keep in mind that most live-ins never marry. . . . If you do marry, divorce may be the price of having lived together first." She then cites a 1985 Columbia University study, which suggests that the people in only one in five cohabiting couples eventually marry each other.

Are you getting the picture? Sexual familiarity before marriage appears to have a negative impact on the long-term prospects of a relationship, pure and simple. And, of course, with the very real dangers of sexually transmitted diseases, it is critical to be concerned about this potentially negative impact on your health.

7

Presenting Yourself Positively

You must gain the respect of the one you want in order to win their complete love. To do that, you have to appear to be an asset. So if you want to be wanted, if you expect to be wanted, you must make sure that you are perceived in a positive light.

LOVE TACTIC #25 Practice Your Presentation

Many people, in their attempts to win the one they want, experience nervousness when they first meet people or try to develop a relationship. It happens all the time, right? So what can you do? Remember the famous (modified) saying, "Practice makes better!" Sure, in some cases, and with regard to certain behaviors, practice may make perfect, but it is a much more realistic goal to keep working to improve your performance than it is to try to be a perfect person— there is no such animal!

Some people may be uncomfortable with this idea, feeling that they're better off being spontaneous. In some cases spontaneity is good, for it keeps you from appearing too "canned" or stiff in your approach. But practicing the way you act and practicing your presentation can help you be much more confident during an encounter. Paradoxically, this growth in confidence from rehearsed preparation will help you to be more spontaneous.

Some people use a procedure called *imagery* to actually envision how they are going to act when they first meet or spend time with someone. Research has shown that this process of visualization can increase the likelihood that you will behave in the way that you have imagined.

If you'd like to use this imagery technique, sit down, relax, and close your eyes. Then mentally play out a scenario of yourself in a certain situation. For example, consider what you perceive to be the potential rough spots when you find yourself in a social encounter, and then visualize yourself the way you'd *like* to behave during these rough times. Keep running this scene through your mind over and over again. This procedure should help you gain enough confidence so that when the time comes, you can act similarly to the way you have mentally pictured it.

In addition to imagery, there are other things that you can practice before going onto the romantic battlefield. For instance, practice saying aloud the words you might use to introduce yourself or to start a conversation. Practice responses to possible questions that may be asked of you. Picture how you carry yourself. Practice the way you smile, walk, and talk. You can even practice the way you yawn!

These techniques will help you demonstrate confidence, although you shouldn't appear to be so sure of yourself that it turns off the other person. As you gain confidence in the way you present yourself, you'll also gain control over the situations you encounter.

Although practicing by yourself has merit, the best practice takes place when you actually enter the "battlefield." Sure, you may make mistakes. But don't be afraid of messing up. There's a song by Billy Joel called "Don't Forget Your Second Wind," which is about how every person, being human, has the right to make mistakes and still come out on top. We all learn from our mistakes.

Practice really does make things better. You have to make mistakes in order to progress. The only way to make mistakes is by experiencing real-life situations and implementing different techniques you've learned. That's the only way to find out what works and what doesn't. And if a technique doesn't work, ask yourself, "How can I do it better?"

The most progress in your abilities to be a "love charmer" will come through an even mix of rehearsing strategies in your mind and actually getting out there and making mistakes in your attempts. Don't spend too much time practicing at home. Too many people sit back and think about their tactics too long. Remember, visualize your strategy in action, then get out there and act! The best way to improve your skills is by blending principle with practice.

LOVE TACTIC #26 Use Bravado as an Attraction

Projecting an air of confidence is one of the most important things you can do to attract other people. One of the charismatic qualities of all great leaders is that they appear to believe in themselves. They show such confidence in their ability to succeed, that others naturally fall in line to follow them.

But now for the grand secret: Rarely can you find people who are truly and absolutely confident in themselves! Everyone harbors doubts! But it's still okay (and even downright desirable) to project bravado or confidence that you don't really feel. Why? People appreciate a person who projects confidence, regardless of what the person is feeling inside.

Try to act confident in the way you carry yourself, in the way you speak, in your body language, and in the way you respond to others. But at the same time, be sensitive to the needs and concerns of the other person as well.

This does not mean you should lie to yourself. Don't delude yourself, while trying to project an air of confidence to others. Recognize your own feelings of insecurity, but don't openly discuss them. It's not "professional," and there's a reason for that expression. Entertainers who are paid for their performances learned a long time ago that audiences would forgive a bad performance much more quickly than they would an entertainer who starts *acknowledging* that his/her performance was bad. So, even if you don't feel confident, make the attempt to appear that way. Don't worry about feeling phony or apologizing because you're trying to appear confident. It's your duty to project confidence even when it may not exist. This will inspire the confidence and enthusiasm of others. *In fact,* you'll be surprised to discover how willing people are to lean on your apparent strength.

Remember two things when trying to exude confidence. Number one is that nobody knows for sure what you're thinking. The second is that even if others suspect that you are not as confident as you appear, they will still respect the fact that you're making the effort! Winning respect should accomplish as much for you as actually feeling the confidence.

Appearing confident can be a turn-on to the person you want to meet. However, there is a thin line between being appropriately confident and appearing boastful. Attract the person with a show of confidence, but keep in mind that showing a little bit of nervousness can still command another person's respect. Too much confidence can be a turn-off.

LOVE TACTIC #27 Smile (and the World Smiles with You)

Abigail Van Buren ("Dear Abby") wrote a column years back in which she said, "The key to being popular is to keep a smile on your face!" Your smile is one of the most important parts of your personality. It is a mirror that reflects the good things inside of you. A warm smile can serve as a magnet to draw people to you. It can help compensate for any other shortcoming that you may be unable to change. By the same token, the lack of a smile may inadvertently keep people away from you.

Practice the art of smiling. Do it in front of a mirror. Although initially you may feel uncomfortable, practicing will help you feel more comfortable with the smile that you're putting on for others. This is helpful not just to improve your attitude, but also to strengthen the muscles involved in your smile!

How do you do this? For sixty seconds each day, stand in front of a mirror and move your face into the biggest smile you can. Feel like you're smiling so hard that your face is going to break! After doing this exercise over and over, your face will begin to assume a more smiling look (even when you're not thinking of anything). Your face will hold on to more of a smile! These exercises will make it easier for you to smile (really!), even when you're not feeling that happy (although the best smiles are when you're feeling good inside).

When practicing the smiling exercise, it may help if you look at yourself and think, "What in the world am I doing? This is ridiculous for me to be doing this, but I'm doing it anyway!" That thought can help you smile all the more!

Becoming more of a frequent smiler will do a couple of things for you. It will make people feel more accepted by you, and it will make you seem to be at peace with yourself. You will appear more confident and, therefore, more attractive. There is also another benefit. To some degree, your emotions follow your physiological initiatives. So if you make an effort to practice smiling, you may find that you actually will become happier.

LOVE TACTIC #28 Don't Be Nervous About Being Nervous

People are nervous about being nervous! But look at it this way. If someone appears nervous when trying to talk to you, be flattered. It means the interaction is important to them. They may feel a little intimidated by you, for whatever reason, but it's still flattering. Admire the person's attempt.

At the same time, if you come across as being nervous, other people may admire you for your courage and for making the effort in spite of your nervousness. In fact, if you come across as being too suave and smooth, the other person may not open their heart to you as easily as they would if you appear somewhat human (insecurities and all). So this can turn out to be a very positive thing, after all.

This is not to say that you should induce any extra signs of nervousness! If you're nervous, it's okay to let a certain amount of it show. That's just part of being yourself. Of course, if you're not nervous, that's fine, too. But more important than being nervous or not nervous is simply being genuine!

LOVE TACTIC #29 Don't Feel You Have to Stand Out in a Crowd

Don't judge your potential for winning the one you want on how much you shine in groups. Don't get discouraged if you feel like a dud at parties. Your popularity, or your ability to be the center of attention in a crowd, has no relation to your ability to win someone's heart in a one-on-one situation! In fact, some of the most spellbinding individuals in romance are completely inept in group situations. Just because you can command the attention of a nation does not mean you can win someone's heart without obeying the fundamental laws of love.

So don't be discouraged if you find yourself sitting quietly among a group of people when the one you want is present. The greatest victories of romance are usually achieved by talking with another person during the quiet times, when nobody else is around. Keep your cool in crowds. Be patient. Remember, your opportunity will come!

Have you ever felt your self-esteem diminish because you feel "alone," even though you're with a group of people? You can be right in the middle of all the action and yet feel like a nothing if the spotlight is focused on someone else long enough. Don't let this get you down! We're telling you the truth. In the end, you're going to win! Let this be your secret source of confidence. Stay calm in troubling moments.

These concerns are normal. But shortcomings in this area don't accurately reflect your true worth as a person or the real power you have to win the one you want. Still waters really do run deep! Even the most successful and popularly acclaimed people often feel insecure and left out.

There is a once-popular story of how, during the height of the Beatles' popularity, Ringo Starr wanted to leave the group. He told Paul McCartney that he felt like the group's outsider. An astonished Paul responded by saying it was he who felt like the outsider. In the end, Ringo stayed with the group.

This story shows that a person can feel unloved and unnoticed, even when that person is showered with attention and adulation. If you experience these feelings, keep in mind that the situation is not as bad as it seems. There are loads of people out there who are willing to love you. Feeling like an outcast is not a true reflection of your lovableness. Just because you don't stand out in a crowd does not mean that you can't stand out in someone's heart.

LOVE TACTIC #30 Don't Let Your Emotions Take the Driver's Seat!

Don't be surprised when the one you want, in the initial stages of trying to win them over, doesn't want you back. Often, during the onset of a relationship, one person's attitude may be completely opposite of the other's. We call this the See-Saw Principle. You might be flying high on romance, while the other person's feet are planted firmly on the ground. When you can think of nothing else but the other person, he/she may not be giving you a passing thought. While you may be desperately wanting that special someone, he/she may be trying to get as far away from you as possible.

It is also a fact that the person whose feet are planted firmly on the ground has more control over the person whose head is in the clouds. Maybe you've heard the saying, "The person who cares least controls the relationship."

What's the point of all this? Until you have the one you want right where you want them, you had better keep control over your heart. Don't let your fantasies run away with you yet, or else you'll be in for a nice see-saw ride. Unfortunately, the other person involved will have complete power to decide when your ride is over! And when they decide to get off while you're still up in the air, watch out! You're going to hit the ground *hard!*

Strive for control of your own feelings. The more restraint you exercise from the beginning the better able you will be to win the one you want. It may help to promise yourself that once you've won the other's heart, you'll allow your feelings a little more latitude. But until then, you've got a job to do. Don't allow yourself the luxury of dreaming too much until your day's work is done.

8
Communicating Effectively

Communication is the central core of love. It's 95 percent of what bonds a love relationship. The main way people communicate is through language. Through words you can attempt to communicate the feelings you have inside.

Although you can never completely understand another human being, the more you are able to understand, the more solid and the stronger the love between you will be. The key to effective communication is to try to understand what the other person is saying. Only after you've shown the other person your attempt to understand should you yourself try to be understood. If the other person does not feel that you understand their position first, it's pointless to go on to the next step. Why? The key to opening another's heart depends on showing that person you care.

LOVE TACTIC #31 Break the Ice

One of the most difficult areas for people who are trying to be more socially successful is in their ability to begin conversations with strangers. This is called breaking the ice.

You've probably noticed plenty of people who seem to be very confident and successful in breaking the ice. They never seem to be uncomfortable or at a loss for words, and they always seem to succeed in getting people to respond to them. If that's not your strength, don't despair. There are things that you can do to improve your ice-breaking ability. Breaking the ice is a skill. If you're not as confident as you'd like to be, follow some of the following suggestions.

First, recognize that all human beings thrive on communication. Even though others may appear aloof and distant when you attempt to get to know them, deep down they still hunger for communication with others.

It is sometimes very difficult to begin a conversation, especially with a stranger. In fact, don't be uptight if the ice doesn't break right away. Don't be discouraged if your first overtures seem to meet with no success.

A guy we observed at a karaoke sing-along at the Tropicana Hotel in Las Vegas tried to strike up a conversation with the girl standing next to him. He was a nice-looking guy and she was a nice-looking girl. He appeared self-confident standing there, but when he spoke to her there was just enough nervousness in his voice to portray that he really just wanted to establish contact with another human being. He asked her how the music was going. She seemed shocked and surprised that he had spoken to her and responded by saying, "Well, I haven't really been here that long." Then she turned away from the guy. It was obvious to us that he was feeling the embarrassment of being rebuffed, so he didn't continue with his effort. However, if he had, she probably would have responded. Because, from our objective viewpoint, it was evident that the girl was flattered by his attention—even a little intrigued—but didn't know how to respond tactfully for fear of looking too anxious and possibly winding up being rejected herself!

Everyone feels a little rejected at times. But remember, people do need you to reach out to them. If you continue to reach out, others will respond in time.

Consider the pattern that often occurs when you try to get a child to warm up to you. You stretch forward your hands and smile at the child, who may look at you and turn away. A few minutes later the child may check to see if you're still looking at him. You simply smile. If he continues to look at you, you may stretch out your arms to him again. He'll probably turn away again! The third or fourth time that this happens, though, most kids will start to come to you. Just don't push it. Relax, and eventually they'll be sitting on your lap, goo-gooing and having a good old time!

Think of this example when you're trying to break the ice with an adult. At first it might seem that things are cold and stiff (as it often does when first communicating with children) and that your efforts are not paying off. But don't appear fazed by the person's unresponsiveness at first. Appear more casual, confident, and relaxed, and continue being friendly and nice. Soon that person will warm up and respond. It won't be long until the ice has completely thawed. (Maybe down the road they'll even sit on your lap!)

So what can you do to "thaw the ice"? First of all, it depends on who it is that you're attempting to talk to. For example, meeting a stranger for the first time is different from speaking to somebody you've known for a long time. But regardless, go slowly. Be bold, but not overbearing. Push, but not too hard. Speak, but then be quiet for a while before, yes, speaking again.

Focus on a neutral topic of conversation. Address the person about casual things. Continue to show interest in the other person. Look the person in the eyes when you talk, and smile. Address that person by name as soon as possible, and use their name a few times throughout the conversation. Don't feel as if you have to address anything in particular. But remember, a person's favorite topic is always him/herself. Show interest in the likes and desires of the other.

When attempting to break the ice, try to ask interesting, open-ended questions. Keep away from questions that have simple yes or no answers. Why? If you're talking with somebody who is shy, a "yes" or "no" may be all you get!

Open-ended questions, on the other hand, ask how a person feels about things—what their opinions are. In this way, you can tap into another person's desire to communicate with another human being. Your questions should be pleasant and motivational. Don't sound like you're giving the third degree. Showing interest in the other person's interests can help bring out a naturally flowing conversation.

Be willing to let the person leave gracefully if you notice any signals that he/she wants to terminate the conversation. But have confidence that, because that person has had a positive experience with you, he/she may come back, desiring future interactions.

LOVE TACTIC #32 Ask Questions to Get Things Flowing

Dale Carnegie pointed out that the subject of greatest interest to every person is him/herself. So the kind of questions you'll want to ask should be about that person. Once you have broken the ice, you can start broadening the subject matter of your conversations.

Follow the Golden Rule—"Do unto others as you would have them do unto you." Think about the kinds of questions that you would enjoy being asked. Ask others those very questions. As long as you show a deep interest and understanding, the other person will probably be very flattered and continue to open up more and more.

Once you have asked a few preliminary ice-breaking questions, you will start to get an idea of the things that interest your communication partner and the things that don't. Tap into those areas of interest further, and avoid the ones that seem to be ill-advised. Remember, you're trying to express genuine interest, to make the other person feel good about talking with you. You don't want to come across as if you are interrogating a witness!

A question such as, "What made you enjoy such and such?" may bring about some interesting answers. Don't express criticism towards any ideas or feelings being expressed by the other person.

If you ask somebody a few questions and their answers are short and succinct, it either means that they are not interested, or that they might be interested but are very shy and reluctant to get involved in a conversation. At that point, you might want to proceed by sharing some personal experience or anecdote to make them feel more comfortable. It is likely that they may follow with a story of their own. If you bring up things about yourself in response to things the other person says, make sure that these tidbits are short and to the point, then immediately focus back on the other person. You don't want to take any attention away from him/her.

Once the ice begins to thaw, try to keep the ball rolling. Remember, above all, that conversations should be pleasant and enjoyable. Avoid arguments or put-downs.

There are times when you may feel your relationship has reached a plateau. In spite of all your work, you may still feel like a stranger with the one you want. What is helpful at times like these is some intimate conversation, alone together, for several hours without interruption.

A great remedy in a case like this is to somehow arrange a trip together in a car. Some of the hardest people to get to know open up when they're out on the interstate.

Just make sure that you are prepared to initiate some conversation. You might even spend a few days thinking of some topics to bring up. Write them down and have discreet access to them during the trip, if necessary.

The best kinds of questions are those about goals, wishes, life memories, and intense feelings. Some examples of conversation initiators are:

1. "If you could do three things before you die, what would they be?"
2. "If you could wish for anything, what would it be?"
3. "Tell me about your elementary-school years . . ."
4. "Who has had the most impact on your life?"

These are just a few examples. There are an infinite number of subjects that could be utilized.

LOVE TACTIC #33 Know What to Talk About and What to Avoid

There are good topics for conversation and there are bad topics. It's always important to be aware of this, especially early in the process of meeting people.

GOOD TOPICS FOR CONVERSATION

Things that bring pleasure to the other person are always good to talk about. People enjoy sharing good things. As long as your questions are not too prying, a pleasant conversation can develop.

When you talk about what the other person does, focus on enjoyable activities. Most people love to talk about where they live, what they do, what their hobbies are, and special interests they may have. Good discussion topics include most things found in the public domain. Good examples include items in the news; health-related issues; television, movies, and music; sports; and predictions.

Once a topic of mutual interest has been found, conversation can then move into more hypothetical areas. For example, there are different types of fun questions that you can ask, such as "If you could be any person, who would you be and why?" Or "If you had a million dollars, how would you spend it?" These can be thought-provoking questions, which, if used at the right time, can deepen a feeling of enjoyable interaction with the one you're interested in.

TOPICS TO CONSIDER AVOIDING

Any topic that elicits a negative or emotionally defensive response from your counterpart is one to avoid. In other words, be sensitive. You can talk about almost anything as long as they seem willing to respond. But if they begin to show distrust or anger, for whatever reason, then change topics as gracefully and quickly as possible.

Be careful in choosing the things you want to talk about, and base this on their ability to handle it. Don't push a topic that they are not enjoying. (Although it's rare to find a topic that a person won't eventually talk about.) Ironically, there are times you will back off from a topic when a person shows a negative response, and within a few minutes you'll find them bringing up the very same topic themselves!

Try to avoid complaints. Yes, if you complain about something, you may evoke sympathy from the other person and that may seem to tighten the relationship. But, in general, you should try to appear confident. Complaining makes it sound like you are less confident than you'd like to be.

Try to avoid any offensive language, comments, or reactions that might present you in a less than positive light. For example, it's not a good idea to use profanity even if the other person does. And don't offer biting criticisms about any people or topics. You never can tell when this may hit a nerve in the other person.

You may not want to start a conversation by talking about the other person's job, because some people may not want to think about work. In addition, if that person happens to be unemployed, the topic can be very embarrassing.

In the beginning, try to avoid sensitive areas such as politics or emotional issues. Try also to avoid conversations about previous relationships, either your own or those of the other person.

Serious topics, such as ones having to do with human tragedy, illness, death, unemployment, or other problems of that nature, may not be beneficial early in a relationship. Sure, these and any other topics may come out in a developing relationship. There are times that serious, relationship-enhancing conversations on these topics may develop almost immediately. In general, though, conversations on topics such as these should take place only after a relationship has developed.

Humor can be a very important part of any relationship, but it should be used carefully. Do not use humor in response to anything said by the other person, especially if you notice that the other person is sensitive to the topic being discussed.

LOVE TACTIC #34 Know the Difference Between What They Say and What They Really Mean

You can't always go by what people say. In fact, *you hardly ever can*, because what people say and what they feel are often two distinct things.

This calls to mind a comic strip that appeared in a newspaper a few years ago:

A couple was sitting together on the couch, he at one end, and she at the other.

She: I'm sorry, John, but I'm just not interested in getting serious with anyone in my life right now. At this stage all I really want, and need, is a good friend.

He: Well, that's fine, Sally. If that's the way you feel . . . all right! I'm happy to just be your friend.

She: Great! Do you know any nice guys for me, then?!

What's the point? If you cultivate a friendship correctly, the one you want will respond, as surely as flowers do to the rain and sunshine, in spite of their protests that they don't need or want a relationship. So while you are in the process of cultivating their love, have faith in this principle. Ignore their verbal protests.

Always remember that within each human being is a person bursting with readiness to love and to be loved. This exists no matter how hardened and apathetic they may seem to you. It may, however, take varying amounts of effort to get through and reach each particular individual's heart.

But keep persisting in the right way. You have to get through to the person's innermost being, the part that needs and wants love. When this happens, their true nature will cause them to reciprocate your love.

LOVE TACTIC #35 Improve Your Ability to Listen

One common factor in most relationships that fall apart is the lack of good, effective listening. In fact, if you're worried about your relationship, just concentrate on improving communication. How? Start listening more (and better)! You'll be surprised at how well the relationship will improve.

Have you ever noticed how, if things fall apart in a budding romance, it seems that the one being let go never fully understands the reasons why? The one doing the letting go almost never fully discloses the real reasons for bailing out of the relationship. And for good reason! The one being rejected usually has a hard time understanding what is going on in the heart and soul of the other person. This is actually the reason for the dissatisfaction felt by the person who wants out of the relationship.

But what is the root of the problem? The rejected lover is unable to get through the communication barriers. If he/she could get the other to spell out the dissatisfactions, doubts, and fears, some of the logical arguments would lose their potency.

There are three important suggestions to keep in mind when trying to improve your listening ability.

First, try to maintain eye contact. There is nothing like eye contact to show that you are listening. Conversely, it can be very upsetting and distracting to the other person if they're talking to you and your eyes are wandering around the room.

Second, when somebody is saying something to you, whether you disagree or not, simply nod your head to signal your willingness for them to continue speaking. However, don't do this all the time or it will look like you have a screw loose in your neck! Rather, focus carefully on what the person is saying, and you'll know when it's appropriate to nod. Remember, this nodding does not offer agreement. It simply offers understanding, and shows your awareness that the other person is saying something important.

Finally, feel free to ask questions about what the person is saying. These questions should not change the topic but should further clarify the meaning of their disclosures. Such questions will clearly demonstrate your sincere interest and effort to understand. Examples of this type of question are, "So, in other words, what you're saying is . . . ?" Or, "Can you help me understand more clearly what you mean when you say such and such?"

Beware, however, of expressions that are intended to be reassuring but often backfire, such as, "I understand how you feel," or, "I know exactly what you are going through." People resent having others presume to know their deeper emotions. It is for them alone to say when they feel understood. The best way to help someone feel understood is to show sincerity in your attempts to really absorb what they are communicating. Learn to listen reflectively. The best you can do is show your willingness *to try* to understand. Miraculously, this willingness is enough to comfort the one you want.

FREUD'S DISCOVERY: THE TRANSFERENCE PRINCIPLE

For the scientific-minded, it is comforting to know that the father of modern psychoanalysis, Sigmund Freud, discovered a consistent rule for getting someone to fall in love with you.

Though not thought to be a very attractive man, Freud discovered that his novel methods of therapy produced a very interesting side effect: Time after time, his female patients fell in love with him! Eventually, Freud came to refer to this phenomenon as "transference." Freud observed that all human beings have a universal bursting of readiness to fall in love. This love inevitably manifests itself towards any person who provides the right "treatment."

And what does this treatment consist of, you may anxiously be asking? It is essentially the opportunity to be alone with someone with whom they can speak freely about very personal, intimate things without fear of cursory judgment.

Freud would sit where his female patients couldn't see him, hoping that this would hinder the falling-in-love process. Eventually, he came to see that this effort was pointless. The falling in love resulted from the unburdening of the soul to a listening ear, not the sight of his bearded face! Freud observed that this tendency in his patients extended to the entire human race. He then went on to say that looks and superficial imagery are totally irrelevant in this type of attachment. It has, instead, everything to do with the bonding process, as a relationship forms through deep, meaningful communication.

So, believe it or not, those long intimate talks you enjoy with the one you want—especially where they are doing most of the talking and revealing their innermost secrets to you—are important steps in getting that person to fall in love with you!

The point of all this is that the very techniques that Freud used are available to every one of us—if we are just willing to invest the time *listening* to the one we want and encouraging their free expression of intimate feelings they are willing to share. As you do this, it is a universal characteristic for people to fall in love with you.

Have confidence in your ability to get another person to fall in love with you! *Listening* is the most powerful key of the psychoanalyst, and it can be just as potent an instrument for you!

LOVE TACTIC #36 Feel Comfortable with Silence

One quality that commands respect is the ability to remain poised at all times. We're referring to "poise" in this context as the ability to remain comfortable in a relationship, even if there are things going on that might threaten your comfort.

One example of something that might threaten your poise is silence. Yes, silence. Many people have difficulty dealing with too much silence in a relationship. They begin to fear they are losing the attention and affections of the other person. Only a person who has confidence in him/herself can remain calm under such circumstances and ride out any periods of silence.

So don't be afraid of silence. Don't feel pressured to keep a conversation going all the time. If silence comes, accept it with grace. In this way, it will contribute to your appearance of poise, and enhance your desirability in the relationship.

LOVE TACTIC #37 Be Honest But Discreet

Don't mistakenly believe that love tactics teach you how to put on airs or be phony. Are the love tactics you're reading really different from how you would normally behave? Probably not. Then try to see the reasons behind our recommendations, and make them *a real part of your regular behavior*. Make the tactics part of the new you, not just something put on for show.

We believe in honesty. But experience teaches that you must be wise in the *disclosure* of your thoughts and feelings. People who go around popping off about every passing impression that crosses their minds are generally perceived to be immature. The wisest people are those who carefully consider the consequences of what they want to say before they verbalize their feelings.

Do not express yourself uncontrollably and unwisely. First, take into consideration what effect the thing you say may have upon the other person. If you don't think it will produce the effect you desire (e.g., get them to fall in love with you), then it might be better left unsaid.

THE MAGIC-OF-BEING-DISCREET PRINCIPLE

Maintaining some degree of mystique about yourself commands more respect than wearing your heart on your sleeve. So practice keeping things to yourself. This is especially important when meeting someone for the first time. It is okay to reveal a little bit about yourself, but too much disclosure early in a relationship tends to turn people away.

Make people pay the price of investing a little time in you, before you start sharing your more intimate details. This is especially true with the one you want, but it is also true when you are introduced to that person's circle of friends and acquaintances.

No matter how proud the one you want may be of you, you have much more to lose by opening your mouth and talking too much when meeting his/her friends for the first time. Remember what Abraham Lincoln said, "It is better to be thought a fool, than to open one's mouth and remove all doubt!" Be friendly and willing to visit, but keep personal details about yourself private until you have gotten to know these people better.

And don't start blabbing about your shortcomings! Everybody has faults, but those who advertise them will feel their consequences more heavily than those who quietly carry on in spite of them.

LOVE TACTIC #38 Don't Shy Away from Anger

Don't be afraid of making the one you want angry. It's far more dangerous to allow them to remain indifferent. According to psychologist Dr. Joyce Brothers, anger and love are much more closely related to each other than they are to indifference. In fact, *indifference* is the opposite of love, while the emotions of anger and love are very similar. Love and anger are both intense levels of emotion.

9

Being Aware of the Other's Needs

There's a big difference between *saying* you are aware of the other's needs and actually *showing* your awareness. There's a saying, "What you do screams loudly in my ears; I can't hear a single word you say." A person cannot be *talked* into feeling cared about. Actually catering to a person's needs for attention, understanding, acceptance, appreciation, and affection may help that person conclude that life is better with you around.

Meeting the needs of the one you want will help them become happier than they have been. As they become happier in their associations with you, and they find themselves less happy when you're not around, they're going to seek out your companionship. After all, it's human nature to pursue happiness.

If you can make your environment one that is nurturing and supportive to others, you'll find you won't have to seek them out. Others will look for you because they feel happy and good around you. Ideally, that's the way it should be in a love relationship.

LOVE TACTIC #39 — Meet the Emotional Needs of the One You Want

Love doesn't happen by accident. There are always definite reasons that a person falls in love. Author and entrepreneur Robert J. Ringer makes the point that love must be bought. Not with money, mind you, but with emotional effort.

We agree. In order to win a lover's heart you must meet his/her emotional needs. You have to meet these needs until it is worth it for that person to give up all other potential lovers to have you and you alone. Committed love comes, in these cases, as the result of the happiness that the person feels you will bring.

Sometimes, in a relationship, you may feel "used." This can be both good and bad news. The good news is that you won't feel used unless you mean something worthwhile to the other. So you can be relatively sure of your value. The bad news about being "used" is that you're being ripped off. You're not getting proper compensation in exchange for what you bring to the relationship. What's the solution to the problem? Don't withdraw yourself from the marketplace by abandoning the relationship, but simply start demanding payment.

This payment is not in the form of money, but in the same kind of emotional payoffs that you are already providing the other person. You are entitled, after all, to your own human needs being met, too; the needs for attention, understanding, acceptance (non-criticism), appreciation (words of praise and validation), and affection. You should not be expected to indefinitely continue a friendship without some reciprocation.

LOVE TACTIC #40 Be Perceptive

Remember in the movie *Superman*, when the hero takes Lois Lane on the surreal flight of her life? Do you recall how overwhelmed she was with the godlike attributes of this super human being, as they flew through the air? During this scene, Lois's thoughts are projected as she and Superman float along above the clouds, under the moonlight. She finds herself trying to talk with him telepathically. She silently wonders if he can read her mind and know the things she is feeling. This scene portrays a common human fantasy—the desire to have someone who can see into our very soul, comprehend our feelings and thoughts, and know us for who we truly are.

The good news is that you can appear to have telepathic abilities if you're willing to work at it! It is easier to read minds than you may realize. People constantly give you clues of what they're thinking. You must simply take the time to notice.

Another way to read minds (or to seem to) is to understand basic human responses to certain stimuli. Have faith that certain situations generally cause basic human reactions.

LOVE TACTIC #41 Be Empathetic, Not Sympathetic

When you give someone sympathy, you're showing that you feel sorry for them. However, people's need for respect is stronger than their need for pity. There is a more effective means of getting your love across, and that is by being understanding without expressing sympathetic judgments or evaluations. You have to show that you're genuinely concerned and interested in what the other person has to say, and what they feel. That's where *empathy* comes in. Empathy is an important part of a good relationship. Think about it. Don't you want the people listening to you to genuinely understand your feelings on a given topic? Everyone prefers being understood and accepted, rather than being agreed with!

People would rather have a listening ear than an agreeing voice. This is a well-understood principle of modern counseling. So remember, you will be much more successful in your relationships with others if you give them a listening ear.

As you become more effective at demonstrating empathy and showing that you genuinely want to understand another's feelings, that other person will feel drawn to you and will appreciate that there is somebody who really cares about their feelings. It is not unlike the attraction a thirsty man in the desert feels for the beckoning oasis. Wouldn't you love to be viewed like that oasis?

LOVE TACTIC #42 Try to Be Aware of How They Feel

A common mistake most of us make at one time or another is to believe that just because we are thinking about another person in a certain way, that person must be feeling the same way towards us. However, especially in the early stages of a relationship before appropriate conditions have been cultivated, there is often nothing further from the truth.

In fact, a comic strip in the paper caught the essence of this truth and made us laugh. In one scene, there's a young man lying in bed, unable to sleep, thinking something like, "I wonder if she's thinking about me right now.... I bet she likes me.... She's probably wondering where I was today.... I bet she can't wait to see me again...."

Meanwhile, in the next panel, the girl is drifting off to sleep and her last thoughts are, "You know ... I really like ... ice cream!"

It can be a shock if you become interested in someone, then learn that that person doesn't have the slightest attraction to you. This can be discouraging. *Don't give up, though!* Love takes time. Confront reality at the *beginning* of the relationship. Facing the truth that you haven't won the person yet is a very important step. It is better to grapple with reality at the beginning of your lives together than way down the road.

Take, for example, the story of the man who was told by his wife after thirty years of marriage that she was divorcing him. "Divorcing me?" he asked in astonishment. "What are you talking about? We've had a *wonderful* marriage!"

"Wrong!" she replied. "*You've* had a wonderful marriage, but *I've* had a lousy one, and now *I want out!*"

Every individual has his own independent perception of things. Don't fall into the trap of believing that the other person necessarily sees and feels things the same way you do. Don't assume that because you're receiving satisfaction in a particular relationship, your partner is, too. If you discover that the one you want is not as excited about you as you are about them, or if you learn that they are not as content in the relationship as you thought, don't let it throw you. Focus on your partner's known human needs rather than your wishful thinking. Never assume you've already achieved the goal of inspiring love in your beloved. This could cause you to quit nurturing the very feelings that need to be attended to!

LOVE TACTIC #43 Be a Mirror

Perhaps you've never thought about it, but you read people's minds every day through their words, expressions, and gestures. The real key, though, is to improve upon this and practice being sensitive, as well as listening reflectively.

One of the authors of this book remembers spending an hour listening to a close friend who confided a problem to him. The author spent the entire time simply paraphrasing the words of his friend in an attempt to clarify and understand what his friend was saying. The author did not repeat anything more than what his friend had told him. But at the end of the hour, the friend earnestly asked, "How do you do that? It's like you're reading my mind!"

People are not used to having others take the time to listen to them. If you can do even a halfway good job at it, they'll feel like you can see into their soul and picture the things they're thinking of.

You can be a mirror by using words, as well as by using body language. If you sit and focus your attention on the one you want, he/she will feel as if you're really on their wavelength. Being a mirror is a great way to reflect your interest and concern. It can work so well that, in many cases, the other person may not even consciously notice that he/she is becoming more dependent on your support.

LOVE TACTIC #44 Try a Little Tenderness

On one occasion, a beautiful young woman shared with us the "list" of qualities she wanted in the perfect man. Her expectations were pretty normal, up until her final "want." Her list included the usual traits of honesty, responsibility, intelligence, sense of humor, and so forth. But the last quality really stood out for some reason: "… and last, but not least," she had stated, "he must *love me tenderly*."

To love someone *tenderly* is to love them the opposite of *forcefully*. When you think of it in this way, the meaning of "loving tenderly" is so much clearer. For when someone attempts to love someone forcefully, doesn't that imply a lack of patience, a desperate attempt to have someone respond right here and now? And doesn't it suggest very little consideration for the other person's wants, needs, cares, and concerns?

This young woman intuitively expressed a need to find someone who would *take the time to cultivate her love, to let it grow naturally and spontaneously*. Loving tenderly may require a lot of suffering, as well as patience, on the part of the pursuer. It means being kind, even if the one you want isn't showing the greatest consideration for your feelings. Why should you be kind, good, and *tender* when the other person gives you no reassurance that your actions are being appreciated?

The answer is just this: Kindness begets kindness. Goodness begets goodness. And eventually, tenderness will penetrate to the heart.

LOVE TACTIC #45   Build Anticipation—It Creates Passion

Here's an important psychological principle: The *anticipation* of possessing or achieving something is almost always more pleasurable than the actual fulfillment of the desire.

Many people have said, "I can't think of anything that's as much fun to own as it is to *look forward* to owning!" We agree. How does this apply to romance? As your relationship begins to warm up, you may sense that the one you want is also beginning to want you back, at last. This is the time for you to exercise a little restraint, rather than surrender right away and abandon your resolve to be strong and independent.

Final victory still depends upon careful restraint. Sure, it's tempting to give yourself over completely to the one you've been working so hard to get. It's a great temptation to lay down your defenses and tell all those things about yourself that you've been hungering to share for so long. Especially now. After all, they're practically inviting you to do so, right? You've worked so hard for this moment and you don't want to partially surrender. You want to surrender completely, but **don't do it!**

Yes, you're getting tired of being alone, and you can't see any sense in enduring a lonesome lifestyle any longer. But the truth is, just because it appears you've won the one you want, *you still haven't arrived yet.* Like a passenger jet that has begun its descent, you may be approaching the runway home, but you haven't quite landed. Not yet. Only after landing, and coming to a complete stop at the terminal, can you pull out the luggage you've hauled with you for many years and let the one you want give you a hand carrying the load. (Phew, what a trip!)

But for now, in the early stages of your victory, it is still a time for restraint and caution. Remember, Patton was killed by carelessness, *after* the war had already been essentially won, but before he was home free, back in the good old USA.

When the one you want begins to show indications of falling for you for the first time, realize that *they* are just beginning to experience the pleasures of anticipation that you may have already been enjoying for quite a while. Don't cheat them of this delicious pleasure now by cutting the time short!

This is the very emotion—passion—that you've been working so hard to get them to experience over you. Maintain it. Bridle your passions *and* keep your mouth in control. Continue to limit your time together. Make sure you continue to use the love tactics that got you this far. You might fear that they may get too frustrated and drop you. Believe us, at this point, they couldn't drop you if they tried. The passions driving them are too strong. The moment you appear, they'll start acting like a thirsty horse near water.

Remember, as soon as the other person realizes that he/she has got you, their more pleasurable feelings of anticipation might begin to diminish. Previously suppressed negative feelings of being cornered and trapped will begin to increase. And if you're not careful, such feelings on their part can grow into an uncontrollable monster before you can even say, "What happened?"

This certainly is not what you want to have happen. It's better to hold off a while. Don't give the other person definite confirmation of your final decisions. Let some suspense reign. Otherwise, you might throw cold water on their passionate flames. Blowing a promising relationship in this way is known as "snatching defeat from the jaws of victory."

Most people who write to us are afraid that if they maintain some emotional distance, their beloved will get discouraged and give up on them. This is almost a totally illusory concern. The very opposite is, in fact, the case. By *not* maintaining some emotional space, the other person may feel that things are "getting too serious" and may try to dump you.

Compare cultivating love to making a piñata. Think of the fragile, temporary inner balloon as love's passion. Longer-lasting plaster of Paris layers of friendship, which have been seasoned with time and experience, are added. You don't pop the balloon as soon as the layers are in place. No, you give the plaster time to get good and hard first so that it can stand up on its own, even when the balloon is burst. Once the plaster of Paris is set, the piñata will maintain its shape even when it is no longer supported by the balloon.

It is the same with love. Passionate attraction keeps couples together long enough to give the real substance of love—friendship—time to set and become strong. But if you burst your beloved's bubble too soon by giving too much reassurance (remember, uncertainty is still a necessary ingredient in the passion recipe), then you will give them a reprieve from having to think about you 95 percent of the day. At the same time, you'll run the risk of having them think, *"What the heck am I getting myself into?!"* If you confirm your undying passion for the other too soon, don't be shocked if he/she starts to get extremely cold feet and walks out on you. You will have brought it on yourself. Don't say we didn't warn you!

LOVE TACTIC #46 Be Enthusiastic

If it seems like there is no zest in your relationship, then you'll have to try to create some. You can do this through your show of enthusiasm.

In a spark plug, a spark is created by electricity having to jump from one electrode to the other. Likewise, your enthusiasm, which is contagious, can jump from you to the one you're with. As you attempt to *act* enthusiastic, it will affect the one you're with. And although he/she may appear resistant at first, your "spark" will eventually get through to the other person.

At the same time, they may realize that if they allow themselves to feel the spark you are emitting, they will get more attached to you than they presently want to be. To prevent this from happening, they may try to use their *will* to overcome their *emotion*, which you are definitely influencing.

They may sit there with a stiff expression and try to outlast you. At this point, it can become a contest of wills. Is your will to maintain this relationship stronger than their will to kill it? Make up your mind to fight on for the one you want. Say, "I will never give up. Never! Never! Never!" But, unless you want to make this a million-year crusade, you had better use some discretion and employ some strategy and tact in your approach to the problem.

Remember, if the one you want thinks that you're not willing to respect their feelings toward you, however reluctant those feelings may be, then that person's heart will remain hard towards you. What you must do is successfully convince the one you want, through the way you act, that your love is true, regardless of what they think, and that your enthusiasm is *independently* generated. Then, if they have no reason to fear hidden motives on your part, they will allow themselves to share and enjoy your enthusiasm. This will, in turn, cause them to open up their heart to you.

10
Interacting in Winning Ways

Books have been written on how to succeed when dealing with people, and how to win friends and influence people. The laws of successful interaction are as well-established as the laws of chemistry!

Behavioral scientists know that positive feelings result when people react and interact in certain ways during certain situations. Since what you're trying to produce are positive feelings in the heart of the one you want, be aware of this fact. Recognize that if you adapt your behavior, and interact in the ways you're advised to do in this book, you'll win in many ways. You'll win because you'll be more popular, you'll get the attention and respect of your peers, and, most important, you'll have a positive relationship with the one you want to spend the rest of your life with.

LOVE TACTIC #47 Interact in Person

The necessity of actually being there in person in order to win the one you want cannot be overemphasized. Too often, people try to develop a relationship through the mail and wonder why it doesn't seem to work out. Developing a relationship is no easy task. It cannot be done effectively from a distance.

Sure, there are stories of people who have successfully used the mail sometime during their courtship and are happily married today. But this is usually effective only in keeping the hopes and interests alive of the one doing most of the writing.

Even Robert and Elizabeth Barrett Browning's celebrated correspondence love affair did not actually blossom until they were able to meet in person. It is true that her love poems for him have become universally acclaimed. But what most people don't know is that she did not show Robert her love poems until *after* they were married!

We want you to understand this principle very clearly now. If Elizabeth Barrett had indiscreetly started sharing her passionate love poems with Robert Browning too soon, there may have never been the team of Barrett-Browning. You have to *win* your love in face-to-face "combat," and not through the mails.

In order to persuade someone to fall in love with you, you're going to have to let them get to know you in person. Remember the expression, "To know you is to love you." This kind of interaction can only occur in personal and direct encounters.

We remember the story of one young man who saw an article in the newspaper about a single young woman who worked with the deaf. He said that he was impressed with the selfless attitude of the young woman as he read the article and thought that she was the kind of girl he'd been looking for. (Of course, the attractive picture of her, which accompanied the news article, didn't hurt any!)

He toyed with the idea of writing a letter to her. After a few days of tormenting himself with the idea, he finally decided to write the letter, feeling that he had nothing to lose! He was pleasantly surprised, though, when she wrote back. Soon, they began corresponding regularly through the mail.

After six months, the young man was completely infatuated with this girl he *thought* he had gotten to know. He was determined to fly to where she lived to finally meet her. What a shock, he later admitted! Yes, she was extremely pleasant and congenial. But in spite of the fact that she was even cuter in some ways than her picture had portrayed, he flew back home disappointed. He realized that she was nothing like the girl his imagination had conjured up during their six-month correspondence.

"I actually found myself grieving on the airplane on the way home," he said. "I suddenly realized that the girl I had fallen in love with was a phantom. She didn't even really exist! It was like having somebody you care about die."

This young man had discovered for himself that there is no substitute for getting to know someone in person.

Letters, telephone calls, telegrams, and handwritten cards are all good ways to keep someone from forgetting about you. Perhaps these things may help maintain an existing relationship, or they may even create a spark of interest. But when it comes down to the real-life, nitty-gritty process of winning somebody's heart, nothing compares with being there in person.

It is said that absence makes the heart grow fonder. This is certainly true, but only if the couple has had a chance to do some psychological bonding first. Then, when there is separation, the one you want will miss what they have already grown accustomed to. This can have a positive effect on the relationship as they will come to appreciate you more. But, even so, separations are only effective in helping the other person become *aware of subconscious attachments* that they have *already* developed for you.

Another important point to remember is that even in well-established relationships (including marriages) *prolonged* separations can cause damage. Human beings are real live creatures needing other real live creatures for emotional nurturing. If they can't get that nurturing from you they'll get it from someone else. Think of your immediate presence in a person's life, along with your emotional interactions with them, as being like food and drink to their soul. Each day you become more a part of them as the experiences you share intermingle. A couple of days without food will not make one's body grow stronger. It *will*, however, make one appreciate the food much more. Keep in mind, though, *prolonged* days without food and water may cause that person to search for it elsewhere.

Once more, we are not saying that you should never use letters, tapes, or phone calls in a relationship. Just don't kid yourself into believing that these methods will ever serve as an adequate substitute for relating with someone *in person*. Admittedly it is always more frightening to give a live performance than to present one you can "pre-record." Remember, however, only the brave will know the thrill of victory, which chickens can never experience.

LOVE TACTIC #48 Love First, and You Shall Be Loved

Perhaps the most powerful aphrodisiac a person has is to arouse another person's romantic interest by gently unveiling his/her own romantic interest first! Believe it or not, if communicated in the right way, this tactic can do more to get things moving (romantically speaking) than just about anything else you can do in a relationship!

To be loved, simply lead the way. Love first, and you shall be loved in return. This truth, that love begets love, is a potent insight that can be used as a guide in your quest for love and romantic fulfillment. Remember that what each person out there is really seeking in a relationship is *to be loved*.

You came into this world as an infant and were attended to and loved by others, which made you happy. As you grew older, this same need continued. As an adult your greatest reward is when someone goes out of their way to take care of *you* and *your* needs. For that reason, when you're trying to win someone's heart, don't expect them to come knocking at your door. You've got to go knocking at theirs. And only after meeting their needs, can you expect that they will begin to meet yours.

The amazing truth is that your love is what kindles the flames of love in another person's heart. Of all the many love tactics one may employ, the most powerful love potion that exists may come from the one you want sensing your powerful desire for them.

Do not misunderstand us here. We are not saying you should force your love on the one you want. However, there will come a time when you can feel comfortable in showing your deeper motives of love, provided you have also demonstrated your ability to function happily and independently whether that person reciprocates immediately or not.

LOVE TACTIC #49 Tap Into the Conscience of the One You Want

All human beings have a conscience. And that conscience tells people, down deep, that they should return love for love and kindness for kindness.

Whenever someone is shown love, something deep down tells that person that they should reciprocate. However, there are numerous barriers that might prevent them from doing so. The main barrier is often the rationalization that your love is not unconditional, but it is self-motivated out of a desire to get something from that person, be it attention, commitment, or something else.

If you decide to make your love truly unconditional, though, eventually this barrier can be overcome. Tap into the conscience of the one you want. Realize that they are fighting an internal battle each time they resist showing kindness and affection in return to yours. The *only* way they can win is if they somehow remain convinced that your love isn't real.

On the surface they may keep up the appearance of being cold and hardened, but underneath they may be wondering how long they can keep up the facade, which is intended to get you to show your true colors.

At this point, the contest of hearts becomes a matter of wills. Whose will is stronger? If you can continue your unconditional attitude of love towards the other long enough, eventually you will win.

Please don't mistakenly think, though, that unconditional love means all give and no take on your part. You can love unconditionally and still insist on being respected.

You can be tolerant of not being put first in that person's life, but you should never allow anyone to mistreat you. By confronting emotional abuse when it occurs, the one you want will realize that your acts of kindness and consideration are free independent choices, and not the offerings of a compulsive, desperate human doormat.

LOVE TACTIC #50 Make a Personal Commitment, Then Hang in There

Maturity is the determination to continue striving toward a worthy goal even after the emotion of the moment has passed. We are reminded of the story of a young woman we know who experienced a divorce after having four children. After picking up the remnants and trying to find some purpose in her life, she wondered if she would ever find a decent man who would be willing to assume the responsibility of caring for her, as well as for her children.

Well, wonder of wonders, such a man actually did come along! But up to the very day of their marriage, doubts continued to plague her. She worried whether or not her knight in shining armor might somehow "regain his senses" and back out. As a result, she constantly expressed her insecure feelings to him. Although generally, it is not a good idea to constantly express your insecurities to your partner, in this case, the woman was lucky. Her fiancé was *truly* committed to her and determined not to be shaken by anything. In order to reassure her, he said, "Honey, I don't want you to worry anymore because, *even if I change my mind, I'm still going to go through with it!*"

That may sound a bit funny, but if you think about it, it is a perfect illustration of what true love and commitment are all about. What this woman's fiancé really meant was, "Even through my frail human emotions may vacillate a bit, there is a more objective part of me still in control . . . you can count on my love. . . ." What a man! What an ideal! Even more, what a tactic!

You evaluate, ponder, and make a decision. Then once you've made a decision, you stick with it—regardless of any transitory feelings along the way—until you've accomplished your undertaking.

LOVE TACTIC #51 Stay Cool

Despite being committed, showing unconditional love first is very important in order to maintain a posture of independence while trying to win the one you want.

Take the story of Sherrill, who was experiencing a typical obstacle in her relationship with Mike. Just when she thought things were going well and the relationship was headed for marriage, she was told that Mike had confided to one of his friends that he had no intentions of getting married.

Still, Sherrill didn't panic. She kept her cool, though the matter was driving her crazy. She kept just enough distance from Mike to keep him in doubt, and one night he proposed. After they were married, he admitted that it was the fear and doubt in his mind that got him over the commitment hurdle.

"I knew all along you were a wonderful woman," he later confessed, "but what did the trick was the fact that *I suddenly got the conviction that another man was going to come along and whisk you away from me.*" He went on, "At that point, I felt it was worth losing my bachelorhood [i.e., freedom and independence] to sew you up before it was too late!" Another thing Mike later congratulated Sherrill on was her style. "I never even felt the hook!" he said with a smile.

This story shows a common mistake that occurs between prospective lovers. When it comes to love and romance, it is a common belief that honesty in a relationship means never holding back your true feelings. Nothing could be more destructive to a developing relationship. Otherwise known as "wearing your heart on your sleeve," this practice of being too open with your feelings in the early stages of a relationship is about the quickest way known to kill a potential romance.

Use discretion. You can be honest without telling everything. What it boils down to is a degree of *openness*, not honesty. Don't tell untruths, but don't volunteer everything, either. Keep some of your feelings in reserve.

LOVE TACTIC #52 Act Paradoxically

In a relationship, there's a definite distinction between being tough and tender, and between being self*less* and self*ish*. It is this very dynamic variability of the human personality that makes it so vibrant, attractive, and alive. It is what gives people the ability to attract others.

Most people tend to be one way or the other, never realizing that the truly whole and complete person exhibits all of these traits at different times during the relationship.

The secret to romantic success is *not* walking the straight and narrow path, which is actually a theoretical line that is infinitesimally thin and impossible to tread. Rather, *cross this line as often as you can!*

There is a time for every purpose. There is a time to be tender, compassionate, and unselfishly caring. There is, as well, a time to be tough, aloof, and insistently concerned with one's own wishes and desires. One's ability to be successful in romance, as well as in other human relationships, is directly related to one's ability to balance these seemingly dichotomous yet desirable personality traits.

LOVE TACTIC #53 Act Unpredictably

Generally, as inconsistent behavior is commonly perceived as a sign of emotional immaturity, many of us may strive to be as consistent as possible in our interactions with others. But the fact is, those who manifest some degree of inconsistent behavior in their actions toward members of the opposite sex quite often have the most success in attracting the ones they want! This is another one of those phenomena of human social response, that we cannot totally explain. But nonetheless, the principle remains true.

So what should you do? You may want to purposely keep the other person off guard by giving mixed signals. Confusing someone gives you an added advantage in your attempts to win their heart. Remember, a question mark, upside down, becomes a hook!

It doesn't seem logical, does it? No, it doesn't. But remember, love is an emotional issue and sometimes acts according to unexpected principles. Who would have ever believed that exhibiting inconsistent characteristics would be touted as a way to success and happiness? Yet, if you don't confuse the one you want, at least a little bit, you may be missing a real opportunity to break through their normally impregnable defenses. And remember, only the ones who are completely at the mercy of the other act in completely predictable ways.

THE DELAYED-AFFIRMATION PRINCIPLE

The Delayed-Affirmation Principle recognizes the fact that the object of your affections responds better, romantically speaking, when you give them mixed signals. People tend to be more attracted to someone who shows enough interest in them to give them hope that there might be feelings there, but who, at the same time, shows enough aloofness to make them wonder.

Let us give you an example. If a certain girl has had her eyes on a certain guy and one night he calls her for a date, of course, she is thrilled to death! Her first impulse is to enthusiastically and immediately agree to whatever his proposal might be.

Inadvertently, though, what this type of reaction almost always does is diminish the pursuer's anxiety, increase their confidence, and start killing off the passion, which is so necessary to keep them coming around. All it might take is a little too much enthusiasm, one too many times on the part of the person being chased, before he/she begins wondering why the person has quit calling. In fact, even the pursuer may disappointedly wonder where all those initial feelings of infatuation went!

On the other hand, what's a pursued person supposed to do? If they turn down the date it may kill the pursuer's confidence and prevent the timid soul from calling again.

This is where the Delayed-Affirmation Principle comes in. This technique combines elements of response that satisfy the human need for both hope and doubt in such a way as to keep your pursuer interested and chomping at the bit! Affirm your interest, but make them wait a bit to get it! How? The following examples will give you an idea.

1. Accept the date but do not be obviously enthusiastic.

2. Ask the person if you could call back with your answer.

3. Accept the date, then call to reschedule or change the time.

4. Accept the date, but be aloof about where to go and when.

There are many other ways to implement this principle, limited only by your imagination. Let's sum it up by saying, "Be nice but be cool."

THE MIXED-SIGNALS PRINCIPLE

As we've been explaining, you can make your best progress winning the one you want by occasionally giving *mixed signals*. Other names for this technique or method might be Pleasing Through Teasing or the Mesmerizing Magic of Frustration.

Basically, though, this technique recognizes the need to mix a little challenge in along with encouragement in your pursuit of another. You should want them to believe there is potential for a relationship with you without giving them too much confidence.

Often, we hear people complain that the person they are involved with indicates "Come, come, come" one moment and "Get away, get away, get away" the next. As frustrating as this scenario sounds, it never ceases to amaze us how enchanted the confused person always feels in spite of their frustration.

So get the one you want a little confused! You don't have to overdo this principle, but just be aware that it is to your advantage to leave the other person wondering occasionally. As much as they may claim that they dislike being disoriented, it will increase their fascination with you.

LOVE TACTIC #54 Do Unto Others *Before* They Do Unto You

We know that this is *not* how the golden rule reads! However, sometimes in love (and sometimes even in life itself) it is important to be the first one to the punch, for the other person's good, as well as for your own!

A few years ago, a close friend of ours was feeling an anxious desire to find a nice girl, settle down, and get married. After a time, he found a young woman who qualified, and he proposed. When he first told us about her, we wondered how committed she really was because, even though she had said yes, he admitted that she had shown quite a bit of reluctance about accepting.

But our friend was just about as perfect a guy as a girl could want. We thought it would all work out because a girl would have to be a downright fool to pass up such a good catch. Apparently she realized our friend's qualities, and that was why she had accepted his proposal in the first place.

Love, however, is an affair of the heart, not of the head. So it wasn't long before there were problems on the horizon. Even though there were many reasons why she should have been thrilled at the opportunity to become his wife, she began experiencing some serious doubts about going through with the marriage.

Our friend was somewhat distraught, and he confided in us that she was having doubts. This was a critical time in the engagement period for him.

"Are you really sure," we asked him, "that you want to marry this girl? Because if you've had any second thoughts yourself or felt any doubts whatsoever, this is your perfect chance to get out of this situation honorably. . . ."

"Oh, no, *no!*" he protested vigorously. "This is *definitely* the girl I want. I really *do* want to marry her with all my heart. There's no doubt in my mind, whatsoever!"

"Well, then," he was told, "if that's true, then you'd better ask for your ring back *now*. Because if *you* take it back from her, ultimately it will save the relationship. She'll be able to clearly see that she wants you, and she will marry you. But if you wait until *she* gives it back, you'll lose her and she'll never marry you!"

Our friend stared in disbelief. "Oh, no, I couldn't do that!" he said. "I'd rather not rock the boat any more than I have to. I'm just going to let her work through this for herself. . . ."

Well, to make a long story short, he didn't take our advice and he *did* let her work it out for herself. As a result, they are both very happily married today. Of course, they are both married to other people.

We believe that, after all is said and done, things worked out for the best. But the fact is, our friend might have been very happily married to his first chosen love if he had taken the initiative to give her the freedom she needed, when she needed it, rather than keep her in a position where she felt trapped and was forced to find her own way out.

The problem may well have been a psychological hang-up on her part more than anything else. She may not have been trying to get away from *him*, as much as she was trying to get out of *the situation*. She perceived him as weak, and he could have changed that perception rather quickly with the right move on his part. If *he* had taken the initiative to remove the cause of her concern, it might have helped her to make up her mind, possibly in favor of choosing him.

The shame of this particular situation was that she was close to being happy with the relationship. The couple had a lot in common and probably would have been very happy together. All this girl needed was a little more reassurance from his independent behavior that he could survive without her, and a suggestion by his unexpected behavior that she might lose him. She was on the fence, as far as decisions go. If he had backed off temporarily, suggesting by his behavior that *she* might be causing *him* to have second thoughts, she might have realized that he was what she wanted.

LOVE TACTIC #55 Take Two Steps Forward, One Step Back

Dan Dunn, editor of the *DFW Singles Magazine*, noticed a pattern of psychological courtship that existed among his readers. He wrote an article entitled "You Can't Win If You Don't Know How to Play the Game!" which discussed an effective strategy in winning another person's heart. The following excerpt, which we agree with, clearly explains this tactic.

Switch roles!... It's simple, but it takes guts and self-esteem.
... The Pursuer holds the winning hand, but only if he knows
how to play his cards. The Pursuer needs to take two steps
forward, then one back! Let your desire be known, then step
back and give the Desired time and room to breathe. Give
them the chance to take a step toward you.

Don't get impatient; Desired [ones] aren't used to walking forward. If the Desired takes a step forward don't be too
eager to step [in response] too quickly. If they don't take a
step, wait awhile and try three forward and two back.

Switch. That's the key. Pursue, then wait to be pursued,
being careful to keep the proper distance between you and
the Desired. If you step [forward] too fast, you will run
over them, which is the greatest fear of the Desired. Yet,
they want a relationship as much as you do. As you pursue
and *back up*, this will give the Desired the time to think and
not feel threatened. Then you can pursue a step further.
Each time, you should advance two steps and retreat one,
each time closing the distance without overcoming the
Desired.

This is a tedious process and must be adhered to. Forgetting your strategies could cost you the relationship. Be careful! You must teach the Desired that you will be there, but
you won't smother them. This will give them the confidence
to give back the love and affection you desire, making you
the Desired. Thus, you have succeeded in the switch!

LOVE TACTIC #56 Take Advantage of Human Suggestibility by Acting Self-Assured

How many of you, when caught in a frustrating, unfruitful relationship, have ever wished you possessed magic powers to cast a spell
on the one you want and mesmerize them with your personality?
Well, you can! One of the greatest lessons taught by professional
hypnotists is that all persons, to one degree or another, are susceptible to suggestion under the right circumstances.

But some people are more suggestible than others. So the one you
want may be more or less suggestible than the average person.
Here's a helpful thing to remember: A key element in exercising

cising persuasion over another human being is the ability to appear to be confident in what you're doing. No person is without self-doubts, however. So don't feel bad if you occasionally feel that you're lacking confidence.

There are two keys to appearing confident. First, *pretend you feel confident*, even though you may not be. (And certainly, don't say that you're not sure of what you're doing!) And second, *continue acting confidently*. Show bravado, or false confidence, even in the face of failure.

This is, in fact, the "magic" of acting. Have you ever wondered what it is that gives movie stars and rock stars their mass appeal? It is this pretended air of confidence, which they manifest on stage. Even when mistakes are made, stars understand that they don't stop and point them out to the audience. That wouldn't be "professional" and it would destroy the magic.

You, too, should act as if you haven't the slightest self-doubts about what you're doing. As a result, others will believe in you, too. Continue to act this way. At first you should aim for satisfactory results, and then begin to raise your standards and work toward better results. This will, in turn, increase your confidence.

LOVE TACTIC #57 Beware of Catering, and of Loving Too Sweetly

Even though some people emphasize their desire for a partner who is sensitive, caring, vulnerable, and open—all positive traits—they clearly need someone who is tough, as well as kind. And, in fact, their initial fascinations will lean towards that person who most seems to have inner-strength, competence, and self-assurance.

So, in your efforts to fulfill someone's needs for friendship, don't neglect cultivating an atmosphere in which you also command respect. Otherwise, you'll run the risk of being like so many others who have found themselves in a predicament where they couldn't understand why they were being dumped, especially after they tried so hard to be there for the other person's every whim!

So listen to what *we* advise. Be strong. Show independence. Be willing to let the one you want maintain some emotional distance, if that's what makes them feel safe. Don't act desperate. And don't be afraid to say no occasionally. Remember, you must not fall into the trap of catering to the other person's every whim.

We're not saying to throw out compassion or good listening skills. Just don't let the one you want treat you like a second-class citizen in the process. Otherwise, your considerate behavior will be taken entirely for granted. You can quote McKnight and Phillips on this one: "If you let them disrespect you, you can kiss your love life good-bye!"

LOVE TACTIC #58 Proceed on Principle, Not Feedback

In order to win the one you want you have to proceed on principle, not reactionary feedback. Otherwise, you will set yourself up for failure. Don't gauge your progress by what the one you want seems to be saying at any given time.

Trust that if you continue to do everything in your power to create good will in the relationship, including cultivation of *friendship*, *respect*, and *passion*, the relationship will progress and eventually reach a point where that person will be in love with you. Remember, the only behavior your can control is your own. By controlling your own behavior in a purely constructive manner, though, you will have a positive effect on everyone around you. Do what is right and let the consequence follow! You will be most pleased with the ultimate result!

11

Praising the One You Want

What roles do praise and criticism have in winning the one you want? We feel that you should use praise liberally, but keep criticism to an absolute minimum.

LOVE TACTIC #59 Use Praise Liberally

Everyone wants to be well thought of. And no matter what position you hold in another person's eyes, they *do* want you to look up to and admire them. You can bet on that.

Oh, sure, if a person has many people giving them emotional strokes, he/she may take your praise and appreciation for granted, but, rest assured, nobody can ever get too much attention and admiration! The need for praise and recognition is like the need for food—constant and enduring. If you had to choose between eating a simple supper every night throughout the year, and eating a sumptuous feast once every month (with nothing to eat in between), which would you choose? Undoubtedly, you would opt for the constant source of nourishment. (You probably wouldn't even survive the first month, otherwise.) In the same way, the one you want will naturally gravitate to that person who meets their need for praise and recognition *most consistently*.

That's one nice thing about appealing to a person's need for admiration and recognition. Yes, it's an ongoing need, like eating. Even if a person is full at the moment, the chances are good that within a few hours they'll be hungry for more. Think of your positive attentions as a gift to the one you want.

DON'T OVERDO—JUST WHET THE APPETITE!

Giving praise doesn't necessarily mean that you should drown the other person in accolades. Let them get the idea that you are just *beginning* to be impressed with them, that you are *almost* an admirer, and that you *think* you see something special in them. Be consistent, but don't pour it on too thick at any given time. Once you have spent more time together, you can begin to show a little more enthusiasm in your positive statements.

If your praise is being taken for granted, then you've said too much too soon. Take a clue. Back off a little bit. Be a little more discreet in what you actually say, as opposed to what you *imply* through your actions. You'll be amazed at the lengths to which a person will go to try and stay in your good graces if they are unsure about your admiration. Eventually, if you offer praise with discretion, you'll have the one you want playing right into your hands.

Just remember, one of our most basic human needs is for recognition and reassurance of our worth. You have the ability to provide it for another person. Just remember, you must be sincere and you must simply be willing to be supportive and reassuring. Proceed on this basis, one small step at a time.

LOVE TACTIC #60 Use Flattery Creatively

One of the needs every human being has is to be praised and appreciated. Because of this need, flattery is something that is hard to get enough of in your life.

In fact, the best flattery is that which touches the areas where praise is most needed. One tongue-in-cheek definition describes flattery as "the ability to tell someone exactly what they think of themselves!"

Flattery comes in many forms and can be offered in many different ways. The following are some common examples.

1. "You know what I like (or love) about you?" Then praise a specific physical trait or quality about the person that you genuinely admire.
2. "Would you like to (take a walk, go for a drive, have dinner, go out, or whatever) with me?" Whether the person wants to or not, they will be complimented.
3. "You've had a great impact on my life and I will never forget you."
4. "You're the best (singer, ice skater, conversationalist, etc.)."
5. "You're so (smart, talented, caring, etc.)."

It is believed that the legendary Casanova's secret of great success with women was that he had mastered the art of flattery. (It is also a well-known fact that Casanova was physically unattractive!)

On one occasion, when a friend asked him how he so easily seemed to charm the women with whom he came into contact, Casanova responded by saying that he had learned to compliment them. The friend protested, saying that he and other men used compliments, but without the same mesmerizing effects as Casanova seemed to have. Casanova then shared that his secret was to compliment the *unexpected* virtues that a woman possessed.

For instance, if a woman was very beautiful and was used to being told so, then Casanova would compliment her on her intelligence, wit, or some other area in which she was, by comparison, hungering for praise. And if a woman was lacking in overall physical attractiveness, then he found some *particular* aspect of her physical appearance that he could sincerely compliment, such as her eyes or her hair. This tactic could not help but make him special in the woman's eyes.

LOVE TACTIC #61 Don't Be Critical

One of our favorite comic strips shows two guys who are drinking at a bar. In the first panel, one of the guys says to the other, "Would you like some constructive criticism?" The next panel shows the guy who had asked the question, dripping wet with his beer mug stuffed over his head. He is answering his own question, "Well, that answers that!"

No one really likes criticism, even when it comes disguised under the pseudonym "constructive." Some of the most cutting, hurtful, painful criticism comes from "friends" who claim to be doing it for a "constructive" purpose, "for your own good"!

Some people may argue that constructive criticism can be a good strategy. In fact, there are experts who believe that criticism is necessary to gain a person's respect. Our response to this belief is *No! No! No!* Criticism, in virtually any form, can be destructive to a relationship.

In addition to direct criticism ("You're wrong, and you should have done this or this"), there are three subtle forms of criticism that can creep in without your even realizing it.

The first form is to use the word "why" when asking a person to explain their behavior. An example is when asking a person, "Why did you do that?" The word "why" is critical. It's an indictment. The person is on trial with you as the inquisitor. This will not contribute to feelings of attachment for you.

Another form of criticism is to give advice. When you give advice, you are actually implying that the person doesn't have the capacity to work out his/her own problems. And that is, in fact, a put-down. We know many of you have never realized that this is what is happening, as it goes on all the time in most human interactions. But now you know. Be a good listener, but avoid giving advice!

The third and most insidious form of criticism is the "constructive" criticism discussed at the beginning of this tactic. Be aware that even constructive criticism can hurt a relationship.

Everyone goes through life receiving positive and negative strokes. The world gives all of us plenty of negatives, plenty of knocks. But when you get together with the one you love, you want to get built up, not knocked down! This may sound a little idealistic. But trust us. The one you're trying to win *is* idealistic about love. And the closer you come to satisfying the ideal, the better chance you'll have of winning their love! It *is* possible to avoid criticism. And you must work to minimize your inclination to criticize, intended or not, if you want your relationship to work. Criticism is one of the most damaging things in your attempts to win and keep the one you want.

LOVE TACTIC #62 Avoid Abuse

A lot of what we're talking about in this book focuses on the definite steps to *build* a relationship. But it is just as important for you to be aware of those definite things that *destroy* a relationship, such as the criticism discussed in Love Tactic #61. This will help you to avoid them!

Two of the most destructive behaviors in a relationship are *dishing out abuse* and, paradoxically enough, *tolerating abuse*. A relationship is designed for growth. As long as abuse is fostered by *either* party of a relationship, the partnership is doomed.

Many people endure being mistreated by their companion. Why? The answer is that they mistakenly think this will allow their companion to get the negative feelings out of their system. Eventually, they believe (hope) the abuse will stop. However, just like children who grow increasingly out of control with permissive parents, the unchecked abuse in a relationship will only get worse. A line must be drawn somewhere and the offending party must realize that the line must not be crossed. If the line is crossed, there will be dire consequences! This must be made very clear!

If your partner is allowed to think they can mistreat, abuse, or take you for granted, without any resistance, then their degree of respect for you will diminish. This will lessen their own romantic satisfaction *and weaken the bonds of attachment that bind the two of you together.*

Know this: A relationship built on *friendship, respect,* and *passion* will eventually bear fruit. When you mistreat your partner, or allow yourself to be mistreated, the relationship will immediately become weak and will continue to degenerate unless the abuse stops.

Emotional abuse in a relationship is a definite sign of trouble ahead. You may allow it to persist, thinking you see a light at the end of the tunnel. But that light is actually just a train that is heading your way. Take immediate action to stop any abuse as soon as you begin to realize it is occurring. This holds true whether you are the victim of the abuse or the abuser.

LOVE TACTIC #63   Use Anger Correctly

Whenever abuse occurs in any relationship, it must be corrected or else the relationship will fall apart. It is just as important to realize that there's no place for hostility in a relationship.

There is, however, a place for anger, but that place is only when your personal feelings are being stepped on by another. If someone is critical of you, you have a right to show anger, solely to make that person back off. Not only is it your right, but it is also your duty. This show of self-respect is a positive step toward winning the one you want.

12
Creating Insecurities

When two people are in love, feeling lucky or blessed is a sign of a healthy, strong relationship. This feeling comes from the recognition of powerlessness to control the other party's love. Therefore, when you're trying to win someone, be aware of this need. Realize that the other person must need to feel lucky to get you. Make sure that the other person is never so secure in the relationship that they take you for granted. As the relationship develops, try to maintain some degree of insecurity in them. In this way, as the relationship is blossoming and growing, they'll be more likely to appreciate you.

LOVE TACTIC #64 Make Them Insecure and Keep Them Humble

Pay attention, now, because this is an important concept: *The same feelings of insecurity that were the source of your intense passionate longing for your chosen heart-throb, will produce the same effect in the one you want!* What does this mean? You have to create an atmosphere in your relationship that will allow the other person to feel insecure.

This may seem harsh to you. After all, when you care about someone, the inclination is to comfort and reassure them. It is only natural to want to rescue the one you want from worries about losing you.

But, be wise here. Recognize that if the shoe were on the other foot and you were the recipient of such feelings of doubt, it would drive you crazy with wild desire. This passion would quench any unrealistic hopes you might have had for the other person and you'd be saying, "Sure they have faults and imperfections! But who cares? This is the one I want!"

Therefore, if you are to win at love, you must get the other person to see you in this way. You must commit yourself to a strategy that causes them to feel insecure about their hold on you. Remember, too much confidence will kill excitement. And it is necessary to sustain this environment of doubt for awhile, even after the other person has started showing overt signs of wanting you.

Of course, over a period of time (this could be many months) you may *gradually* give them a growing number of reasons to hope you might be in the process of being won over. But you must always be sensitive to too much cockiness on their part, even to the end of your lives together.

A good friend once described the ideal relationship of his grandparents. They remained very much in love all the days of their lives. His grandfather told him the secret of their successful marriage was that his grandmother was never absolutely sure that if she ever betrayed him he wouldn't be out that door and gone.

Do you want a real brain-twister? Think about this one. In order for someone to really feel intense passionate longing for you, they're going to have to experience the intense pain *of not having you completely*. In other words, if someone's not hurting over you, then they're not wanting you very badly, either. So if you want someone to really want you, you've got to be willing to hold off from reassuring them long enough to give them a chance to experience some pain over you! If the one you want doesn't have the power to make you miserable, they don't have the power to make you happy, either!

LOVE TACTIC #65 Create Some Distance

If you sense that you're not making a lot of headway in your relationship, this tactic may prove to be helpful. Your partner might be feeling some guilt for encouraging your feelings while not equally reciprocating. In order to alleviate their guilt, they may try to put their foot on your brake pedal.

They may not want to do anything to encourage you to fall for them any more than you already have. This would make them feel obligated to reciprocate, which would, in turn, cause them to get the feeling of "being cornered." Yet, they really do like you, and don't want to tell you to get lost. They just don't want to be trapped. They want to keep their freedom.

Before the relationship gets to this point, you've got to put on your own brakes first.

With this scenario in mind, here is what you should do: Call the person on the phone and tell them you can sense that things are getting a little bit too serious. Suggest that it might be a good idea to take a break from each other. For at least a month.

At least, that's what you should say. But that doesn't mean you have to follow through with it. Know perfectly well that you can call to say hello after a few days or drop by and see the person. You could even ask them to do something with you. Assure them that the separation is still in force, for the most part, but that this is just an exception. Tell them if they don't want to get together you'll understand.

In all probability, this strategy will elicit a favorable response. However, even though you will be spending time with them, keep up the appearance that, for the most part, you have no further expectations than this one get-together exception. You can squeeze a lot of mileage out of this "just-this-once" routine.

LOVE TACTIC #66 Break Off to Make Your Love Better

Often a person's resistance to you can be overcome by breaking off the relationship, and then resuming contact once again.

Don't shrink from conflict just because you're afraid of getting the one you want angry at you. The course of true love really never does run smooth! Just because the going gets tough, it does not mean the relationship is over. It's only over when you quit. So don't be afraid to take a tough stand from time to time, to scold if necessary, or even to break off contact with the one you want and drop them for awhile. But, just as important, don't forget to resume contact and pick up the banner of love again after the smoke clears.

After the first edition of *Love Tactics* came out, we learned of an experience from a woman who admitted that when she had first read our counsel to strategically drop somebody (temporarily) if they are taking you for granted, she was appalled. But then, after reflecting on her own marriage of more than twenty years, she realized we were right. She shared the following story.

I have to share something with you from my own life. When I was younger, I was one of those people who took their suitors for granted. When I started dating my future husband, he was so good to me that I guess I couldn't stand it. He showered me with attention and gifts, and I guess you could say I treated him pretty badly. I'll never forget one day when my girlfriends and I were driving down the street and I took off a bracelet he'd given me and threw it out the window. My friends were shocked that I would do such a thing, but I told them that it just didn't mean anything to me. . . .

Then one day, out of the clear blue, he just quit calling me. Just like that! Without any warning! Well, the first couple of days it was no big deal. I was sure he'd be back pestering me soon enough. At first, I was relieved that I didn't have to constantly deal with him. After all, who wants somebody who is *that* crazy about them?

But he didn't call, amazingly enough. And after a few more days of not hearing from him, I found myself actually beginning to miss him and wishing he would call. Then I began to doubt whether he was ever going to come back at all. I started chastising myself for having taken him for granted, and I was soon very sad and remorseful. I realized for the first time that I really did have strong feelings for him; but alas, it seemed too late to do anything to repair the situation. . . .

Well, about two weeks after not hearing from him, the telephone rang. I picked it up and suddenly heard his voice on the other end of the line speaking my name. A thrill went down my spine with an intensity I had never experienced before, and I'll never forget thinking, "I'll never let him go again! Never, no, never!"

He admitted, after we were married, that the whole thing had been a calculated move on his part to try to win me.

In the intervening years, though, she had forgotten how well the tactic had worked, until she was reminded of it by reading *Love Tactics*.

LOVE TACTIC #67 Don't Be Afraid to Let Go

In *Love Tactics*, we discussed the story line from the play *The Music Man*. We couldn't resist the temptation to use it again to illustrate a very important principle.

The Music Man is the story of a flim-flam salesman who breezes into River City, Iowa, masquerading as a music professor. His plan includes romancing Marian, the town music teacher, to gain credibility with the townspeople. At first, however, Marion refuses to be romanced and soon discovers that the Professor is a fraud. Just as she is ready to expose him, however, she begins to feel that there is something very good and wonderful underneath his mask (something even the Professor doesn't see). She starts to fall for him.

The Professor, not knowing that Marian knows he is a fraud, gets her to meet him at the town footbridge. His plan is to "score" with her before he skips town. The Professor thinks that if Marian knew he was about to leave her, she'd be clinging to him and begging him to stay (just like the girls in the last hundred and two counties).

But Marian surprises him. First, she makes it clear that she has no future expectations. Then, she tells him that she knows he is a fraud, but that she loves him for what he is underneath the facade. The greatest act of love, though, is her understanding of his need to leave. She tells him she is grateful for the memories he left behind. From that moment on, the Professor is in love and, in fact, powerless to leave her. You see, it is an ironic principle of love that the act of letting someone go is sometimes the very act that makes them cleave to you all the more.

THE IT'S-NOW-OR-NEVER PRINCIPLE— THE ULTIMATE ULTIMATUM

Every salesman knows that as long as a buyer can put off making a purchase, a sale cannot be consummated. Thus, a buyer has to be given a reason to buy *now*. It is human nature to postpone commitments. Basically, people do only what they *have* to do.

That is why there comes a time in a relationship when a person needs to be convinced that time is running out, and that the option of having you will not always be available to them. Of course, you should not resort to this ultimate level of influence until you have invested much time in the relationship and have formed a good solid foundation of friendship and respect.

The It's-Now-or-Never Principle, as you may have deduced, is designed to produce *passion* in the relationship. All you need is a spark, but when a person realizes they are about to lose you, that spark of anticipatory pain should be sufficient to bring all the other positive qualities of your relationship to mind. And this will help them make the decision that will bring you down the aisle together.

13
Rebounding from Setbacks

Not only should you know how to make your relationship move forward, you also need to know how to deal with the myriad of problems that will inevitably rise with any developing relationship.

Part of the experience of growth in life comes from making mistakes and then learning from them. The most powerful thing you can learn in life is that a mistake is never really a mistake unless nothing is learned from it. Therefore, don't look upon your failures in love as indications of powerlessness. Rather view them as stepping stones toward growing and becoming a more perfect person, a person who will be able to succeed in those areas of a relationship that may have failed in the past.

A lot of people go for years making the same old mistakes. What your attitude as a "love tactician" should be is to learn from the mistakes that you make, then come back harder than ever. When you try to put a round peg into a square hole and realize that it doesn't fit, don't keep pushing. Persistence does not mean continuing to try to pound that round peg into the square hole. It just means that once you know it doesn't fit, you'll try to find a peg that more closely approximates what is needed to get through the hole. That's the correct kind of persistence, *to continually try something new when something else hasn't worked.*

This is how Thomas Edison invented the light bulb. He didn't just get a bright idea (sorry about that!) and then come up with the first light-bulb filament out of thin air. He took existing ideas and tried to improve upon them. Ultimately, that's how the light bulb came to be. That's also the way it is with most great inventions and all great successes.

This theory is particularly true in relationships with people. If one approach doesn't work, try another, and then another. Use the approach that gets the best results.

LOVE TACTIC #68 Understand the Reasons for Setbacks

One principle we want you to keep in mind is that *every* setback has a cause. You may not always know what the cause is at first, but if you examine the problem long enough, eventually you will understand what is missing. Then you'll be able to fix it! You are not inherently powerless. In fact, you are inherently powerful.

The answer, the knowledge of what to do, and thus, the power, actually lies within you. Sometimes somebody else, like the authors of this book, can help bring out this knowledge. But you'll recognize that we're not really telling you anything you don't already know. For the same reason, there is also an infinite well of knowledge and understanding still untapped within you. You have the answers to thousands of as yet unasked questions. And that is where your power lies.

Believe it or not, you can win the person of your dreams because you are infinitely powerful, more than you may have ever previously believed. But first you have to believe that there's a solution! And you have to believe it strongly enough to look for it each time you encounter an obstacle.

Rest assured of one thing: All mistakes are made due to ignorance. They are not because you are inferior. They are not because you don't have what it takes, except perhaps in the area of needing a little more experience. Ignorance is not due to inferiority. It is due to inexperience. And *that* is always fixable.

But once it becomes clear to you, really clear, what you have been doing wrong, it will be relatively easy for you to correct the problem.

LOVE TACTIC #69 Hold a Steady Course

Don't be discouraged if it seems like your first attempts to win the one you want are without effect. Remember, love is an emotion that is subconsciously based. It takes a while to warm up someone's emotions.

Think of people as hot-water faucets—they take a while to warm up once you've turned on the tap! If you get discouraged because the one you want doesn't reciprocate your feelings right away, you may give up unnecessarily and turn off the tap (and they'll never have a chance to get warmed up!). Remember, you've got to keep doing the right things according to correct principles. Ultimately, other people's feelings and actions towards you will be determined *by how you behave towards them!*

When Tyler was dating Colleen he began to feel like she was the girl for him. Colleen sensed this, however, and began to feel that she'd better tell Tyler that he was not the one she had been waiting for all her life. (Are you beginning to recognize this pattern yet? One person begins to like another. The other starts to feel trapped and tries to discourage that person.)

Tyler later confided that his first reaction was, "Oh no! This can't be happening again!" as he had been on this route with other girls before. But by now his experience was beginning to get the better of him, and so was his stubbornness. He thought, "Well, who cares? I have just as much right to keep dating her as anybody else!" And so, instead of licking his wounds and going to his corner, he continued to date her and worked to win her over. Eventually, Cupid's arrow flew and found its target in Colleen's heart.

People are not inclined to reject you as a friend, you see, as long as they feel there are no strings attached. They're more likely to reject you if they feel they're becoming obligated, which limits their future options. You'll be surprised how many people will keep the door open to you once they've laid down their own ground rules and you agree to abide by them. Often, the most crucial ground rule they want to get across to you is "just friends" and "not serious stuff."

Accept someone telling you that they are not physically attracted to you but think you're very nice. If you can handle this crushing news with dignity, and continue to show a sincere active interest in continuing the friendship, even they will soon be surprised at how differently they feel towards you. Eventually this may ripen into actual feelings of love for you on their part! And then they *will* be physically attracted!

By the way, this pattern is quite common. One person has a stronger interest in the other. This makes the other take that person for granted and start to brush them off. However, guess what usually happens when there is enough persistence on the part of the pursuer? After they've shown that they don't shake easily, the pursued, disinterested person will bring out the big guns. As gently as one can shoot a cannon into someone else's face, they tell the person that there is no hope. They care a lot about them as a friend, they will say, but it would be cruel to lead their pursuer on with "false" hopes.

Most of the time, the pursuer would be so crushed by this information that they would drop out of the race. After all, it's not easy to stay poised when getting a bomb blown up in your face. However, it doesn't have to be this way if you are a persistent suitor! Hang in there, even if you've been told straight out that there is no possibility of the one you want ever wanting you. If you do, the odds are even more in your favor that the one you want will eventually eat their words and want you in the worst (or best) way.

LOVE TACTIC #70 Don't Be Discouraged by Your Beloved's Attempts to Deter You

What does it mean when the one you want tells you, "I love you—but I just need some more time"? You can be sure that they have not yet developed sufficient feelings of emotional longing toward you. The reason they want more time, whether or not they admit this to themselves, is that they want more time to find somebody better.

That's right. They are stalling with the hope—sometimes conscious, sometimes subconscious—that somebody else will come along and then they can dump you.

Obviously, the solution here is not to give the one you want more time! Why? The very reality they are stalling for may come to pass if you are not careful! What's the best thing to do? Recognize their symptoms of inadequate satisfaction, and make the necessary corrections.

This doesn't mean, however, that the person is looking for more attention, more catering to, or other *friendship* needs. They know, by now, that you're their friend. What they actually need more of, at this juncture in the relationship, is *doubt*.

You read that right! By this time, you two have already travelled that long path of *friendship* together and have established a decent, solid relationship. What you are currently facing is a *wall* that blocks your pathway, a psychological obstacle called the *commitment hurdle*.

So how do you get past this obstacle? You must find a way to go directly around it, over it, or under it. Think of your love interest, the one you want, as a person about five to six feet tall, and the *commitment hurdle* as a brick wall about nine feet tall. Under ordinary circumstances, it would be almost impossible for a human being to get over such an obstacle.

But with the proper motivation, it *can* be done!

So how do you motivate an unmotivated "friend" to decide they want you badly enough to commit to you? Employ the formula: *Friendship + Hope + Doubt = Passion*. They already have enough friendship and hope, in this situation. What they need is a little more doubt! That is accomplished by backing off a little bit. Then start being a little more mysterious in your actions and expressions. Be a little aloof. Create a little doubt.

LOVE TACTIC #71 Expect Adversity

In your strategy to win the one you want, learn to expect and plan to overcome adversity. Plan for the worst; the best will take care of itself!

Prominent spiritual leader Boyd K. Packer said in a 1963 address to the student body of Brigham Young University, "There is a strange phenomenon involved in courtship that is as strange as anything in human behavior. When a boy and a girl start to relate to one another, if the boy feels a heavy attraction for a girl and pursues her too strongly, surely he will be repulsed . . . while it is absolutely necessary that this deep attraction takes place, if one or the other of the partners makes an expression of it too soon, the relationship is destroyed . . ."

A twenty-eight-year-old friend shared an experience with us. In church one day, he spotted a girl who piqued his interest. The problem was that she was already involved with another guy (who was temporarily out of the country).

When she realized that our friend had become very interested in her, she tried doing everything in her power to avoid him. One day, in fact, she walked into church and saw him before he had noticed her. She actually dropped to her knees and tried to crawl away behind the long church benches before he spotted her. He approached her before she had a chance to get away.

Many guys would have considered her avoidance as an indication of disinterest and would have given up. But not this guy! Rather, his motto seemed to be, "I have just begun to fight!"

He continued to hang in there, and she could not help but respect his determination and self-motivation, because it was certainly obvious she wasn't giving him any encouragement.

To make a long story short, he won out. And when he did, her devotion and love for him was unparalleled.

We hope you realize the moral of this story. Heroes don't give up at the first sign of rejection. In fact, they don't really start making progress until they actually experience rejection. In Olympic circles they call the success threshold the "pain barrier." It is understood by all true champions that triumph comes only by persisting through the pain. In this case, our hero persisted and won the one he wanted.

Don't be discouraged because the one you want tries to turn you away initially. Don't try to force yourself on anyone. But don't give up, either. Use some strategy. Use some creativity. The one you want is just waiting to be won!

LOVE TACTIC #72 Handle Rejection with Patient Self-Assurance

Consider the case of a friend who not only experienced the trauma of being told it was over, but was also informed that the girl he wanted was going to move four hundred miles away to a college town where she had some other romantic interest. Talk about pain! And powerlessness! How could he ever win her if she was four hundred miles away?

However, the rejected young man maintained contact with her by phone. He checked in every few weeks to see how she was doing. Ultimately, when things didn't work out, she moved back home and married him, because she realized that his caring ran deep enough to pay the price of patience. And deep, sincere caring is what it takes to get another person's true love hormones stirring!

A STRONG DEFENSE DOESN'T NECESSARILY MEAN IT'S OVER

When Don first began dating Miriam, she was struggling alone to raise her young family after the death of her husband. Sure, she liked Don well enough, but her older boys, who were in high school at the time, were not all that keen on having a new man in the house. They put pressure on Miriam to make a choice between them.

Don never knew what happened. All of a sudden, Miriam stopped taking his calls, and she wouldn't answer the door when he came over. She had succumbed to the pressure from her kids, and had decided to make a clean break. Don couldn't even get her to come to the phone to discuss the problem.

After going on like this for weeks, Don finally drove his car on the same highway that Miriam used to drive home from work. He pulled his car off the side of the highway, stopped, got out, and raised the hood. When Miriam drove by and realized that it was Don who was stopped on the side of the road, she pulled over to help him.

"The car is fine, Miriam," Don said.

"Well, why are you on the side of the road like this?" asked a puzzled Miriam.

"Because it's the only way I could see you," Don admitted. "Miriam, I've been trying to talk to you for weeks!"

Miriam was a "goner" after that. Today, Don and Miriam have been happily married for twenty years, and we don't know of a more devoted couple.

Sometimes, the reason you face adversity when you're so close to victory is that people often put up their strongest defenses when they realize they haven't got much fight left. Hang in there when the fighting gets toughest. You may find a sweet, sweet surrender around the corner!

LOVE TACTIC #73 Don't Worry About First Impressions!

You've heard it before. "You can't change a first impression!" "You never get a second chance to make a first impression!" "Don't blow it, because your first impression is your lasting impression!"

One of the biggest things people worry about when first meeting someone or when attempting to initiate a relationship is that they will make some little slip and permanently blow their chances from then on.

Poppycock! Of course it's nice to make a good impression on someone. But every day is new, and every impression you make is new. It's true that someone may misjudge you at first. As a result, it may take a little time for them to see you in a more favorable light. Don't let these worries concern you.

Contrary to popular myth, the attitudes people develop towards you are not set in concrete with a single encounter. Rather, people tend to look at you in the context of their *entire accumulation* of experiences with you, not some momentary flash in the pan. Stick with it. You'll find yourself winning the one you want over time by having many possibly unimpressive yet positive interactions. These add up!

How many couples do you know who were not attracted to each other when they first met? If you haven't had this experience, then here's your assignment for today: Ask several happily married couples you know if they experienced love at first sight. Find out what their first thoughts of each other were. You'll soon start to get the picture!

There is one outstanding couple we know that has been married for over forty years. Still very much in love to this day, they are an inspiration to all who know them. She confided that she had not really been all that impressed with her husband when she had first met and dated him over four decades ago.

"I remember coming home from our first date," she said. "I was twenty at the time and he was twenty-eight. My mother was still up when I came in and she asked me how I liked him. 'Nothing special,' I told her."

Nothing special? You should see them today! The light that appears in her eyes whenever he is around her is enough to assure anyone of the irony of those first impressions! So don't be discouraged or dismayed if you don't feel like you've made a good first impression. Remember this: The only impression that really matters is the lasting one!

Most relationships do not begin with immediate feelings of love. Former President George Bush recalled his courtship with wife, Barbara.

He referred to their romance as "a classic love story." But Mrs. Bush more candidly remembered, "It wasn't love at first sight, but we enjoyed each other's company. . . ." Love, you see, is something that takes time.

Another young couple we know described their struggle to fall in love. The young man, who was severely overweight, found himself falling head over heels for a beautiful young girl in his church singles crowd. They became friends and he started calling her, but she refused to see him unless it was with the group, and she never let him pay her way anywhere. She was not interested in getting tied down to him. There were many very physically fit young men she found herself much more attracted to. He became discouraged, but continued making as much contact as she would allow. This eventually built up to a phone call a day, which she enjoyed and began to look forward to.

Months later, she went on a vacation with her family that lasted several weeks. During that time, she realized that she missed that daily phone call from her friend. She discovered that she had fond feelings for him and looked forward to talking with him again.

Upon her return, she called and told him how much she had missed him while she was gone. She then told him he could start paying her way when they went places. When he heard that, he knew he had begun to win her over!

Nonetheless, he didn't show her how overjoyed he felt. He continued to play it cool, and didn't wear his heart on his sleeve. He waited until her newly discovered feelings had had a chance to become second nature to her. Today they are an ideal, happily married couple.

LOVE TACTIC #74 Don't Get Discouraged ('Cuz You're Gonna Win in the End!)

Don't be discouraged if the one you want indicates that the relationship is never going to mature and blossom. Don't believe it! Consider the following story.

Nat admitted that when he first started dating Janine, he liked her very much, but felt that she lacked some of the essential qualities he *had* to have in a wife. Today, however, he is one of the happiest men alive, married to the very girl he was sure at the beginning didn't measure up to his standards.

What happened here? Did Janine somehow change? In this case, not really. What happened was that their love was nurtured and continued to grow. Eventually the feelings Nat came to have were strong enough to overcome all other obstacles. This is known as *bonding*. Love matured and strengthened with time.

Always remember: *Emotion is stronger than any logic ever devised or created!* At first, what may seem to be a disadvantage, such as an unimpressive first appearance, can actually turn out to be an even greater blessing, if the situation is handled right. A slow starter can be an impressively strong finisher!

Another common mistake among aspiring lovers is believing everything their partner says. When you elevate someone to the status of a worshiped idol, it's natural to assume that every word they speak is a revelation from heaven. This, of course, is not true. In many cases, they don't even know the real depth of their own feelings.

This is especially true if they tell you that the relationship doesn't stand a chance. Undoubtedly, they even believe this in most cases. However, you must maintain confidence that if you pursue this relationship in the right way, it can only get better and better until you have won them over.

LOVE TACTIC #75 Make Rejection Work for You

Being rejected can offer a great opportunity for you to gain respect and love from the one you want.

A common complaint among many women concerns the way men ask them out. They complain that men commonly beat around the bush to avoid taking responsibility (and possible rejection) for the invitation.

For example, women claim a man might say, "What are you doing this weekend?" The problem is that the man remains uncommitted in his question, while the woman must commit herself in the answer. If she says, "Nothing. What did you have in mind?" then it looks like she has nothing better to do.

On the other hand, if she doesn't want to let the guy know she has no plans, she might say something like, "I'm going to the county fair with my friends . . . why?" The guy will be forced to respond, "Oh, I was just wondering . . ." An opportunity to go out together has been missed because the guy, afraid of possible rejection, has not been straightforward in his request.

What is the best way to ask someone out? Be direct and bite the bullet, so you will be able to withstand possible rejection. That is true assertiveness and will ultimately result in true respect, because it shows your ability to stand tall, no matter what the other person's response is.

Ask simply, "Will you go to the movies with me Friday night?" Astonishingly, this is one of the hardest questions for one human being to ask another. It is, however, reflective of one of the main lessons taught in any salesmanship course: *In order to get the sale, you have to ask for it!* Too often, because of the pain experienced when one is turned down, along with the feelings of rejection that invariably accompany (and cause) this pain, you may find yourself subconsciously going to great lengths to avoid asking the simple but effective question, "Will you . . . ?" Instead, you hint around, hoping to give the other person enough encouragement to do the asking for you.

The term for this cowardly method of trying to get a commitment before giving one is called the Wimp Approach. This method inspires disrespect, the very thing you *don't* need when trying to win your true love's heart.

So, whoever you are, male or female, when you ask someone to go out with you, go in headfirst. After all, what's the worst thing that can happen? Sure, the person may say no. Or the person may say yes. Their answer is not as important as the fact that you asked.

Your ability to weather rejection is an attractive quality. That person who most appears to let the opinions of others have little effect upon him (like water running off a duck's back), displays a wholeness inside—an independence of soul—that commands the respect of those who observe it.

Ironically, this particular strength can be displayed only when there is a rejection to begin with! So what you need is a person who is *not* that impressed with you at first or, at the very least, not intimidated by you. This will give you the chance to show that person your ability to go right on living as happily as ever in spite of their rejection. That can help you to *win* their respect. Maybe this is why so many good marriages started out with one of the parties having to overcome the initial rejection of the other.

TAKE HEART! THE COURSE OF LOVE
NEVER RUNS SMOOTH!

Many times, people are afraid they have blown their chances for a successful relationship when things don't go as well as they once did. Resistance and rejection indicate that they can never win the person who is resisting them.

Contrary to this perception, resistance, rejection, breakups, and other setbacks in relationships are a natural part of the trip. They are not the end of the road! Most people in happy and stable marriages can recount tales of obstacles that they had to face and overcome during their courtship.

In other words, just because a horse tries to buck its first rider, that does not mean it won't make a great working horse when it's finally broken. In fact, as any cowboy will tell you, "Them horses that bucks the hardest, rides the best once they've reconciled themselves to their fate!"

If a farmer went out into his cornfield after watering the new plants for a week and expected to find a fully mature harvest, he would be sadly disappointed. Yet how many people are like foolish farmers who, upon their first visit to the crops after only a week of watering, say, "What scrawny little things are these? This isn't what I've been hoping for!" And they mercilessly stomp the disappointing harvest back into the ground!

But you know what's really funny? Hopeful suitors go back into the same field of potential relationships week after week in this same self-destructive frame of mind, and they continually destroy the tender young plants, which, if nurtured long enough, would have eventually given them more reward than they could receive in any other way. Premature harvests in relationships inevitably lack substance.

LOVE TACTIC #76 Be an Injured Martyr

The one you want has a conscience. In all our discussions with people who have jilted lovers, we have never talked to one who bragged about their ability to hurt somebody. What we're saying here, though, is that sometimes you should allow your pain to show. Don't overdo it, however.

On a limited basis, showing your pain can be beneficial at times. It can help the other person see you in a way that may soften their heart towards you. Compassion, after all, *is* love. And once some love has gotten its foot in the door, the rest will follow more easily.

When someone hurts you it is often because they themselves are feeling pain—the pain of not feeling understood. When this happens they really just want to communicate to you some of the pain they are feeling.

Most people can only hurt you so much before they begin to make it up to you, especially if they feel that you understand their reasons for hurting you.

Allow that person to see that they have hurt you. This will cause them to lose the inclination to hurt you further.

A friend of ours shared the following story of his courtship with the girl who eventually became his wife.

When Diane first started dating Jack, she showed a little bit too much enthusiasm toward him. This eagerness quickly diminished his interest, so he stopped dating her.

However, Diane wouldn't give up. She kept showing up in places where he was, hoping he would ask her out again. Although Jack was polite to her, he tried not to lead her on in any way. The thing that frustrated Jack was that Diane didn't seem to take his hints (which meant he was not being understood). In other words, she appeared insensitive to his uncomfortable feelings.

Then one day Diane showed up at Jack's apartment and told him that she was going to fix him a special lunch and bring it to his office that day. *That* really did it! Now Jack was starting to feel trapped! So he told her nicely, but *very firmly*, that he didn't want her to make the lunch. The message was obvious, and suddenly, for the first time, she got the message.

Immediately, Diane's hurt became very apparent. Her eyes clouded, her shoulders dropped, and her voice became submissive as she said, "Oh, okay . . ." Then she quickly turned and walked away.

Jack's conscience suddenly got to him, though. He realized he had hurt someone who had been nothing but nice to him from the start. His need to feel understood suddenly had been satisfied, for he knew that Diane finally realized the frustration he had been feeling.

Jack ran after Diane and apologized. He tried to explain that he hadn't meant to be harsh, but he had made other arrangements for lunch that day. She sweetly accepted his explanation, but the hurt within was obvious.

Jack suddenly became a different person where Diane was concerned. He decided to take her out just one more time. Well, they were married within a year, and you can be sure that he didn't marry her out of pity. In fact, if anything, by the time they were married, he was absolutely crazy about her.

So don't discount the power of letting the one you want see your pain when the time is right. We're not telling you to be a crybaby, but don't feel like you should never show any hurt, either. You just may miss out on an opportunity.

LOVE TACTIC #77 Don't Fall for a Stall

People want to get married. They really do. They want to love and be loved forever. So when people appear to have reservations about getting married, don't be deceived into thinking that their reservation is about marriage, as much as it is about whom they are going to marry.

The real reason marriage is entered into reluctantly (or avoided completely by the person having the final say in the matter) is that the man or woman secretly harbors a suspicion that they might still be able to get someone better. They're not really sure that the person they've got is the best to be had.

So what they do is stall and hope that something better will come along in the meantime. What happens then? The person who is being put on hold is, in effect, being used. This is a horrible truth. It means that if somebody comes along who has a little bit more of what your partner is looking for than you have, *you will be dropped like a hot potato!* Don't kid yourself into believing otherwise.

So what is your protection? You must command their loyalty! Don't let them string you along indefinitely. But don't condemn them for doing this, either. They're only human. It's *your* responsibility to convince them that you are the best one for them!

Authors Mickie Silverstein and Teddi Sanford shared a classic story in the *National Singles Register*. A young woman named Pam had been put on hold for three years by Gordon, her boyfriend. During that time, Gordon vacillated in his decision to marry her.

Finally Pam reached a point where she was determined enough to go for broke. She decided to use a strategy to maximize her chances for success.

One night, after an especially delectable dinner, which Pam had prepared, she told Gordon she had something to discuss with him. She took his hand, looked him directly in the eyes, and informed him that she had decided to end the relationship unless he was willing to marry her.

Gordon, as most men would in this situation, took it calmly and coolly because his experience told him she wouldn't have the strength to follow through with this ultimatum. He went through his usual list of reasons why he couldn't commit to anything at that time. Pam patiently waited for him to finish, then she firmly emphasized that she was serious about what she had said. She told Gordon that her mother was going to be visiting her in three weeks. If they were going to get married, it would have to be then. And if not then, then never, and they were through.

Gordon, of course, tried to buy some time, saying he needed to think things out. Pam calmly asked how much time he needed, but Gordon was (characteristically) noncommittal. She firmly told him that she needed an answer in one week. If he couldn't make up his mind by that time, then it would be too late.

Of course, Gordon still didn't believe she was serious. Pam had to show him that her strength ran deeper than her words. She told him not to call her or see her until he had come to his decision. Then she asked him to leave.

Some who have suffered in similar situations may never comprehend how she did it. After Gordon left, she turned on her answering machine while she bawled like a baby. He tried to call an hour later, but Pam let the machine run. She also refused to take his calls when she was at work.

Three days later, she found Gordon nervously waiting outside her office. He begged to talk to her. Pam simply asked if he had made his decision yet. When he hemmed and hawed around, she simply said that they had nothing to talk about. The next day she didn't hear from Gordon at all.

The following day, a balloon bouquet was delivered to Pam along with a message that read: Call your mother and invite her to a wedding. I love you, Gordon.

When you've established a good solid foundation for a lasting relationship, know that you're in a strong enough position not to be put on hold. Insist on being taken seriously.

LOVE TACTIC #78   Confront the Dragon Face to Face and It Will Die

Confrontation is one of the most effective techniques in keeping the lines of communication open. And, as you know, good communication is crucial to a successful love relationship.

One common characteristic of almost all relationships that fall apart is a lack of good, effective communication. In fact, if you're worried about your relationship, concentrate on improving the communication. You'll be surprised at the difference it makes.

Good communication can overcome almost any problem you might encounter in achieving intimacy in friendship. If you don't understand what's bugging the other person, then good communication is missing.

On the other hand, no matter how bad your relationship may be in other ways, if you really understand how the other person feels, and if that person feels understood by you, then it's a sure bet that good communication exists between you (in spite of whatever other differences may exist). In the final analysis, this is the real essence of a loving, romantic relationship.

The person who wants out of the relationship almost never fully discloses the real reasons why. And for good reason! They feel if they disclosed their true motivations or dissatisfactions, the other person would be devastated.

Here's the challenge. Even though it may hurt you to hear it, you must get your partner to tell you his/her true reasons for wanting out. Paradoxically, this is the key to keeping the relationship intact.

In this type of situation, most people don't really want to hear the truth. It's difficult to hear about your inadequacies or imperfections, and so you allow the other person to keep his/her true feelings from you. This, in turn, only reinforces their reasons for ending the relationship.

Most people who do the breaking up almost always believe that the reason they are rejecting the other person has to do with logical reasons of incompatibility. They believe they are not compatible with the character imperfections of the other person. But the truth is often something that they themselves are completely unaware of. Too often the real reason the person wants to end the relationship is because of the other person's inability to insist upon the truth, even if it hurts. In other words, the main problem is actually the inability of the rejected one to get through the communication barriers that exist.

So, what to do? The person being rejected needs to get the other person to lay all of his/her doubts, fears, and dissatisfactions on the table. These negatives will begin to seem petty and insignificant compared to the comforting sense of being loved and understood.

LOVE TACTIC #79 Drive with a Purpose, a Plan, a Design

Do you know what one of the hardest parts of winning the one you want is? It's temporarily accepting their lack of enthusiasm in the beginning, and maintaining your own willingness to persevere in spite of this lack of reciprocation. If you can pass the test and overcome this tendency to give up, then there is no heart you cannot ultimately persuade to be yours!

Most people are not willing to set aside their own feelings and needs for immediate reciprocation long enough to plant the seeds and cultivate the harvest. You must be different. Remember, human beings are like mirrors. They reflect the attitudes that they think others have of them. You are no exception to this rule. The first time a lack of reciprocation slaps you in the face, you will experience how difficult it is to continue feeling enthusiasm for that person. You'll feel like rejecting them in return. You must not do this, however! Their initial lack of interest in you does not mean that they won't be a very loving and committed companion to you down the road.

There are many examples of couples very much in love with each other where either or both of the partners had no romantic interest in the beginning. You undoubtedly know many yourself.

When the one you want does not take the initiative and ask *you* for a date, then the responsibility for inviting falls back on you. The important thing is that you ask. At this point it doesn't matter so much whether they accept or not. It is a greater extension of yourself to spend ten seconds asking the person to go out with you, than it is to spend hours with them in casual conversation (although that is important, too).

Yes, extending yourself *is* the right thing to do. It cannot help but create some form of goodwill. Eventually, through such willingness to make yourself vulnerable to rejection, you will be able to obtain a toehold in your effort to get the other person to willingly spend some time with you. Don't be distressed if it isn't much time at first. In fact, there is something you can do. In subsequent efforts and invitations, simply scale down the magnitude of your request. Make it so humble and minuscule that they cannot reasonably refuse you.

For example, let's say you begin asking the person to accompany you on a nature walk for a few hours. He or she turns you down. The next time you phone, call on the spur of the moment and say something like, "How about meeting me for a quick ice-cream cone tonight at 9:00? I promise that you will be home by 9:30."

The idea here is to keep scaling back your requests until you can get your foot in the door and finally get that person to spend a few minutes with you. As long as you adhere to the Love Tactics principle of being the first to say good-bye, even though you may have initiated the contact, you should be able to increase the amount of time spent together.

LOVE TACTIC #80 Work to Improve Your Relationship

As long as at least one person is willing to do whatever is necessary, a relationship can always be made stronger and better. No matter where your relationship is today, you must recognize that it can always be improved.

Every interaction has an effect. For example, if you lie to someone, you can be relatively certain that when that person finds out, it will weaken their trust in you. If you criticize or insult someone, you can be sure that your remarks will hurt that person and weaken the bond of affection.

The key is to do things that build the relationship up faster than it can be torn down. The ideal, of course, is to eventually eliminate all of your negative behaviors. Remember, you have the power, through your actions, to strengthen or weaken your relationship.

LOVE TACTIC #81 Wear Their Resistance Down (By Building the Relationship Up!)

An important premise to always remember is that willpower wins out in the end. Persistence empowers! The following story is an example of true willpower.

In September 1970, young Will Stoddard returned to college after an absence of three years. One night he stopped at a friend's apartment to borrow a history book. It was there that he first laid eyes on Carol, his friend's roommate.

Will sensed, right off the bat, that this girl was special, and he wanted to get to know her better. After a few minutes of conversation, he asked Carol if she would go with him to his class reunion the following week. She immediately turned him down.

Many guys would have become disheartened at that rejection, but not Will. He understood the principle that "no" does not necessarily mean "never," and he took Carol's answer to mean, "not right now." So he asked her again. This time he had more earnestness in his voice. But again, Carol turned him down flat and intimated (misleadingly) that she was engaged to someone else.

Will ran into Carol three days later. He decided to give it one more good old college try.

"I'm going to give you one more chance," he teasingly/seriously said. "Now, will you go out with me this weekend?" Once again, Carol made some excuse and said no.

By now, Will had been turned down three times, but he was not ready to give up. He definitely had what you call "Will" power.

Will decided that maybe he could soften Carol up a little if he talked to her on the phone. The only problem was that she avoided his calls. Finally, after dodging his phone calls for several days, she gave in and talked to him.

"I'd really like you to go out with me," Will pleaded. Carol told him that she had already made plans to go out with her roommates that Saturday night. "But that's Saturday," Will persisted. "You can still go out with me on Friday night."

Finally, Carol relented. There is just so far a person can go to try and get out of a date. Well, one date led to another, and another . . . Today, Will and Carol are happily married and the parents of four children!

For every story like Will's, there are a thousand more about relationships that were abandoned prematurely. Will's example is a good one for every person who thinks that "no" is the end of the road. Remember, "no" doesn't necessarily mean "never." It simply means "not this minute."

LOVE TACTIC #82 Deal with Mistakes

Often, in the pursuit of winning the one they want, people make some real mistakes. It is very easy to do something that can turn away the one you want. Have you ever had this experience? Don't let it get to you!

We've had lots of people write to us, wondering if they could correct mistakes that had already been made in their relationship. That's the beautiful thing about this world. Nothing is permanent, and that applies to mistakes as well.

Begin each day anew, applying the lessons you've learned from the previous day's mistakes. In doing this, your success ratio will increase each day. You've heard it before—a mistake is never really a mistake unless nothing is learned from it. How does this apply to romance? Remember that the human heart is not something that can be hardened against you forever.

Let's say you have made a mistake in your relationship, and any time you try to encounter the other person, you are met with resistance. If you continually show evidence that you have changed—as a result of learning from your mistake—it will become increasingly difficult for the other person to resist you. Make sure you don't repeat the same old mistakes that got you into trouble in the first place. Show that you *are* trying to realize where you need to change, and *are* actually incorporating those changes into your approach.

LOVE TACTIC #83 Avoid Common Mistakes

There are a number of common mistakes made by aspiring lovers. Let's discuss some of them.

Mistake #1
Giving Up Prematurely.

What do you do when one approach doesn't work? Many people give up, thinking that it's hopeless. It's not hopeless. *But it does require some adaptability on the part of the suitor!* That man or woman who is most capable of trying something new and different is best positioned for future success.

And here's something else to think about. Many married couples have reported that it took sometimes more than twenty dates before they began to feel love for each other! Don't give up because the one you want doesn't seem to be in love you after one date. Persistence in your attempt to develop the relationship could make a world of difference in the final outcome.

Mistake #2
Trying to Rush Romance.

Have you ever tried to force the other person to show signs of reciprocated commitment far too early in the relationship? That's why it can be advantageous to let the relationship take the form of a *platonic friendship* for a lengthy period of time at first, without any pressures of commitment.

This relaxed relationship often blossoms into romantic love. Try to allow the friendship to take its natural, unimpeded course. Trying to extract a commitment at the wrong time can actually hurt even a platonic friendship. After all, how many of your good friends, your closest ones, require commitments from you? And if they did, what would your reaction be? We'll bet it would be to put some emotional distance between you.

Mistake #3
Not Meeting Basic Emotional Needs of the Other.

There is an obvious difference between a casual acquaintance and a close, intimate friendship. The latter, of course, is the kind of friendship you are striving to cultivate. A true friend anticipates the needs of others. A true friend extends him/herself to help satisfy those needs.

True friendship often requires reaching out to the other person. It also requires a willingness to gracefully back off, temporarily, when the person seems to have other priorities. If the person wants to interrelate with you, it will require a willingness on your part to listen empathetically. And it will require a whole new way of thinking when it comes to giving advice and making suggestions.

People need this kind of relationship in their life, but few ever obtain it. You, however, are in a position to provide it, if you so choose. You can make a point to tell the other person good things that you've noticed about them, and reassure them that they are special! These are the kinds of emotional needs that people crave to have met every single day. And why shouldn't you be the one to fulfill those needs? It will make you indispensable to that person.

Mistake #4
Being Too Agreeable.

Many people make the mistake of surrendering their individuality in order to be the kind of person that the other one wants them to be. Some people may find this exhilarating, but it is absolutely the wrong thing to do when trying to win someone's heart.

People should be attracted to you by the image of *independence* that you project, not your *neediness*. Also, be aware (and here's an image to remember) that *vultures are attracted to weakness and vulnerability*. Yes, there will come a time when your lover will want you to share your vulnerabilities, but don't put the cart before the horse. If you show your weak, dependent side (everyone has one) too much, or too soon, you will suddenly find the one you want turning away from you (or preying on your weakness).

Be independent-minded and *act* independent, as well.

Mistake #5
Tolerating Emotional Disregard or Mistreatment.

If may seem amazing, but the one you want will eventually try to see how much they can mistreat you and get away with it. Even the nicest people do this. It is human nature to test your limits, especially with someone you care about.

After awhile, the person you are involved with may wonder (subconsciously, mind you) if all of the tender consideration and loving kindness that he/she has been getting from you is deserved. They may feel that you show kindness because you are afraid to display anything else.

So then (still not realizing what they're doing or why) they may do something inconsiderate or unkind to you. At first, of course, it will be very subtle. If you allow the unkindness, you can count on more and more flagrant types of inconsiderate behavior. In some cases, the person may even become verbally or physically abusive.

If you want to command respect *and* keep the one you want happy in their love for you, it is absolutely essential that you draw a line early in your relationship. You must insist on being treated considerately. Let the other person know that you will be more than happy to meet their needs for consideration and kindness; but at the same time, you must insist upon your own needs being met as well. By demonstrating that you won't tolerate being treated with disrespect, you show respect for yourself. This, in turn, will raise your esteem in the eyes of others. It will make them want you more.

Mistake #6
Being Too Available.

The very key to making someone desire you is to maintain a certain degree of unavailability. Never forget: *People want what they can't have!* This does not mean that you can't or shouldn't be partially available as the relationship progresses. Be aware, however, that if the other person senses that you are available at their every beck and call, they will probably start to lose interest in you.

Many insecure suitors, however, feel that if they make themselves *at all* hard to get, they will wind up losing the very one they want. Nothing could be further from the truth!

If your partner in the relationship exhibits some signs of doubt, *don't panic!* It is imperative for you to back off and let your partner catch his/her emotional breath. Know that the worst thing you can do is shower that person with more attention. Any increased attention will make your partner (who is already feeling a bit closed in) feel trapped and even more determined to drop you.

Part III
WINNING BACK THE ONE YOU HAVE LOST

Many of our readers write to us about damaged or broken relation-ships—even marriages—and wonder if there are tactics that can help restore the love that once was there. Can former loves be won again? The answer is yes! But read this whole section before you start jumping up and down for joy.

Nothing in life ever comes without a price. The harvest of love does not come spontaneously. It requires a time for planting and a time for cultivation. Where severe damage has occurred to a crop that once existed, time must be taken first to clear the field. Only then can one start recultivation.

So the main difference between restoring a broken relationship and beginning a new one is that it may take longer to restore the broken one. Time is needed to undo weeks, months, or even years of damage that have taken their toll on the relationship. As we have already pointed out, the only lasting mistake you can really make is to quit trying.

Remember, part of the process of cultivating deep, lasting love normally includes going through rotten, difficult, insecure times. Wisely did Shakespeare say, "The course of true love never did run smooth."

For some reason, rocky roads actually make relationships stronger, once they have been successfully travelled together. People who withdraw from the challenge each time the going gets a little rough never get to enjoy the fruits of accomplishing something truly wonderful. Always remember, when the going gets tough, the tough get going! It's worth going through some pain for the things in life that are worthwhile. True love means *commitment*. You have to decide if you are really committed to making the relationship work (preferably long before you actually begin engaging in battle for it). So don't think that just because you're going through some rough sailing you're necessarily going to sink. The trick is to fight to keep your ship on course.

As baseball great Yogi Berra said, "It's not over till it's over!" And in love, there's no umpire except you. It's not over until you say it's over. That gives you all the power. If the relationship has fallen apart, think about what went wrong. Re-evaluate. Are there changes you can make? Are you willing to make those changes? Making positive changes will help you make personal progress in becoming a better person . . . someone more capable of giving and receiving love. There is no reason in the world why you should ever believe the one you've lost is irretrievably lost. However, it may be easier to start over with someone new. Only *you* can decide whether it's worth it or not to try to fix a damaged relationship. *More Love Tactics* gives you power through knowledge, but you must be practical and use common sense.

Even though, ideally, you can win if you hang in there long enough, sometimes it's just not in your best interest to do so. This is the question that every decision in life ultimately comes down to: When should you keep trying, and when should you throw in the towel? Keep in mind the words of the famous Serenity Prayer: "God, grant me the serenity to accept the things I cannot change, the courage to change the things I can, and the wisdom to know the difference." This prayer, which is a good guide to live by, is the motto of a growing army of empowered human beings in twelve-step groups around the world.

Yes, in time you can win almost anyone's heart using the correct love-inducing methods. But don't ever believe that you can ever really change the person! No, even though you may win a heart, you will never have the power to remake it or change its nature. You must *truly* be willing to ultimately accept the other person just as he/she is! The irony of knowing more love tactics is that if you are not very careful, you may win someone's love only to realize it does not bring the fulfillment for which you had hoped.

So what's the point? Be sure you want a person who truly would be your best choice, rather than wanting someone simply because they are momentarily unobtainable. It's quite a decision, and one you must ultimately make by yourself.

14

Learning How to Win Back a Lost Love

After the publication of our first book, *Love Tactics*, our most popular reader comment was, "I wish I had read your book sooner. Is there any hope for me to win back the person I lost?"

The answer is yes, there is always hope. You must go back and apply the knowledge learned from correct love tactics. Don't be afraid of failure. Effective strategies for winning back the one you have lost are found throughout *More Love Tactics*, as well as in the original book *Love Tactics*. You hold the keys for success.

Like any skill, it takes practice to properly implement love strategies. Practice consists of trying and failing, trying again and failing a little less, trying still once more and finally getting the hang of it, and finally succeeding on a consistent basis. But none of this will happen unless you get out there, do your best, and refuse to accept any negatives.

LOVE TACTIC #84 Determine the Potential for "Repair"

When attempting to decide whether you should cut your losses and start over or not, we suggest the following thought process:

• *Assess the damage, then determine the effort needed for repair.*
The first thing you need to do when determining how much damage you may have caused in your pre-existing relationship is to consider

how serious the damage was and for how long it occurred. J.B. spent over ten years emotionally abusing his wife. She eventually hardened her heart toward him and left. The big shock for J.B. was that he didn't see it coming until the day she walked out on him.

Love can conceivably be restored in a relationship, even where abuse has occurred. But in J.B.'s case, it may take a long, long time.

In the second part of your damage assessment, honestly review your role in the relationship. For instance, how much time did you spend showing consideration and kindness by listening to your partner? How often were you critical? Did you build up your companion with words of praise and appreciation? Were you excessively permissive in the relationship? Did you insist, for the good of the relationship, that your own needs, as well as your partner's, be met? Each of these questions must be addressed objectively.

Was there a good balance of selflessness and selfishness? Did you let your partner take you for granted? Did you speak up when you were hurt and show anger if your pain was disregarded? Did you withhold the pleasure of your company when your partner continued to show disrespect for your feelings? Before you can start correcting the things that you've been doing wrong, you first need to know what the problems are.

The third part of this assessment process is to determine how much effort will be needed on your part to restore the relationship. Just because you know what to do doesn't necessarily mean you have the intestinal fortitude to pull it off successfully! There is no sense wasting your time hoping to change a relationship if you're not willing to make the necessary changes.

Even though you may have an ideal goal, human weakness will always prevent you from reaching absolute perfection. Still, you should try to be as perfect as you can. You may not hit the bull's eye, but you certainly can get close.

- *Determine if restoring the relationship is worth the effort.*

Once you realize the price that must be paid in order to win back your partner, a question must be faced. Are you willing to pay that price, whatever it may be? Are you willing to endure, without reward, for as long as it may take? If so, then this is an undertaking that's worth the effort. The best of luck to you!

However, if you find yourself wanting to re-establish the relationship, but not willing to change or work to rebuild the broken ties, then wake up and face the real world! You are simply not willing to pay the price. Write the relationship off to experience and look for another. Just remember, never shortchange what any relationship requires or you'll fail every time.

• *Know how to let go.*

If the relationship has ended and there is no possibility of reconciliation (for whatever reason), you may still have to face another problem. Although logically you know you must give someone up, emotionally you may not be able to do so. It's not that you're *unwilling* to give up the person, it's that you're *not able!* Or at least it *seems* that way.

Here's some good news. Time really does heal all wounds. And time can help you even more effectively if you help it along. Keep your mind occupied. Get involved in worthwhile activities while you come to grips with your loss. Diverting your mind can relieve a lot of the pain and restore your emotional strength.

A young woman who had been through several broken relationships shared her prescription for getting over a heartache. She called it her Get-a-New-Dog Theory. If you lose a pet, some people believe it will help if you get another. In some ways, relationships with people are similar. True, you may never totally forget or replace the one you've lost. But getting a substitute can help.

Make sure the replacement for your lost love has as many desirable qualities as possible. Take your time narrowing the field. If you don't, and you become dissatisfied with your new love, you may drift back into long periods of sad contemplation and comparison. But when you choose wisely, and select someone who is capable of meeting your emotional needs for love, you'll be surprised how healed and comforted you can still feel in spite of an earlier loss.

LOVE TACTIC #85   Know When to "Cut Your Losses"

Any person's heart can be won eventually, since every human heart responds to being loved. However, some hearts are not worth the time it takes to win them. There are often many other opportunities that may be better for you.

Does it make sense to spend years cultivating a harvest in barren ground, when a more fertile field lies just next door? (And often it does!) Does it make sense to spend years walking on eggshells, having to watch every word you say, when you could be enjoying those years with a person who nurtures and comforts *you*?

Although you should want a prize that you have to work for, don't be fooled into spending your time trying to win something that is attractive solely due to its unavailability! Remember, you have to continue living with this person once you have won them over. Some basic personality traits don't change. Be cautious of wanting someone who isn't considerate.

On the other hand, beware of getting involved with neurotic people-pleasers, who go overboard in their attentiveness toward others. This personality type can actually smother you, quenching your flames of desire. So be careful not to jump into a committed relationship with such a person.

15

Showing
a Willingness
to Change

Let's assume that you are not giving up on the relationship. You want to give it one more concerted try. Let's discuss some of the strategies that can help you.

One of the most essential attitudes necessary in applying the suggestions in *More Love Tactics* is to realize that no one is perfect. However, you're working to progress as much as you can towards perfection.

Understand that change is a lifelong process. As you learn the lessons life has to teach you, you should apply those lessons by showing a willingness to change. This requires humility. It requires knowing that you're not perfect. It requires acknowledging faults.

But take comfort. There is no such thing as a person without faults. If you learn the lessons life has for you, and make the changes necessary to apply those lessons in the future, you'll ultimately come out on top. Recognize that you *can* make changes, and that those changes can help you become a better and happier person.

LOVE TACTIC #86 **Assess Your Strengths and Weaknesses**

It is helpful to understand that the one you want may feel that you are not the person of their dreams. That's okay. It's okay to be imperfect. It's okay to be resistible. It does not necessarily mean that you will lose the person that you want. You must, though, be honest. Recognize your strengths and weaknesses. When you face a weakness, acknowledge it then accept it. (This, ironically, transforms that weakness into a strength!) You'll become a more attractive person through this honest acceptance.

How can you use this process to help you win back the one you have lost? Remember that facing your own weaknesses will make you stronger emotionally. There's a certain peace, serenity, and glow that comes with accepting yourself for who you are. This will result in a charismatic magnetic attraction towards you. It is not something you have to advertise. Rather, it is something that will radiate from you.

LOVE TACTIC #87 Be Willing to Change and Grow

Everybody should be willing to change. Anybody who is unwilling to make changes, stagnates. This is certainly not good for a relationship. But the fact is, there is only one person in this world that you can change and that is you! So reconcile yourself to the fact that if you want your relationship to grow and become better, you must focus on making changes in yourself.

Gently try to show, mostly by example, how certain changes may benefit both of you. Make sure that you're not resistant to change. After all, you're the one trying to win back the other person. That person has left you because of a lack of satisfaction in the relationship. The only way that can change is if you change.

Of course, this doesn't mean that change is easy, but this is one of those instances where you have to make the choice. Should you stay the way you are and risk the permanent loss of the relationship? Or should you attempt to make certain needed changes, which are comfortable for you and will, hopefully, increase the likelihood of reconciliation? Don't feel that you have to change in impossible ways. Make slow but steady changes in a direction that can make you more desirable in the eyes of the one you want to win back.

Considering all this may make you angry. You may feel that you shouldn't be the one changing, the other person should! Remember, you are the one who is trying to win the other person. So you are the one who has to take the first step. But fear not, if you do a good job with that first step, other steps will follow (and you won't be making all of them yourself).

Use a scientific approach to make change. The first step is to try to see what is going on. Try to observe it as clearly and as objectively as you can. What are the reasons that led to this relationship dissolving? What have you done? What has the other person done? What other variables are involved? Take a sheet of paper and write down every conceivable idea that comes into your mind.

The second step is to try to figure out what can be done. What are the changes that can be made? How can you make certain changes? How can you gently encourage the one you want to be willing to make certain changes? Again, it is a good idea to jot down all the thoughts that come to mind.

Step three is to implement your plan. Make sure that you proceed in a way that is comfortable for you, as well as for the other person.

LOVE TACTIC #88 Create Some Excitement

Boredom is a factor that is often found in relationships that have fallen apart. Either or both of the individuals may have become so locked into certain patterns and routines that the spice of the relationship is gone. Try to create some excitement. Figure out things that will interest and entice the other person. Do things that will make that person realize that there are more good things that can evolve out of the relationship.

Variety is the spice of life! If companionship is the cake, excitement is the icing. So it's essential to create excitement in your relationship by seeking to grow, having new experiences, and being unpredictable.

You take a positive step in your relationship when you try to create excitement and have new experiences. Your efforts will further endear you to the one you want. It's so important that you try, even if you fail in the attempt. A good attitude about trying to develop new experiences in life will cause you to become more attractive.

Excitement can be created in several ways. Having a positive attitude and showing enthusiasm (even when it is not strongly felt) is one way of creating an air of excitement. Another way is not to get caught up in a routine. Try to change and add a little variety to your everyday life. Don't always go to the same places. Try new restaurants, vacation spots, or even a different skating rink. Get out of the house. Don't sit around all the time. Try cultivating new friends.

16
Evaluating Communication Skills

The biggest part of any relationship is friendship, and the core of friendship is communication. Whether you're trying to win back the one you have lost or are attempting to win somebody for the first time, communication is of utmost importance. Losing a love indicates that there were problems between you in the communication area. Therefore, if you want to win this person back, you'll have to look closely at past communication problems.

There's a saying that goes, "Facts not frankly faced have a way of coming back around and stabbing you in the back." That's what happens in a lot of relationships. If you are afraid to take the bull by the horns and communicate frankly and freely, eventually the relationship will fail. Accordingly, you need to have good communication skills, and you need to correct them if they've been the source of losing the one you want.

SO WHAT HAPPENS?

What are some of the ways in which the communication in your relationship has broken down? Conversation may no longer be meaningful. Important feelings that have to be shared may not be. New, interesting topics are never brought up. Either one person or the other becomes bored, disgusted, angered, or annoyed with the other (yet these feelings may not be discussed). Either individual may look elsewhere for satisfaction.

Another problem with a breakdown in communication is that, because the relationship is in jeopardy, feelings should be expressed more than ever. Yet it's often at this very point that feelings are expressed *less* frequently. This often accelerates the falling apart of the relationship.

Virtually every single communication-improving tactic found in this book is relevant in trying to win back the one you've lost. They may simply require some modification to make the technique work now, given the precarious state of your relationship. In addition to the tactics presented in this chapter, you may find it helpful to reread the communication tactics discussed earlier in this book. Ask yourself, "How can I use this technique to win back somebody who has turned away from me, is hostile toward me, is not interested in what I have to say, or has moved on with his/her life?" Combine those tactics with the ones that follow.

LOVE TACTIC #89 Start a Healing Conversation

Good communication is a key to re-establishing a positive relationship. Initially, you may have to settle for *any* type of interaction when trying to communicate with the other person. Even expressing anger, for example, can be a step in the right direction.

There are times when you may be reluctant to express your feelings because you feel as if you're walking on eggshells. You may feel that if you say anything more it will further damage the relationship. However, this may be the wrong approach. Evaluate your relationship. If it seems to be going nowhere, then you may have nothing to lose. If the relationship is going to end anyway, why not give it one last shot?

Start a conversation. Say whatever you have to in order to draw out that person's feelings. Try, try, try! Then listen, listen, listen! Show consideration but be persistent. Show a genuine interest in what they have to say, even if you don't like hearing it.

Getting a conversation going under these circumstances is like pushing a stopped car. The hardest part is getting it moving in the first place. Once it is moving, though, pushing it becomes a lot easier (in spite of the fact that you may be pushing a two-ton piece of machinery). However, anticipate uphills as well as downhills in these discussions. Be prepared and show that you're interested.

LOVE TACTIC #90 Keep Interactions Warm

Don't be hostile. In your conversational efforts, try to be as calm and as supportive as you possibly can. The other person may get angry or hostile, but don't let this happen to you. Maintaining control is essential. You're treading on thin ice already, so don't risk sinking into the icy waters where there is no communication at all!

A perfect example of maintaining control comes from an episode of the television classic *The Honeymooners*. Ralph and his wife Alice had gotten into a fight in which he had called her names. She had stormed out of the house and went to live with her mother. Once Ralph had cooled down, he and his good buddy Ed Norton decided to send Alice a recorded message in the hope that she would melt when she heard it and come back to him.

He began the recording by being very warm and loving. However, as the recording continued, he became angrier. He ended the recording by losing control completely, calling Alice some of the very same names he had called her when she stormed out!

Norton immediately jumped in, calmed him down, and began a new recording. This time Ralph maintained control and was able to express his feelings in a very loving and endearing way. Even Norton was brought to tears!

Norton was then given the responsibility of delivering the recording to Alice. As you might have guessed, Norton gave Alice the wrong tape. You can imagine the consequences of such a grievous mistake!

So what's the moral? Maintain control. By remaining calm and expressing your feelings in a warm, loving, supportive way, you can increase the likelihood of developing a conversation in which an exchange of ideas is comfortable.

LOVE TACTIC #91 Understand, Don't Just Agree; Listen, Don't Just Hear

This tactic relates to giving feedback. When you express agreement or disagreement, you are implying that you understand what the other person is feeling. But that is really not your judgment to make. Only the other person can judge whether or not you are understanding correctly. Your objective is to listen responsively in such a way that *the other person feels that you understand them.*

How do you do that? Continue to give feedback by seeking clarification, as well as by implementing the reflective listening techniques we talked about in Part II. Your goal is for the other person to sense that, yes, you're aware of the doubt, the dilemma, the negative feelings that they're experiencing. By sharing those feelings, they will feel more bonded to you.

Good relationships are based on understanding and empathy, not on agreement. Why? You can have disagreements with somebody, but as long as each person understands the other person's point of view, and understands the right of the other person to have that point of view, the conversation will constructively build up the relationship.

It's far more important to show respect for a person's feelings than it is to simply agree with their ideas. Five minutes of empathy and reflective listening does far more to join two people together than twenty-four hours of agreement does.

Don't become defensive if the other person becomes critical of you. One of the surest ways for the lines of communication to break down is to become defensive and retaliate with painful retorts. Don't do that. Rather, sidestep any verbal javelins that may be thrown your way, allow them to land harmlessly, then respond in a way that is designed to add to and enhance communication.

LOVE TACTIC #92 Show That Positives Outweigh Negatives

All relationships have both positives and negatives. When a relationship is moving along nicely, the negatives are nothing more than unpleasant events that have to be endured. However, when the relationship is in trouble, it seems like the positives are fewer and farther apart. In addition, most of the attention seems to be focused on the negatives.

It is important to get the other person to focus on the positives. Help that person put unpleasant past experiences into proper perspective by working to make as many positive experiences as you can. Giving clear examples of the potential for positives can overshadow any of the negatives that inevitably occur in a relationship.

At the same time, though, you should focus on changing yourself. It will show that you are aware of the negatives that have turned the other person off to you.

LOVE TACTIC #93 Keep on Stroking

Regardless of the discouragement you may feel in the relationship, try to sprinkle in a liberal amount of praise and positive comments. Everybody likes to be stroked, even somebody who may be so upset with you that they want to end (or have already ended) the relationship. By including a generous amount of praise in your conversations, and by emphasizing the good, positive qualities of the other person, you can increase the likelihood that they will listen to the other things you have to say. Focus on positive, praiseworthy topics, and shy away from being critical.

However, remember that too much honey can be too sweet. Try to be realistic in your use of praise. Otherwise, it may choke the other person. Too much praise may be overwhelming and may appear as though you're trying to cover up the real issues in the breakup of the relationship. So keep things in balance. Some praise can go a long way, but too much can go nowhere.

LOVE TACTIC #94 Defuse Their Resistance

Here's a way to keep a conversation going at those times when it may otherwise seem impossible: Don't disagree with things the other person is saying. Even if he/she is airing all of your faults, don't contradict what's being said. Why? It will take the wind out of their sails. (And remember, contention only stirs up the storm!) As it's your intention to discuss how things can be changed, you

must begin by having an awareness of the problem. By your willingness to hear what the other person says, you're showing your sensitivity to their feelings. (Sure, there may be times that you silently
disagree, but you do want things to improve, don't you?)

This tactic accomplishes a couple of important things. It helps
the other person get his/her feelings out in the open. It shows that
you are willing to respond to their needs. And it encourages the
other's faith in you because you are willing to listen. This can
facilitate increased communication, especially on those topics that
have contributed to the rift in your relationship.

LOVE TACTIC #95 Focus on Areas of Mutual Agreement

Find an issue on which you and your ex-partner agree. Any issue,
whether it's positive or negative, can serve this purpose, as long as
your views are in agreement. Even an area of mutual dislike can
provide some common ground for discussion, despite the relationship still being very fragile.

Remember, the other person may feel that the two of you have
absolutely nothing in common, and this may be why the relationship
is ending. Demonstrate that there are certain areas on which the two
of you agree.

LOVE TACTIC #96 Keep Interactions Constructive

When the two of you discuss things that are bothering you, try to
guide the conversation so that these sensitive points are presented
in a constructive way. Both of you should offer suggestions on how
to improve these bothersome areas.

For example, let's say the other person brings up one of your
negative qualities. Listen for a little while, but then try to redirect the
conversation. Ask him/her what you can do to make it better. You
can make a lot of progress by showing your willingness to change,
rather than fighting it.

The same holds true when you present your concerns to the
other person. Don't just criticize. Try to offer suggestions or ideas
for things that you would like to see. Use "I" messages, such as "I'd

like to see ..." or "It would make me feel better if we ..." This makes the criticism less threatening to the other person, enabling him/her to think about your point more clearly.

One mistake often made in failing relationships is the tendency to take things for granted. For example, you may get into a much-needed conversation with the other person, airing some hurt feelings and other grievances that needed to be aired. Then after a particularly productive session, either or both of you might assume that there's nothing more to talk about. Wrong! Continue to have these constructive discussions on a regular basis, even if it seems like there's nothing that needs discussion. For your relationship to have gotten to the point where it was on the verge of breaking up, or did in fact break up, there are so many underlying issues that need to be discussed that regular conversations are the only way to really eliminate these obstacles. This is another important aspect of being persistent and consistent.

LOVE TACTIC #97 Stress the Importance of Mutual Listening

You know by now how important listening is as a component of good communication. Not only is it essential for you to be a good listener, it is equally important that your partner is, too. During conversations, try not to accuse the other person of not listening to you. Rather, present important points in short bursts, a little at a time, and pause to make sure the other person is listening before you continue.

It's easy to tell if the other person's mind is wandering. When this happens, pause and wait before proceeding to your next important point. But do it in a gentle, tactful way. Ask for feedback from time to time. Don't be condemning if the other person seems unwilling to listen. They may not be emotionally capable of providing you with a listening ear. If this is the case, you may want to reconsider whether this is the right person for you.

LOVE TACTIC #98 Avoid Making Assumptions

If you're not sure how the other person feels, ask. Don't assume anything. Mind reading can create anger in the other person, especially if what you're suggesting is totally different from what he/she is actually thinking!

At the same time, avoid making the other person read your mind. How do you do that? If there is something important that you want to communicate, make sure you express it. Don't assume the person understands.

LOVE TACTIC #99 Call a Truce

If you're trying to reestablish a relationship that is falling apart, recognize that the state of your relationship may be so fragile that virtually anything that is said or done can further widen the rift. Consider calling a truce. Ask that person, for a specified period of time, to avoid saying or doing anything that might be perceived as negative and promise that you will do the same! Then try to fill the relationship with such quality goings-on that the truce will end up being a long-term one as the relationship grows stronger. In other words, agree to set aside less-important issues of irritation temporarily for the sake of the many positive things you both have going for you.

Although this technique can work well, there's a time that it can be inappropriate. If the one you are trying to win back wants to communicate an issue that may be unimportant to you but is definitely important to them, calling a truce now would show a total disregard for that person's feelings.

An ideal time to use this tactic would be when you're trying to get a point across to that person, and you sense that he/she is becoming irritated. Then you may want to put the whole discussion on hold and try to do something that would be interesting and stimulating.

Calling a truce does not mean that you will never return to the issue(s) that have been put on hold. But an enjoyable diversion should provide more of a solid footing on which to resume the discussion when the time comes.

LOVE TACTIC #100 Insist, Don't Plead

In addition to working on your communication techniques, you must also demonstrate your confidence. A common reason for losing the one that you want is that you may not seem to be as confident as you once were. Don't appear to be a wimp. Be in control. Begging or pleading indicates a lack of power, and it does nothing to gain the respect of the other person. On the other hand, if you insist on certain things, you will appear more confident in what you are saying. If a lack of respect was one of the things that contributed to the breakup of the relationship, insistence may be one of the things that will restore it.

A girl we know, Joanne, came to us for counseling. She described how ideal her love relationship was in some ways, but how frustrating it was in others. Her boyfriend constantly took her for granted. She pleaded with him on numerous occasions to stop taking advantage of her in this way, but he either didn't respond or he blew it off. The behavior continued.

Joanne soon realized that her pleading came across as weak and nagging. She learned that if she really wanted her boyfriend to stop taking advantage of her she had to *insist* that he stop. And she had to be willing to back up her insistence with a consequence.

When you insist on something, you must be prepared to follow up with an actual consequence. And if you're not prepared to follow up, don't nag! It will come across as whiny and will create disrespect in the relationship.

Remember, you don't have the right to change someone simply for the sake of change. You do, however, have a real right to insist that the other person does not hurt you in any way.

17
Using Attention Wisely

One of the most widely used concepts in raising children is that attention affects behavior. Attention is not the only factor, but it is certainly the dominant one.

It's the same with adults. The basis of the human emotional diet is attention. No person can get enough. Therefore, if you provide a person with quality attention, they will blossom and grow in a relationship with you.

LOVE TACTIC # 101 Demonstrate the Advantages of You

Watch any effective sales presentation and notice that the salesperson points out benefit after benefit before mentioning the product's special low price. The price of the product is never given first. It's the same way in relationships. You must remind the person of the benefits before focusing on the normal responsibilities that go with the relationship. Focus on the benefits, not the costs.

In the game of love, you should realize that you are selling yourself. You have to show the other person why it is in their best interest to maintain a relationship with you. The operative word here is to show or demonstrate. Don't just talk about the benefits. Telling a person that you love them, that you care about them, and that you're committed to them, is not nearly as effective as being

297

in a relationship and showing these things to the person. You should do as little talking and as much showing as possible.

In trying to win someone back, remember that some or all of the advantages, positive characteristics, or traits that were initially part of the relationship may have faded or been replaced by other, less-desirable characteristics. Part of your demonstration should include assertively showing the other person that those good qualities still exist and that you are willing to reestablish them in the relationship.

LOVE TACTIC # 102 Give Freely of Your Love

There are two kinds of love: unconditional love and conditional love. Unconditional love is given purely without expectation of reciprocation. Conditional love is given in expectation of receiving something in return. Conditional love is more common, although throughout your life, you must be willing to give a certain amount of love unconditionally.

The need to give unconditional love is especially important if you're trying to reestablish a relationship. You have to be able to show the person that you have the capacity, the strength, and the desire to give without expectation of something in return. And as you do that, the other person will open their mind to the thought of continuing to receive the benefits of reconciling with you.

LOVE TACTIC # 103 Spend Money Wisely

Finances and money are often central issues on which the smoothness of a relationship rests. It has been shown that one of the greatest reasons people break up is because of problems over money. Realize that moderation is the key in all things. You can be too foolish and too easily parted with your money, which can cause problems. Being miserly or too tight with your money can cause problems, too. So look for a moderate compromise where you earn and spend your money with maximum intelligence. Try to make sure that you are financially wise and prudent. In doing so, you can eliminate one of the most common difficulties involved in breakups.

Money can be an advantage *or* a disadvantage, depending on how it is put to use. The question is, which is which? Should you spend money on trying to win back the one you have lost?

When relationships are falling apart, one of the things that people tend to do is buy gifts for their partner. Financial means are used to influence and interest the one that they may be losing. There are cases in which this can be a very beneficial thing to do. But if you're going to do it, make sure to do it wisely.

Gift giving or spending money on the one you want to win back may not seem like the most pleasant or rewarding of ideas. However, it can work wonders if done judiciously. You must be careful not to let the other person think that you are simply trying to buy their love. Rather, you want your money to speak as loudly for you as your words might if you had the opportunity.

Any gifts that you give should be personal gifts, useful gifts, not ones that have no clear use. Money spent on activity-related gifts should include things that (hopefully) you can be part of. Tickets to a concert or show, as well as a gift certificate for dinner in a special restaurant, are all good choices.

Try not to spend money beyond your means. If you do, the discomfort that you may feel will negate any positive benefits to come out of spending the money in the first place.

LOVE TACTIC # 104 Share Quality Time

Compared to money, time spent with the other person is infinitely more important. So the greatest sacrifice you can make to assure a person of your love and commitment is to give of your time. Of course, quality time means positive time. This involves meeting the other person's emotional needs for attention, understanding, acceptance, appreciation, and affection. If you're not meeting those needs, then you're not giving quality time.

There is a big difference between quality time and quantity time. All too often relationships go sour when, regardless of the amount of time you spend with somebody, there is no quality in that time.

For you to be able to determine what quality time is, take yourself out of your own desires. Focus on the other person. Think of what that other person may have communicated to you in the past. What things did they want from you (time-wise), or did they just want you to be available? And exactly what did that mean to them? This is what defines quality time for them, and this is what you want to show to that person.

When you decide on things to do, make sure that you are extra sensitive to what you think the other person wants. All too often, one's own interests take precedence. These priorities tend to overwhelm the other person's desires. A relationship can fall apart if a person feels that his/her interests are not being enjoyed. Try to focus as clearly as possible on those important activities, those interesting events, that the other person would enjoy. Make yourself an integral part of those activities.

If the one you want to win back has, for a long period of time, wanted you to try a particular activity, try it. Even if it's something that you never wanted to do before, and even if the other person knows of your lack of interest, sincerely express your interest in trying it.

Quality time often involves being alone with the other person. Larger get-togethers can sometimes take away from that quality time. Quality time is time spent in constructive discussion, sharing thoughts and ideas with each other and patiently listening to each other's words. Compare this to time spent silently staring at the television or a movie screen. Talking during commercials is not necessarily quality time. But substantive reflective listening, especially if the one you want is hurting, is an example of quality time.

LOVE TACTIC # 105 Share Burdens and Responsibilities

A major motivation for getting married is the fact that life is difficult. Life is tough to go through alone. It's easier when you have someone to share it with. Ponder the Oriental saying, "Shared joy is double joy, shared sorrow is half sorrow." Life's joys are more joyful and lows are less painful when they are shared with a true companion. Show the other person your willingness to share not only the joyful experiences but the burdens as well. This can be a very important strategy for winning back the one you have lost.

Be helpful. One of the things that can create a rift in a relationship is the feeling that somebody has to bear his/her burdens alone. Try to show sensitivity to their feelings and try to bring about change. Try to share the burdens. Find out what the most unpleasant things are for them, then help out as much as you can. The minimal amount of time that this involves on your part will reap great rewards.

Keep the following thought in mind: People don't run from being loved. They run from being enslaved or committed to things. Of course, the other person has a responsibility to the relationship as well.

Often in a relationship, both people fall into their own routines. One person makes the plans, the other person follows. This can be fine if they are getting along well and the relationship is thriving. But if the relationship is falling apart, consider the fact that the one you want may be tired of his/her role. Try to assume more of the responsibility for that role.

LOVE TACTIC # 106 Flex Your Emotional Muscles

If there is a problem in a relationship, emotions are probably very heavily involved. Recognizing the emotional concerns on each side of the fence is very important. Being able to tap into the emotions of the other person may be one of the keys to winning back that person.

If the one you lost is depressed, for example, being aware of that person's depression is important. Try to figure out a way to help them deal with the depression. The same thing goes for anxiety, guilt, boredom, loneliness, or any of the other emotions that the person may experience. Flex your own emotional muscles. Show that you're strong, compassionate, and willing to help. Show a sensitivity to the emotions of the other person. This can help reestablish positive thinking in the other person's mind, and can lead to a reconciliation.

Remember that every person looks for someone to lean on. Demonstrate that you have the emotional strength to help another person through difficult times. Show that you have the capacity to be there for them, without being drowned by the emotion or the pain that they are experiencing.

Share their pain. By seeing your emotional strength, the other person will become confident that they can lean on you in times of need. And this will further enhance the relationship by increasing not only their desire, but their hope that the relationship can work.

Here's another thing to think about. There may be times during your attempt to win back the one you have lost when the situation seems hopeless. It may seem that there is nothing that you can say or do that's going to have any impact. This is the time to flex your emotional muscles. The one true asset that you have, the most important factor in your efforts to win back the one you have lost, is your strong feeling for that person. After all, you wouldn't be going to this extent to try to reestablish a relationship if it weren't so important to you. Use that as a basis for flexing your emotional muscles. Share your feelings. Pull out all the stops. Make sure that you communicate how important the person is to you.

Remember the saying, "All's fair in love and war." If your assertiveness creates guilt or anxiety in the other person, then so be it! If it can get the person to consider what you're saying, and look toward what might be worked out for the future, isn't it worth the effort?

Although it is very beneficial to be assertive, it is just as important *not* to overdo it. Too much aggression can cause the other person to return to you out of fear. Eventually, when the fear fades, that person will regret having gotten back into the relationship.

18

Being a Successful Competitor

If you are trying to win back the one you've lost, you may be involved in intense competition. This may be because your former love is no longer interested in you, or because there is another person pursuing them.

If the one you want to win back has already entered a relationship with somebody else, you will have a much more difficult road to travel. This doesn't mean that your task is impossible, but you have to be aware that the person may be less receptive to your tactics.

There's a saying, "Never let them see you sweat." This applies when the entry of a rival affects your relationship or your efforts at winning back the one you have lost. Remember that true strength is shown by those who are capable of looking failure squarely in the face and not flinching.

Ultimately you must prepare yourself for the possibility of failure, even though you have maximized your possibilities for success by using these love tactics. Try not to fear failure. It can be counterproductive to fear the loss of the one you love to someone else. It is better to face the always-present possibility that you may lose that person, and know that you'll go on and survive anyway.

Isn't this negative thinking? No! What you're really doing is trying to strengthen yourself to become ready for these possibilities. Your strength will be conveyed to the one you want. Isn't this better than your fear being evident? Evidence of fear can actually weaken your possibilities with the other person. Your ability to communicate confidence is one of the strongest elements you can introduce in your attempts to win back the one you want.

Never fear your rival. Always have confidence in the Love Tactic principles. If you treat the person in the best possible way and meet their emotional needs, ultimately you can come out on top.

LOVE TACTIC #107 Face Your Rival

You must be able to face your rival in any situation and still show the ability to handle the complete loss of the one you want to that rival. If there is any chance for your success, it is through this course.

If you know who the other love interest is, don't show fear. Don't present yourself as being inferior to that person or in awe of that person. Always show yourself as a pillar of strength.

It's normal to feel jealous. It's normal to feel insecure. It's normal to feel intimidated. But don't speak negatively of your rival to the one you want. Rather, speak of that person respectfully (if you have to refer to them at all).

It's better to just ignore the competitive situation as much as possible. Pretend that you are not affected one way or another. Don't demonstrate jealousy. It will make the other person feel closed in, trapped, and inclined to try to get away from you. Jealous actions won't get you back together.

LOVE TACTIC #108 Withhold What They Want

When you feel your partner drawing away from you, it is instinctive to cling tighter. Remember one of the paradoxes of love: You draw closer to that which evades you, and try to escape that which chases you.

This calls to mind the story of the little boy who went with his father to fly a kite. His father showed him how to let the string out so the kite would rise. By the time the string was out all the way, the kite was flying high. The little boy excitedly jumped up and down because he had never seen such a thing before. He said, "Daddy, let the string go. The kite will go all the way up to the sun." The father responded, "If we let the string go, the kite will go off course, fly about wildly, and eventually crash to the ground. Remember, son, sometimes it is the thing that holds you down that keeps you up."

In romance, it's the same kind of paradox. Sometimes, the things that you think have an adverse effect on the relationship can actually have a positive effect. So if the other person shows signs of drawing away from you, you may want to draw a little bit away from them. Show a little independence. As you do that, you may suddenly become desirable to them.

When you're trying to restore a relationship, it's very easy to forget this rule, especially at the first indication that the person may be coming back to you. But realize that you must still withhold some of yourself. The more totally you give of yourself, the less desirable you become.

LOVE TACTIC # 109 Be Persistent and Consistent

Persistence is the key to accomplishing all things. Consistency is simply proving your integrity through your behavior and remaining true to the principles that have been presented in *More Love Tactics*.

You won't be able to apply the principles perfectly, but you must continue in your efforts to the best of your ability. Learn from your mistakes. Persistence does not mean that you keep trying something that does not work. Rather, try something, evaluate the portion that doesn't work, and learn how to reapply it in a better way. Persistence just says, "I don't give up, I will find a way . . ."

Remember the saying, "Slow and steady wins the race." Don't be abnormally aggressive in any phase of your attempts to win back the one you have lost. Rather, be persistent and consistent. Continue to do the things that you feel are going to help your relationship, and show that you are ready, willing, and able to change.

LOVE TACTIC # 110 Suggest Conditions for Reconciliation

Don't suggest conditions for reconciliation before the other person is ready. It may be a turn-off if they feel that you're trying to sew them up, and it may drive them away. The best approach? Give freely of your love until they clearly want you back.

It's probably better to let the other person indicate areas of change that they would like to see. This may be done in a testing manner at first, without any commitment. The implication, however, is that if changes are made, they'll be happier with you and they'll want to be back in a relationship with you.

Remember, throughout all of these discussions, that your competitor may be lurking in the background, waiting for something to go wrong. Make sure you keep this in mind, especially when you start discussing your own terms for reconciliation.

Sometimes, especially if you're the one trying to win the other person back, you're better off starting with very few demands. Don't give a lengthy list of things that have to be changed. You're in no position to be demanding when you are the one who is on thin ice to start with!

In preparing the groundwork for reconciliation, try to listen very carefully and take very seriously every concern that is expressed by the other person. Don't belittle their concerns. What are the most important things that the person wants from you?

Make sure that both of your needs are being addressed. Don't make it seem like everything that's being done is for the other person at this point. You are involved, too! Don't allow yourself to become a doormat.

It's very important not to press for a commitment. Reflect the other person's feelings back to them. Then follow up on their suggestions by showing your acceptance and understanding through your subsequent behavior. Show, through your actions, that you're actually making the changes that they had hoped for. Let them know that you're really listening to them and are sensitive to their needs.

Continue to focus on the reasons for the split so that you can make sure the same mistakes don't happen again. Part of the conditions of your reconciliation may be to have continued discussions that focus on the areas of your incompatibility. It may take some time before the other person is willing to take a chance on a commitment with you again. Remember that positive things existed in the original relationship, and you must look to reestablish them.

All of the tactics we've described need to be continued in a successful ongoing relationship. Don't feel like the only way that there can be a reconciliation is if you do everything for the other person. Yes, you must be willing to change, but a good strong relationship requires flexibility, compromise, and willingness on both sides. So, while striving to meet the other person's needs, don't allow them to walk on you in the process.

If there seems to be a desire to reconcile, make sure that you maintain a long-term perspective, where all efforts focus on that reconciliation. Try not to plan on an immediate full reconciliation. In other words, don't say to yourself, "We'll be back together in a week." You can be sure that there will be some problems that will occur after a week.

Try to focus on a reconciliation effort of six months or longer, where both people must work to overcome the obstacles that set the relationship apart in the first place. Remember, the relationship did not go bad overnight (although it may have seemed to). It will take awhile to recultivate the relationship.

In your discussions on reconciliation (or on anything for that matter), sound confident and constructive in the things you say. Don't whine or beg. This behavior won't inspire interest from the other person.

LOVE TACTIC # 111 Give the Other Person a Vacation from You

Sometimes, after all you have done or have attempted to do, it may seem like you're still not having success. At this point, you may need to let the other person experience life without you. Let that person realize that you're capable of living happily without them. Give that person a vacation from you.

This doesn't mean that you're giving up. What it does mean is that there's a limit to how much you can continue to bang your head against the wall. After you back off for awhile, the other person may be more open to a new encounter with you. A vacation from you might open their eyes to what they're missing.

This vacation can be a week, a month, or even longer, depending on your particular situation. Don't ever feel that this is the end. Make this a specific strategy, in which you plan how much time will elapse before your next contact. Prepare yourself for how you'll respond if the person contacts you, and what you plan to do the next time you contact them. Your whole purpose in doing this is to show them that their life will not be as complete without you in it.

LOVE TACTIC #112 Consider a Professional, Third-Party Viewpoint

There may be times when, despite everything you've tried to do, you don't succeed. Or, you may find that although your relationship might have a chance of getting back together, you're not able to do it yourself.

Getting professional help can be a very important asset at a time when it seems like nothing else is working. Getting objective feedback from a trained professional may help you to eliminate the last obstacles that may be keeping you from winning the one you want. Besides, we all need moral support, and sometimes it's just plain nice to know we have someone on our side! If you do seek professional help, make sure you work with somebody who is qualified and experienced in the field of human relationships.

LOVE TACTIC #113 Evaluate Who Is Winning the Game

Don't take it personally when the one you want seems unable to respond to your romantic overtures because they're already preoccupied with another love interest. When a person is already involved in another fulfilling love relationship, it does not leave a lot of room for your pursuit.

What it all comes down to, though, is how successful your rival suitor is in his/her ability to satisfy all three of the fundamental romance needs of *friendship, respect,* and *passion* in the life of your mutual love object. Realistically, your competitor is at a disadvantage, unless he/she has read *Love Tactics* or *More Love Tactics*.

Until the one you want is married, anything is still possible. However, as a practical matter, if the one you want is already in love with someone who is doing a fairly good job of meeting their basic love needs of *friendship, respect,* and *passion,* then that relationship is fairly secure for your rival.

Don't be discouraged by your seeming powerlessness in a situation like this. It has nothing to do with your being an inferior rival, or with an inability to apply love tactics skillfully. It is simply a matter of arriving on the scene after the window of opportunity is tightly closed. Yes, it can be a bit painful, but be assured that there are others who will be inspired by your ardor.

This is the one situation where your best alternative may be to find someone new. Yes, some people actually do choose to wait it out indefinitely, but we recommend you find someone new and not to take it personally. Look to the future. There are other options.

Remember, where there was one person you could want, there will be others. There's nothing wrong with beginning again. And what's more, you have *More Love Tactics* to help you from the beginning!

LOVE TACTIC # 114 Don't Settle for a Relationship That Requires Force

If you work hard enough, there isn't anyone you can't ultimately win over. But beyond a wholesome application of the principles outlined in this book, don't attempt to force the one you want to respond the way you need them to, or else you'll be sorry. If you have to go beyond reasonable efforts to achieve your goal, it is an indication that things are not going to run smoothly. You will probably spend the rest of your life fighting to keep your head above water.

Real estate magnate Donald Trump wanted to buy the Plaza Hotel in New York City. He *had to have it*, and he was willing to pay more for the hotel than it was worth. Because he was carried away with the emotion of wanting, instead of thinking things out logically, the normally clear-thinking Trump broke his own rule and overpaid for the Plaza. The hotel expenses eventually outran the income and helped cause the downfall of Trump's financial empire.

The same type of thing can happen in pursuit of a love relationship. The costs of the relationship, in terms of emotional output, can sometimes far outstrip the emotional rewards. You may win the person but lose the battle for a fulfilling life, so be careful. You can't change the basic nature of the one you want simply by capturing that person's heart (and don't ever fool yourself into thinking otherwise). Do your best to make a relationship work out but don't feel obligated to go beyond that. Don't force it. In emotional terms, make a fair offer by doing the things this book suggests, but if the other person remains hesitant about meeting your emotional needs, then seriously consider withdrawing from the relationship altogether.

The most rewarding, fulfilling relationship you can ever experience is the one that allows you to stretch your capacities and skills to make it work, but not to the point that makes you snap. Be willing to throw in the towel if the other person's heart requires extreme measures on your part to stimulate a loving response. It is a sign that their ability to meet your ongoing emotional needs is too underdeveloped and conditional to ever bring you the fulfillment and happiness you deserve (even if they do marry you). It is an unhealthy obsession for you to stay involved in a relationship that cannot and will not bring you the consummate fulfillment that you desire.

The greatest happiness results from choosing someone who not only keeps you on your toes, but who also gives you the love you need in return for the love you give.

Sometimes the difference between the two options (i.e., choosing someone who loves you enough to meet your needs and choosing someone who does not) may be razor thin, but it makes a world of difference in the ultimate outcome. In business, you must show a cumulative profit, and you can't do that with continual losses. It is the same in romance. Emotional deficits will eventually result in romantic bankruptcy.

For you to make a good decision, you must be emotionally strong enough to "take it or leave it," based on the objective assessment of whether or not you can get a fair return of love on your investment of time and self. Cutting your losses and changing pursuit of an object are not indications of your inabilities, but of a realistic assessment of the maturity level of the one you want. You can win their conditional love, but if they don't have an adequate supply of unconditional love to meet your needs *then you just ain't gonna get it!*

Do what is right, then let the consequences follow. The irony of finding the inner strength to let a bad relationship go is that you will be able to find true love so much more easily. There is someone out there who is really good for you, someone who can bring you a sense of fulfillment and great happiness. Don't compromise and settle. Wait for the "right" person, one who is able to give you the love you need.

Frank Bettger, a phenomenal salesman of the 1930s, shared the secret of his success in his classic *How I Raised Myself from Failure to*

Success in Selling. After analyzing his first year's sales, Bettger discovered that 70 percent were made on the first interview, 23 percent on the second interview, and 7 percent on the third. His greatest revelation was that he spent half of his time going after that last 7 percent! When he realized this, he began concentrating his efforts on those first interviews and nearly doubled his income overnight!

In similar fashion, when pursuing the love of your life, you should be willing to let go when it's *obvious* that your needs for loving attention are not being met after you've made a reasonable effort to love the person the best you can. What's reasonable? When you have pretty much exhausted your best understanding of the principles in this book, you have more than satisfied this requirement.

If you're spending all your time trying to carve a square peg to go through a round hole, it's just not worth the effort. We assure you that the world is full of round pegs just waiting for you. Don't feel obligated to take one you don't want, either. If a blue peg is what you want, then don't settle for a green or a yellow. Keep sorting until you find your blue peg. But don't get stuck on a square peg just because it's blue. It may cause you to miss your opportunity for a partner who has everything, including the ability to meet your very real emotional needs.

We have interviewed many people who have spent years fruitlessly trying with all their might to make an existing relationship work. After finally cutting their losses and going on alone, they eventually met someone else. This was not because the pursuer had suddenly become more attractive or smarter. He/she wasn't working any harder at the relationship; however, the pursuer was now relating with a person who was developed enough to appreciate his/her qualities.

Don't fall for the deception that once you lose somebody, you will never be able to find anybody else you will want as much. It may require some scratching in the barnyard, but there are more pickin's out there!

In summary, give it your best. Do your part to cultivate a relationship with the one you want. But if experience proves that the one you want remains hardhearted to you even after you have given it your all, then wish them the best and get on with finding somebody who *will* reciprocate your love after a reasonable effort. True love is still waiting out there for you.

LOVE TACTIC # 115 Proceed with Faith

The one element that we have saved for last is, for many, the most important: Let your life be guided by faith. It is comforting to believe that all of life's experiences are part of a greater plan. Successes and accomplishments, as well as disappointments, all add color and texture to the tapestry of your life.

Believe in the strength of a higher power that is armed with goodness and a loving hand to guide you purposefully through life. Trust in God. By trusting that everyday happenings are not without design or reason, you will gain strength and confidence when facing challenges.

In all areas, including love, have faith that each twist and turn has a purpose. Believe that a seemingly negative experience can bring about something positive, and keep in mind that when one door closes, another one opens.

If you maintain a strong faith and trust that there is a purpose for the things you experience, it will be easier to overcome difficulties. Remember that any suffering you may encounter along life's way is only temporary and, in some way, may be the cause of future happiness.

Final Words

So there you have it! Love does not just happen. It has to be cultivated. When this truth finally sinks into your heart, it will open doors of unlimited power to you.

A person who is truly in love feels about 90 percent *friendship*, 9 percent *respect*, and about 1 percent *passion* for the other person (although it is that 1 percent of which we are most conscious). Ideally, both people in a relationship should feel this balance toward each other.

One-hundred percent *passion* may be exciting for a short while, but it's not enough. If the core of your relationship is not *friendship*, where you can count on your long-term emotional needs being met, you will eventually become as sick as a kid who eats nothing but icing from a birthday cake. Icing is nice, but not when you make an entire meal out of it. We want you to have your cake and eat it, too!

If you get nothing else from this book, let it be this: Every time you utilize a Love Tactics principle, you'll be creating a more positive relationship than you had before. As long as you do *something* to further cultivate one of the areas of *friendship*, *respect*, and *passion*, you cannot help but improve the love between you. And even if this improvement is not enough to elicit the commitment you want today, keep working on it. Someday it will be.

While this book, as well as the original *Love Tactics*, has explored various methods of cultivating each of the three important elements of love, it's up to you to evaluate your current relationship and what it lacks. If the one you want enjoys your friendship but mistreats you and seems to take you for granted, then you need to take steps to increase the *respect* in the relationship.

On the other hand, if the other person fears you more than trusts you, then concentrate on doing things to improve *friendship*. Remember to cultivate what you *lack* in the relationship! Your relationship can only be as strong as its weakest link in this three-link chain.

You may not need a lot of *passion*, but you do need some! Frankly, though, this should be your lowest priority in building a successful relationship. You shouldn't worry about getting the one you want crazy with passion until everything else is in place first. Then, when the *friendship* is solid, and the *respect* is firmly established, you can ignite the whole powder keg in one fell swoop. This will foreverafter be known as "the moment he/she fell in love with you."

Many love tactics have been offered in this book. They have been presented in a way that we hope will enhance your efforts at winning the one you want or winning back the one you've lost. It is virtually impossible to cover every possible variable that may occur, each scenario that may exist, or every obstacle that you may encounter. Many of our readers have discovered additional tactics that have worked well for them. We invite you to contact us, in care of the publisher, with any new tactics that you've found to be successful for you. We may even include your ideas in future books.

We wish you the best in your quest for love. It is the greatest crusade man or woman can embark upon in this world. Our best wishes go with you!

Index